LONDON

CONTENTS

Key to Map Symbols 3

Key to Map Pages................................... 4-5

Central London Maps 6-7

Map Pages 8-42

Index to Street Names 43-91

Published by Collins
An imprint of HarperCollins*Publishers*
77-85 Fulham Palace Road, Hammersmith, London W6 8JB

www.collins.co.uk

Copyright © HarperCollins*Publishers* Ltd 2004
Collins® is a registered trademark of HarperCollins*Publishers* Limited

Mapping generated from Collins Bartholomew digital databases

London Underground Map by permission of Transport Trading Limited
Registered User No. 05/4084

The grid on this map is the National Grid taken from the Ordnance Survey
map with the permission of the Controller of Her Majesty's Stationery Office.

All rights reserved. No part of this publication may be reproduced, stored in
a retrieval system, or transmitted, in any form or by any means, electronic,
mechanical, photocopying, recording or otherwise, without the prior written
permission of the publisher and copyright owners.

The contents of this publication are believed correct at the time of printing.
Nevertheless, the publisher can accept no responsibility for errors or
omissions, changes in the detail given, or for any expense or loss thereby
caused.

The representation of a road, track or footpath is no evidence of a right of
way.

Printed in Hong Kong

ISBN 0 00 7171560 Imp 001   QM 11625   ADM

e-mail: roadcheck@harpercollins.co.uk

KEY TO MAP SYMBOLS

3

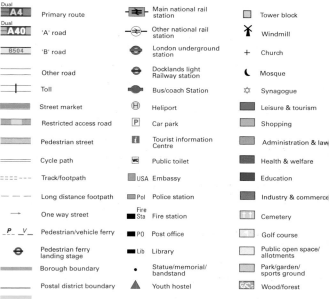

Dual A4	Primary route	Main national rail station
Dual A40	'A' road	Other national rail station
B504	'B' road	London underground station
	Other road	Docklands light Railway station
	Toll	Bus/coach Station
	Street market	ℍ Heliport
	Restricted access road	ℙ Car park
	Pedestrian street	𝒊 Tourist information Centre
	Cycle path	wc Public toilet
	Track/footpath	USA Embassy
	Long distance footpath	Pol Police station
	One way street	Fire Sta Fire station
P V	Pedestrian/vehicle ferry	PO Post office
	Pedestrian ferry landing stage	Lib Library
	Borough boundary	• Statue/memorial/ bandstand
	Postal district boundary	▲ Youth hostel

	Tower block
✶	Windmill
+	Church
☾	Mosque
✡	Synagogue
	Leisure & tourism
	Shopping
	Administration & law
	Health & welfare
	Education
	Industry & commerce
	Cemetery
	Golf course
	Public open space/ allotments
	Park/garden/ sports ground
	Wood/forest

Central London congestion charging zone

The reference grid on this atlas coincides with the Ordnance Survey National Grid System

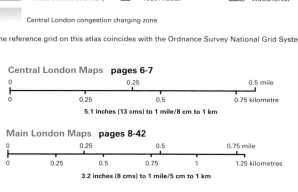

Central London Maps **pages 6-7**

0		0.25		0.5 mile
0	0.25	0.5		0.75 kilometre

5.1 inches (13 cms) to 1 mile/8 cm to 1 km

Main London Maps **pages 8-42**

0		0.25		0.5		0.75 mile
0	0.25	0.5	0.75	1		1.25 kilometres

3.2 inches (8 cms) to 1 mile/5 cm to 1 km

4

KEY TO MAP PAGES

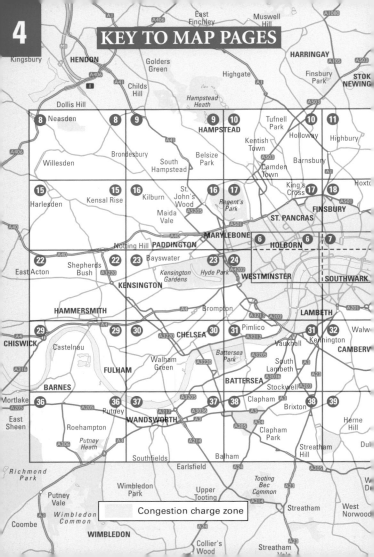

East Finchley
Muswell Hill
A1080
A406
A1
Kingsbury
HENDON
Golders Green
HARRINGAY
A503
A1
M1
A1
Highgate
Finsbury Park
STOK NEWING
Dollis Hill
A406
A41
Childs Hill
Hampstead Heath
A503
A1

8 Neasden
8
9
9
HAMPSTEAD
10
Tufnell Park
10
11
Willesden
Brondesbury
A41
Belsize Park
Kentish Town
Holloway
Highbury
A1
South Hampstead
Camden Town
Barnsbury

15
15
16 Kilburn
St. John's Wood
16
17
King's Cross
17
18
Harlesden
Kensal Rise
A205
Maida Vale
Regent's Park
A501
FINSBURY
Hoxto
A50
A40
Notting Hill
A40
PADDINGTON
MARYLEBONE
ST. PANCRAS
A40
6
6
7
HOLBORN

22
Shepherds Bush
22
23 Bayswater
23
24
A202
A501
East Acton
A3220
Kensington Gardens
Hyde Park
WESTMINSTER
SOUTHWARK
KENSINGTON

HAMMERSMITH
A4
Brompton
A4
A3213 A202
LAMBETH
A201

29
29
30
A3220
CHELSEA
30
31 Pimlico
31
32 Walw
CHISWICK
Castelnau
A4
Walham Green
A3212
Vauxhall
Kennington
CAMBERV
A316
Battersea Park
A3205
South Lambeth
A3
A23
FULHAM
A3220
BATTERSEA
A3036
BARNES
Stockwell
A203

Mortlake
36
36
37
37
38 Clapham
38
39
East Sheen
A205
Putney
WANDSWORTH
A3036
A3
Brixton
Herne Hill
Roehampton
Putney Heath
A214
Clapham Park
Streatham Hill
Dul
Southfields
Balham

Richmond Park
Earlsfield
A24
Tooting Bec Common
A214
A205
Putney Vale
Wimbledon Park
Upper Tooting
Streatham
West Norwood
A3
┌─────────────────────────────┐
│ Congestion charge zone   │
└─────────────────────────────┘
Coombe
Wimbledon Common
A3
WIMBLEDON
A24
Collier's Wood
Streatham
A23

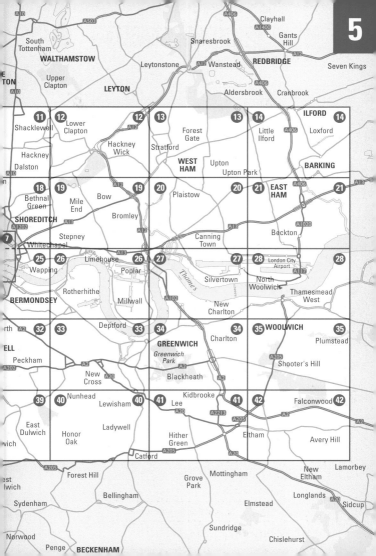

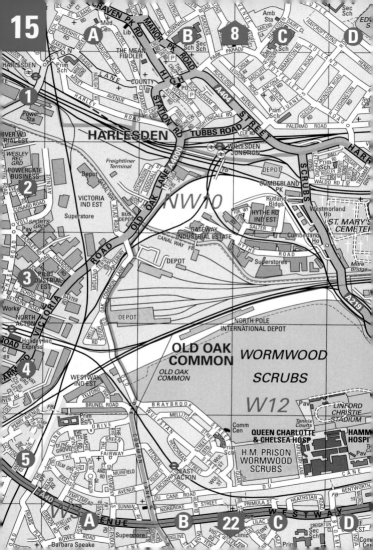

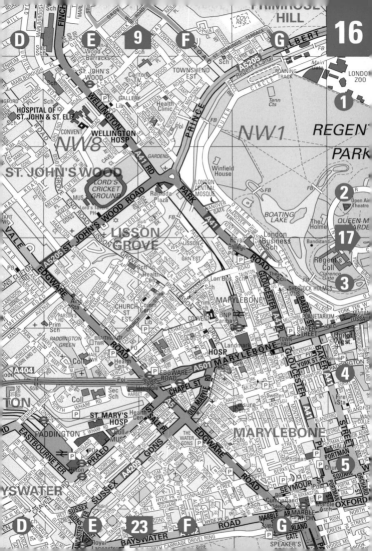

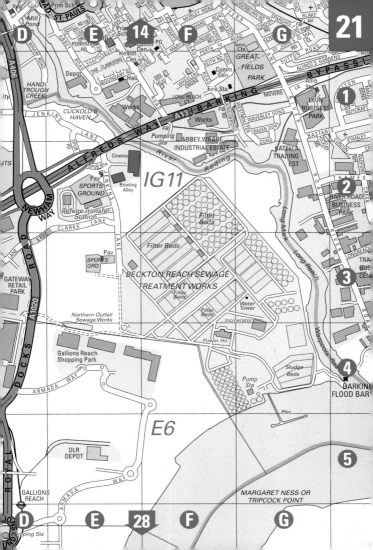

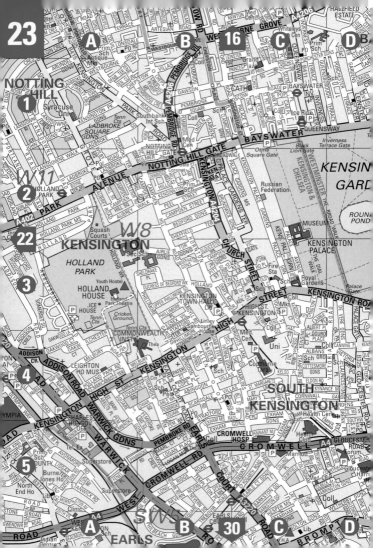

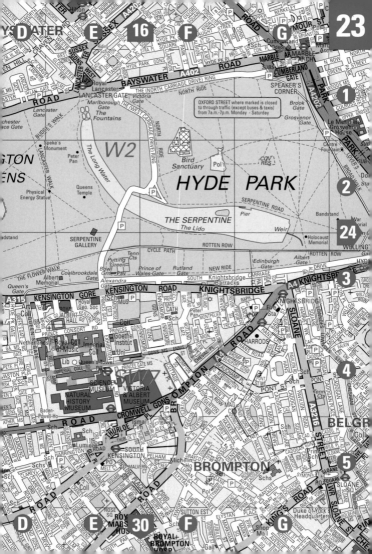

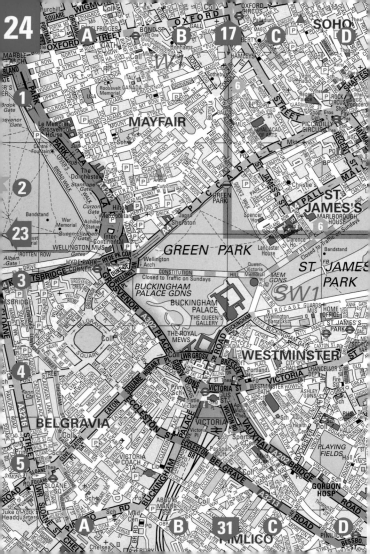

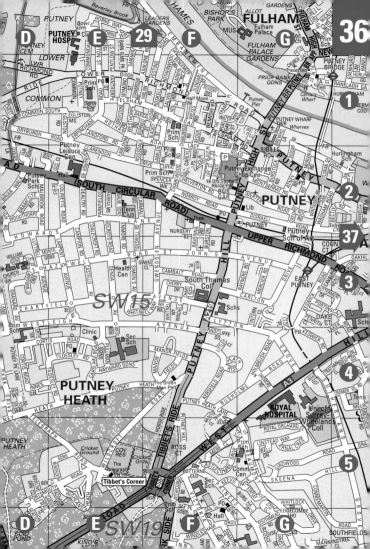

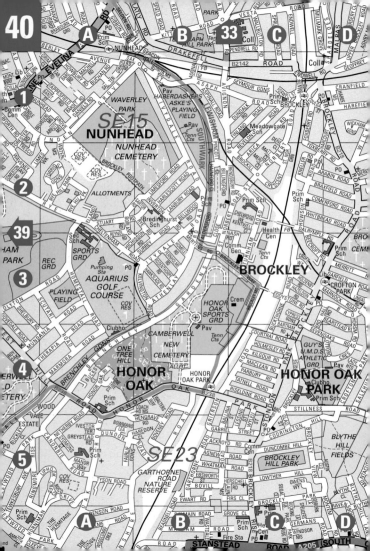

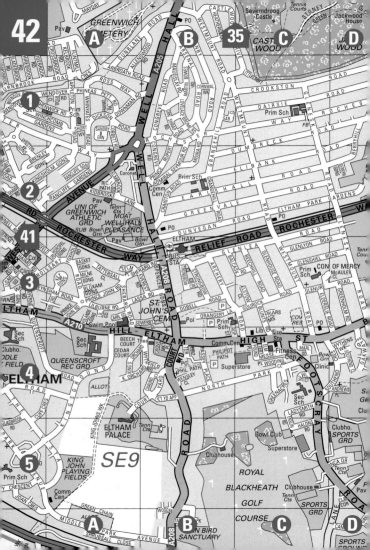

INDEX TO STREETS

General Abbreviations

All	Alley	Dws	Dwellings	Hts	Heights	Ri	Rise
App	Approach	E	East	Ind	Industrial	S	South
Arc	Arcade	Embk	Embankment	Junct	Junction	Sch	School
Av	Avenue	Est	Estate	La	Lane	Shop	Shopping
Bdy	Broadway	Ex	Exchange	Lo	Lodge	Sq	Square
Bldgs	Buildings	Fld	Field	Mans	Mansions	St.	Saint
Br	Bridge	Flds	Fields	Mkt	Market	St	Street
Cen	Central, Centre	Fm	Farm	Mkts	Markets	Sta	Station
Ch	Church	Gdn	Garden	Ms	Mews	Ter	Terrace
Chyd	Churchyard	Gdns	Gardens	Mt	Mount	Trd	Trading
Circ	Circus	Gra	Grange	N	North	Twr	Tower
Cl	Close	Grd	Ground	Par	Parade	Vil	Villas
Cor	Corner	Grds	Grounds	Pas	Passage	Vw	View
Cotts	Cottages	Grn	Green	Pk	Park	W	West
Cres	Crescent	Gro	Grove	Pl	Place	Wd	Wood
Ct	Court	Gt	Great	Prec	Precinct	Wf	Wharf
Ctyd	Courtyard	Ho	House	Pt	Point	Wk	Walk
Dr	Drive	Hos	Houses	Rd	Road	Yd	Yard

Abbreviations of Post Towns

Bark.	Barking	Ilf.	Ilford	Sid.	Sidcup	Well.	Welling

Notes

The figures and letters following a street name indicate the Postal District, page and map square where the name can be found. Street names shown as **bold entries** can be found on the central London pages, 6 and 7.

A

Aaron Hill Rd E6 21 C4
Abbeville Rd SW4 38 C4
Abbey Cl E5 11 F1
Abbey Cl SW8 31 D4
Aberfeldy St E16 26 A5
Abbey Gdns NW8 16 D1
Abbey Gdns W6 29 G2
Abbey La E15 19 G1
Abbey Orchard St SW1 24 D4
Abbey Retail Pk, Bark. 14 D5
Abbey Rd E15 19 G1
Abbey Rd NW6 9 C4
Abbey Rd NW8 16 D1
Abbey Rd, Bark. 14 D4
Abbey Rd Est SW9 30 C5
Abbey St E13 20 D4
Abbey St SE1 25 D4
Abbey Wf Ind Est, Bark. 21 F1
Abbotsbury Cl E15 19 G1
Abbotsbury Ms SE15 40 A1
Abbotsbury Rd W14 22 G3
Abbotshade Rd SE16 26 B2
Abbots La SE1 7 J6
Abbots Manor Est SW1 24 B5
Abbot's Pl NW6 9 C5
Abbot's Rd E6 13 G5
Abbotstone Rd SW15 36 C1
Abbot St E8 11 E3
Abbotswell Rd SE4 40 D3
Abbotswood Rd SE22 39 D2
Abbott Rd E14 19 G4
Abchurch La EC4 7 G3
Abchurch Yd EC4 7 F3
Abdale Rd W12 22 D2
Aberavon Rd E3 19 C2
Abercorn Cl NW8 16 D2
Abercorn Pl NW8 16 D2
Abercorn Way SE1 32 F1
Abercrombie St SW11 30 F5
Aberdare Gdns NW6 9 C4

Aberdeen La N5 11 A2
Aberdeen Pk N5 11 A2
Aberdeen Pk Ms N5 11 B1
Aberdeen Pl NW8 16 E3
Aberdeen Rd N5 11 B1
Aberdeen Rd NW10 8 B2
Aberdeen Ter SE3 34 A5
Aberdour St SE1 25 D5
Aberfeldy St E14 19 G5
Aberford Gdns SE18 35 A4
Abergeldie Rd SE12 41 E4
Abernethy Rd SE13 41 B2
Abersham Rd E8 11 E2
Abery St SE18 28 G5
Abingdon Rd W8 23 B4
Abingdon St SW1 24 E4
Abingdon Vil W8 23 B4
Abinger Gro SE8 33 D2
Abinger Rd W4 22 A4
Ablett St SE16 26 C5
Acacia Cl SE8 26 C5
Acacia Pl NW8 16 E1
Acacia Rd NW8 16 E1
Academy Pl SE18 35 B4
Academy Rd SE18 35 A4
Acanthus Dr SE1 32 F1
Acanthus Rd SW11 38 A1
Achfold Rd SW6 30 C4
Achilles Cl SE1 32 F1
Achilles Rd NW6 9 B2
Achilles St SE14 33 C3
Acklam Rd W10 16 A4
Ackmar Rd SW6 30 B4
Ackroyd Dr E3 19 D4
Ackroyd Rd SE23 40 B5
Acland Cres SE5 39 C2
Acland Rd NW2 8 D3
Acol Rd NW6 9 B4
Acorn Wk SE16 26 C2
Acre Dr SE22 39 F2
Acre La SW2 38 C2
Acris St SW18 37 D3
Adpar St W2 16 E3
Adrian Ms SW10 30 C2
Adys Rd SE15 39 E1
Afghan Rd SW11 30 F5
Africa Rd SE16 25 G4
Agamemnon Rd NW6 9 A2
Agar Gro NW1 10 C4
Agar Gro Est NW1 10 D4
Agar Pl NW1 10 C4
Agar St WC2 6 E4
Agate Cl E16 20 G5

Adam St WC2 6 F4
Adam Wk SW6 29 E3
Ada Pl E2 11 F5
Ada Rd SE5 32 D3
Ada St E8 11 G5
Adderley St E14 19 G5
Addington Rd E3 19 E2
Addington Rd E16 20 B3
Addington Sq SE5 32 B3
Addison Av W11 22 G2
Addison Br Pl W14 23 A5
Addison Cres W14 22 G4
Addison Gdns W14 22 F4
Addison Gro W4 22 A4
Addison Pl W11 22 G2
Addison Rd SE6 40 E5
Aden Gro N16 11 C1
Aden Ter N16 11 C1
Adie Rd W6 22 E4
Adine Rd E13 20 E3
Adler St E1 18 F5
Adley St E5 12 C2
Admaston Rd SE18 35 E3
Adelina Gro E1 19 A4
Adeline Pl WC1 17 D4
Adelphi Ter WC2 6 F4
Adeney Cl W6 29 F2
Admiral Cl W8 6 B1
Admiral Seymour Rd SE5 32 B2
Admirals Gate SE10 33 F4
Admiral Sq SW10 30 E4
Admiral St SE8 33 E3
Admirals Way E14 26 E3
Admiral Wk W9 16 C3
Adolphus St SE8 33 D3

Adam & Eve Ct W1 6 B1
Adam & Eve Ms W8 23 B4
Adams Ct EC2 7 G1
Adamson Rd E16 20 D5
Adamson Rd NW3 9 E4
Adams Row W1 24 A1

Agave Rd NW2 8 E1
Agdon St EC1 18 A3
Agincourt Rd NW3 9 G1
Agnes Av, Ilf. 14 D1
Agnes Cl E6 28 C1
Agnes Rd W3 22 B2
Agnes St E14 19 D5
Agnew Rd SE23 40 B5
Aileen Wk E15 13 C4
Ailsa St E14 19 G4
Ainger Rd NW3 9 G4
Ainsdale Dr SE1 32 F1
Ainsley St E2 18 G2
Ainslie Wk SW12 38 B5
Ainsty St SE16 26 B3
Ainsworth Rd E9 12 A4
Ainsworth Way NW8 9 D5
Aintree Av E6 14 A5
Aintree St SW6 29 G3
Airdrie Cl N1 10 F4
Airedale Av W4 22 B1
Airedale Rd SW12 37 G5
Airlie Gdns W8 23 B3
Air St W1 6 B4
Aisgill Av W14 30 A1
Aislibie Rd SE12 41 B2
Ajax Rd NW6 9 B2
Akehurst St SW15 36 C4
Akenside Rd NW3 9 E2
Akerman Rd SW9 32 A5
Alabama St SE18 35 F3
Alan Hocken Way E15 20 B1
Alanthus Cl SE12 41 C4
Alaska St SE1 6 J6
Albacore Cres SE13 40 F4
Albany W1 6 A4
Albany Ctyd W1 6 B4
Albany Mans SW11 30 F3
Albany Rd E12 13 G1
Albany Rd E15 32 C2
Albany Rd SE5 32 B1
Albany St NW1 17 B1
Albatross St SE18 35 G3
Albatross Way SE16 26 B3
Albemarle St W1 24 B1
Alberta Est SE17 32 A1
Alberta St SE17 32 A1
Albert Av SW8 31 F3
Albert Br SW3 30 F2
Albert Br Rd SW11 30 F2
Albert Embk SE1 31 E1
Albert Gdns E1 19 B5

Albert Gate SW1 23 G3
Albert Pl W8 23 C3
Albert Rd E16 28 A2
Albert Rd NW6 16 A1
Albert Sq E15 13 B2
Albert Sq SW8 31 F3
Albert St NW1 10 B5
Albert Ter NW1 10 A5
Albert Way SE15 32 G3
Albion Av SW8 31 D5
Albion Dr E8 11 D1
Albion Est SE16 26 B3
Albion Gro N16 11 D1
Albion Ms N1 10 G5
Albion Ms W2 16 F5
Albion Pl EC1 18 A4
Albion Pl W6 22 D5
Albion Rd N16 11 C1
Albion Sq E8 11 E1
Albion St SE16 26 A3
Albion St W2 16 F5
Albion Way SE13 40 E1
Albrighton Rd SE22 39 D1
Albury St SE8 33 E2
Albyn Rd SE8 33 E4
Aldbourne Rd W12 22 A1
Aldbridge St SE17 32 D2
Aldebert Ter SW8 31 E3
Aldeburgh St SE10 34 D1
Alden Av E15 20 C2
Aldenham St NW1 17 D1
Aldensley Rd W6 22 D4
Alderbrook Rd
SW12 38 B4
Alderbury Rd SW13 29 C2
Alder Cl SE15 32 E2
Aldermanbury EC2 7 E1
Alderney Ms SE1 25 C4
Alderney Rd E1 19 B3
Alderney St SW1 24 B5
Aldersey Gdns,
Bark. 14 F3
Aldersford Cl SE4 40 B3
Aldershot Rd NW6 16 A1
Alderton Rd SE24 39 B1
Alderville Rd SW6 30 A5
Alder Wk, Ilf. 14 E2
Alderwood Rd SE9 42 G4
Aldford St W1 24 A1
Aldgate EC3 18 E5
Aldgate High St EC3 18 E5
Aldine St W12 22 C2
Aldington Rd SE18 27 G4
Aldred Rd NW6 9 B2
Aldridge Rd Vil W11 16 A4
Aldsworth Cl W9 16 C3
Aldworth Rd E15 13 B4
Aldworth Rd E15 13 B4
Aldwych WC2 6 G3
Alestan Beck Rd E16 20 G4
Alexander Av NW10 8 D4
Alexander Cl, Sid. 42 G3
Alexander Pl SW7 23 F5
Alexander Sq SW3 23 F5
Alexander St W2 16 B5
Alexandra Av SW11 31 A4
Alexandra Cl SE8 33 D2
Alexandra Cotts
SE14 33 D4
Alexandra Pl NW8 9 D5
Alexandra Rd E6 21 C2
Alexandra Rd NW8 9 D4
Alexandra St E16 20 D4
Alexandra St SE14 33 C3
Alexis St SE16 25 F5
Alfearn Rd E5 12 A1
Alfreda St SW11 31 B4
Alfred Ms W1 17 D4
Alfred Pl WC1 17 D4
Alfred Prior Ho E12 14 C1
Alfred Rd E15 13 C2
Alfred Rd W3 22 B1
Alfred's Gdns, Bark. 21 G1
Alfred St E3 19 D2

Alfreds Way, Bark. 21 E2
Alfriston Rd SW11 37 G3
Algernon Rd NW6 9 B5
Algernon Rd SE13 40 F2
Algiers Rd SE13 40 E2
Alice Gilliatt Ct
W14 30 A2
Alice La E3 12 D5
Alice St SE1 25 D4
Alice St E1 18 E5
Alison Cl E6 21 C5
Aliwal Rd SW11 37 F2
Alkerden Rd W4 29 A1
Allard Gdns SW4 38 D3
Allardyce St SW4 38 F2
Allcroft Rd NW5 10 A2
Allen Edwards Dr
SW8 31 E4
Allen Rd E3 19 D1
Allen Rd N16 11 D1
Allensbury Pl NW1 10 D4
Allen St W8 23 B4
Allenswood Rd SE9 42 A1
Allestree Rd SW6 29 G3
Allfarthing La SW18 37 C4
Allhallows La EC4 7 F4
Allhallows Rd E6 21 A4
Alliance Rd E13 20 F5
Allingham St N1 18 B1
Allington Rd W10 15 G1
Allington St SW1 24 B4
Allitsen Rd NW8 16 F1
Allnutt Way SW4 38 D3
Alloa Rd SE8 33 B1
Alloway Rd E3 19 C2
All Saints Dr SE3 34 B5
All Saints Rd W11 16 A4
All Saints St N1 17 F1
Allsop Pl NW1 16 G3
All Souls Av NW10 15 D1
Alma Cro SE1 25 E5
Alma Gro SE1 25 E5
Alma Rd SW18 37 D3
Alma Sq NW8 16 D2
Alma St E15 13 A3
Alma St NW5 10 B3
Alma Ter NW5 10 B3
Almeida St N1 11 A4
Almeric Rd SW11 37 G2
Almond Cl SE15 32 F5
Almond Rd SE16 25 G5
Almorah Rd N1 11 C4
Alnwick Rd E16 20 F5
Alnwick Rd SE12 41 E5
Alperton St W10 15 G3
Alpha Gro E14 26 E3
Alpha Pl NW6 16 B1
Alpha Pl SW3 30 F2
Alpha Rd SE14 33 D4
Alpha St SE15 25 E5
Alpine Business Cen
E6 21 C4
Alpine Gro E9 12 A4
Alpine Rd SE16 26 A5
Alpine Way E6 21 C5
Alsace Rd SE17 32 D1
Alscot Rd SE1 25 E5
Alscot Way SE1 25 E5
Altenburg Gdns
SW11 37 G2
Althea St SW6 37 C1
Altmore Av E6 14 B4
Alton St E14 19 F4
Alvanley Gdns NW6 9 F2
Alverstone Rd E12 14 C1
Alverstone Rd NW2 8 E4
Alverton St SE8 33 D1
Alvey St SE17 25 D5
Alvington Cres E8 11 E2
Alwold Cres SE12 41 E4
Alwyne Pl N1 11 B3
Alwyne Rd N1 11 B3
Alwyne Sq N1 11 B3
Alwyne Vil N1 11 A4
Alzette Ho E2 19 B2

Ambassador Gdns
E6 21 B4
Ambassador's Ct
SW1 6 B6
Ambergate St SE17 32 A1
Amberley Rd W9 16 B4
Ambleside Rd NW10 8 B4
Ambrosden Av SW1 24 C4
Ambrose Ms SW11 30 F5
Ambrose St SE16 25 G5
Amelia St SE17 32 A1
Amen Cor EC4 7 C2
Amen St EC4 7 C1
America St SE1 7 D6
Amerland Rd SW18 37 A4
Amersham Gro
SE14 33 D3
Amersham Rd SE14 33 D3
Amersham Vale
SE14 33 D3
Amethyst Rd E15 13 A1
Amhurst Pas E8 11 F1
Amhurst Rd E8 11 G2
Amhurst Rd N16 11 F1
Amhurst Ter E8 11 F1
Amiel St E1 19 A3
Amies St SW11 37 G1
Amity Rd E15 13 C4
Amner Rd SW11 38 A4
Amor Rd W6 22 E4
Amott Rd SE15 39 F1
Amoy Pl E14 19 E5
Ampton St WC1 17 F2
Amsterdam Rd E14 26 G4
Amwell St EC1 17 G2
Amyruth Rd SE4 40 E3
Ancaster St SE18 35 G3
Anchorage Pt Ind Est
SE7 27 F4
Ancona Rd NW10 15 C1
Ancona Rd SE18 35 F1
Andalus Rd SW9 38 E1
Anderson Rd E9 12 B3
Anderson St SW3 30 G1
Anderton Cl SE5 39 C1
Andover Pl NW6 16 C1
Andre St E8 11 F2
Andrew Borde St
WC2 6 D1
Andrewes Gdns E6 21 A5
Andrews Crosse
WC2 6 J2
Andrews Pl SE9 42 D4
Andrew's Rd E8 11 G5
Andrew St E14 19 G5
Anerley St SW11 30 G5
Angel Ct EC2 7 G1
Angel Ct SW1 6 B6
Angelica Dr E6 21 C4
Angel La E15 13 A3
Angell Pk Gdns
SW9 38 G1
Angell Rd SW9 38 G1
Angel Town Est
SW9 38 G1
Angel Ms N1 17 G1
Angel Pas EC4 7 F4
Angel St EC1 7 D1
Angel Wk W6 22 E5
Angler's La NW5 10 B3
Anglesea Av SE18 28 D5
Anglesea Rd SE18 28 D5
Anglia Ho E14 19 C5
Anglia Wk E6 14 B5
Anglo Rd E3 19 D1
Angrave Ct E8 11 E5
Angus Rd E13 20 F2
Angus St SE14 33 C3
Anhalt Rd SW11 30 F3

Ankerdine Cres
SE18 35 C3
Anley Rd W14 22 F3
Annabel Cl E14 19 F5
Anna Cl E8 11 E5
Annandale Rd SE10 34 C2
Annandale Rd W4 22 A5
Annandale Rd, Sid. 42 G5
Anne Compton Ms
SE12 41 C5
Annesley Rd SE3 34 E4
Annette Rd E13 20 D3
Annette Rd N7 10 F1
Annie Besant Cl E3 12 D5
Annis Rd E9 12 C3
Ann La SW10 30 E3
Ann Moss Way
SE16 26 A4
Ansdell Rd SE15 28 F5
Ansdell St W8 33 A5
Ansdell St W8 23 C4
Anselm Rd SW6 30 B2
Ansleigh Pl W11 22 F1
Anson Rd N7 10 C1
Anson Rd NW2 8 F2
Anstey Rd SE15 39 F1
Anstice Cl W4 29 A3
Anstridge Path SE9 42 F4
Anstridge Rd SE9 42 F4
Antelope Rd SE18 28 B4
Antill Rd E3 19 C2
Antill Ter E1 19 B5
Anton St E8 11 F2
Antrim Gro NW3 9 G3
Antrim Mans NW3 9 F3
Antrim Rd NW3 9 G3
Apollo Pl SW10 30 E3
Apothecary St EC4 7 B2
Appach Rd SW2 38 G4
Appleby Rd E8 11 F4
Appleby Rd E16 20 D5
Appleby St E2 18 E1
Appleford Rd W10 15 G3
Applegarth Rd W14 22 F4
Appleton Rd SE9 42 A1
Apple Tree Yd SW1 6 B5
Applewood Dr E13 20 E3
Appold St EC2 18 D4
Approach Rd E2 19 A1
April St E8 11 E1
Aquila St NW8 16 E1
Aquinas St SE1 7 A6
Arabella Dr SW15 36 A2
Arabin Rd SE4 40 C2
Aragon Twr SE8 26 D5
Arbery Rd E3 19 C2
Arbour Sq E1 19 B5
Arbroath Rd SE9 42 A1
Arbuthnot Rd SE14 33 B5
Arbutus St E8 11 D5
Arcadia St E14 19 E5
Archangel St SE16 26 B3
Archbishops Pl
SW2 38 F4
Archdale Rd SE22 39 E3
Archel Rd W14 30 A2
Archer St W1 6 C3
Archery Cl W2 16 F5
Archery Rd SE9 42 B3
Arches, The WC2 6 F5
Archibald Ms W1 24 B1
Archibald Rd N7 10 D1
Archibald St E3 19 E2
Arch St SE1 25 B4
Archway Cl W10 15 F4
Archway St SW13 36 A1
Arcola St E8 11 E2
Ardbeg Rd SE24 39 C4
Arden Cres E14 26 E5
Arden Est N1 18 D1
Ardgowan Rd SE6 41 B5
Ardilaun Rd N5 11 B1
Ardleigh Rd N1 11 D3
Ardmere Rd SE13 41 A4
Ardwick Rd NW2 9 B1

Argon Ms SW6 30 B3
Argyle Pl W6 22 D5
Argyle Rd E1 19 B3
Argyle Rd E16 13 B1
Argyle Rd E16 20 F5
Argyle Sq WC1 17 E2
Argyle St WC1 17 E2
Argyle Way SE16 32 F1
Argyll Rd W8 23 B3
Argyll St W1 6 A2
Arica Rd SE4 40 C2
Ariel Rd NW6 9 B3
Ariel Way W12 22 E2
Aristotle Rd SW4 38 D1
Arklow Rd SE14 33 D2
Arkwright Rd NW3 9 D2
Arlesford Rd SW9 38 E1
Arlingford Rd SW2 38 G3
Arlington Av N1 18 B1
Arlington Ct SE13 41 A4
Arlington Cl, Sid. 42 G5
Arlington Lo SW2 38 E3
Arlington Rd NW1 10 B5
Arlington Sq N1 11 B5
Arlington St SW1 6 A5
Arlington Way EC1 17 G2
Armadale Rd SW6 30 B3
Armada Way E6 21 E4
Armagh Rd E3 12 D2
Arminger Rd W12 22 D2
Armitage Rd SE10 34 C1
Armoury Rd SE8 33 F3
Armoury Way SW18 37 B3
Armstrong Rd SE18 28 E4
Armstrong Rd SW7 23 E4
Armstrong Rd W3 22 B2
Arnal Cres SW18 36 G5
Arne St WC2 6 F2
Arne Wk SE3 41 C2
Arngask Rd SE6 41 A5
Arnhem Pl E14 26 E4
Arnold Circ E2 18 E2
Arnold Est SE1 25 E3
Arnold Rd E3 19 E2
Arnould Av SE5 39 C2
Arnside St SE17 32 B2
Arodene Rd SW2 38 F4
Arragon Rd E6 13 G5
Arran Wk N1 11 B4
Arrow Rd E3 19 F2
Arsenal Rd SE9 35 B5
Arsenal Way SE18 28 E4
Artesian Rd W2 16 B5
Arthingworth St E15 13 B5
Arthurdon Rd SE4 40 E3
Arthur Rd SW18 28 E5
Arthur Henderson Ho SW6 30 A5
Arthur Rd E6 21 B1
Arthur Rd N7 10 F1
Arthur St EC4 7 G4
Artillery La E1 18 D4
Artillery La W12 15 C5
Artillery Pl SE18 28 B5
Artillery Row SW1 24 D4
Artizan St E1 7 J1
Arundel Ct E15 13 B3
Arundel Gdns W11 23 A1
Arundel Gt Ct WC2 6 H3
Arundel Gro N16 11 D2
Arundel Pl N1 10 G3
Arundel Sq N7 10 G3
Arundel St WC2 6 H3
Arundel Ter SW13 29 D2
Arvon Rd N5 10 G2
Ascalon St SW8 31 C3
Ascham St NW5 10 C2
Ascot Rd E6 21 B2
Ashbourne Gro SE22 39 E3
Ashbourne Gro W4 29 A1
Ashbridge St NW8 16 F3
Ashburn Gdns SW7 23 D5
Ashbourne Gro SE10 33 F3

Ashburnham Pl SE10 33 F3
Ashburnham Retreat SE10 33 F3
Ashburnham Rd NW10 15 E2
Ashburnham Rd SW10 33 D3
Ashburn Pl SW7 23 D5
Ashburton Av, Ilf. 14 G1
Ashburton Gro N7 10 G1
Ashburton Rd E16 20 D5
Ashbury Rd SW11 37 G1
Ashby Gro N1 11 B4
Ashby Ms SE4 33 D5
Ashby Rd SE4 33 D5
Ashchurch Gro W12 22 C3
Ashchurch Pk Vil W12 22 C4
Ashchurch Ter W12 22 C3
Ashcombe St SW6 30 C5
Ashcroft Rd E3 19 C2
Ashdene SE15 32 G4
Ashdon Rd NW10 8 A5
Ashdown Wk E14 26 E5
Ashenden Rd E5 12 B2
Ashentree Ct EC4 7 A2
Asher Way E1 25 F1
Ashfield Rd W3 22 B2
Ashfield St E1 19 A4
Ashford Rd E6 14 C3
Ashford Rd NW2 8 F1
Ash Gro E8 11 G5
Ash Gro NW2 8 F1
Ashgrove Rd, Ilf. 14 G1
Ashington Rd SW6 30 A5
Ashland Pl W1 17 A4
Ashleigh Rd SW14 36 A1
Ashley Cres SW11 38 A1
Ashley Gdns SW1 24 C4
Ashley Pl SW1 24 C4
Ashley Rd E7 13 F4
Ashlin Rd E15 13 A3
Ashlone Rd SW15 36 E1
Ashmead Rd SE8 33 E5
Ashmere Gro SW2 38 E2
Ashmill St NW1 16 F4
Ashmole Pl SW8 31 F2
Ashmole St SW8 31 F2
Ashmore Gro, Well. 42 F1
Ashmore Rd W9 16 A3
Ashness Rd SW11 37 G3
Ashridge Cres SE18 35 E3
Ash Rd E15 13 B2
Ashton Rd E15 13 A3
Ashton St E14 26 G1
Ashwin St E8 11 E3
Ashworth Rd W9 16 C2
Askew Cres W12 22 B3
Askew Rd W12 22 B2
Askham Ct W12 22 C2
Askham Rd W12 22 C2
Asland Rd E15 13 B5
Aslett St SW18 37 C5
Asmara Rd NW2 8 G2
Aspen Gdns W6 29 D2
Aspenlea Rd W6 29 F2
Aspen Way E14 26 E1
Aspern Gro NW3 9 F2
Aspinall Rd SE4 40 B1
Aspinden Rd SE16 25 G5
Aspley Rd SW18 37 C3
Assembly Pas E1 19 A4
Astbury Rd SE15 33 A4
Astell St SW3 30 F1
Aste St E14 26 G3
Astle St SW11 31 A5
Astley Av NW2 8 E2
Aston St E14 19 C5
Astoria Wk SW9 38 G1
Astrop Ms W6 22 E4
Astrop Ter W6 22 E4
Astwood Ms SW7 23 D5
Asylum Rd SE15 32 G3
Atalanta St SW6 29 G3
Athelstane Gro E3 19 D1
Athenlay Rd SE15 40 B3

Atherden Rd E5 12 A1
Atherfold Rd SW9 38 E1
Atherstone Ms SW7 23 D5
Atherton Ms E7 13 C3
Atherton Rd E7 13 C2
Atherton Rd SW13 29 C3
Atherton St SW11 30 F5
Athlone Rd SW2 38 F5
Athlone St NW5 10 A3
Athol Sq E14 19 G5
Atkinson Rd E16 20 F4
Atkins Rd SE12 38 D5
Atlantic Rd SW9 38 G2
Atlas Gdns SE7 27 F5
Atlas Ms E7 10 F3
Atlas Rd E13 20 D1
Atlas Rd NW10 15 A2
Atley Rd E3 12 E5
Atney Rd SW15 36 G2
Atterbury St SW1 24 E5
Attwood Rd W6 22 D5
Aubert Pk N5 11 A1
Aubert Rd N5 11 A1
Aubrey Rd W8 23 A2
Aubrey Wk W8 23 A2
Auburn Cl SE14 33 C3
Aubyn Sq SW15 36 C2
Auckland Rd SW11 37 F2
Auden Pl NW1 10 A5
Audley Cl SW11 38 A1
Audrey St E2 18 F1
Augusta La E13 20 E2
Augusta St E14 19 F5
Augustine Rd W14 22 F4
Augustus Rd SW19 36 C5
Augustus St NW1 17 B1
Auriga Ms N16 11 C2
Auriol Rd W14 22 G5
Austen Ho NW6 16 B2
Austin Cl SE23 40 D5
Austin Friars EC2 7 G1
Austin Friars Pas EC2 7 G1
Austin Friars Sq EC2 7 G1
Austin St E2 18 E2
Australia Rd W12 22 D1
Austral St SE11 25 A5
Autumn St E3 12 E5
Avalon Rd SW6 30 C4
Aveline St SE11 31 F1
Ave Maria La EC4 7 C2
Avening Rd SW18 37 B5
Avenons Rd E13 20 D3
Avenue, The NW6 9 A5
Avenue, The E4 13 C3
Avenue, The SW4 38 A3
Avenue, The SW11 37 F5
Avenue, The SW18 37 A5
Avenue, The W4 22 A4
Avenue Cl NW8 9 F5
Avenue Gdns SW14 36 A1
Avenue Rd E7 13 E2
Avenue Rd N6 9 E4
Avenue Rd NW3 9 E4
Avenue Rd NW8 9 E4
Avenue Rd NW10 15 B1
Averill St W6 29 F2
Avery Hill Rd SE9 42 F4
Avery Row W1 24 B2
Aviary Cl E16 20 C4
Avignon Rd SE4 40 B1
Avis Sq E1 19 B5
Avocet Ms SE28 28 F1
Avondale Pk Gdns W11 22 G1
Avondale Pk Rd W11 22 G1
Avondale Ri SE15 39 E1
Avondale Rd E16 20 B4
Avondale Rd SE1 32 F1
Avonley Rd SE14 33 A3
Avonmore Rd W14 23 A5
Avonmouth St SE1 25 A4
Avon Rd SE4 40 E1
Axe St, Bark. 14 E5
Aybrook St W1 17 A4
Aycliffe Rd W12 22 B2
Aylesbury Rd SE17 32 C1

Aylesbury St EC1 18 A3
Aylesford St SW1 31 D1
Aylesham Cen, The SE15 32 F4
Aylestone Av NW6 9 G5
Aylmer Rd W12 22 B3
Aylward St E1 19 A5
Aylwyn Est SE1 25 D4
Aynhoe Rd W14 22 F5
Ayres Cl E13 20 D2
Ayres St SE1 7 F6
Aysgarth Rd SE21 39 D4
Aytoun Pl SW9 31 F5
Aytoun Rd SW9 31 F5
Azalea Cl, Ilf. 14 D2
Azania Ms NW5 10 B3
Azenby Rd SE15 32 E5
Azof St SE10 27 B5

B

Baalbec Rd N5 11 A2
Babmaes St SW1 6 B4
Baches St N1 18 C2
Back Ch La E1 25 F1
Back Hill EC1 17 G3
Bacon Gro SE1 25 E4
Bacon St E1 18 E3
Bacon St E2 18 E3
Bacon NW5 10 A2
Baddow Wk N1 11 B5
Baden Rd, Ilf. 14 D2
Badminton Rd SW12 38 A4
Badsworth Rd SE5 32 B3
Bagley's La SW6 30 C4
Bagshot St SE17 32 D1
Baildon St SE8 33 D3
Bailey Ms SW2 38 G3
Bainbridge St WC1 6 D1
Baizdon Rd SE3 34 B5
Baker Rd NW10 15 A5
Baker Rd SE18 35 A3
Bakers Hall Ct EC3 7 H4
Bakers Row E15 20 B1
Baker's Row EC1 17 G3
Baker St NW1 16 G3
Baker St W1 16 G4
Bakery Cl SW9 31 F4
Balaam St E13 20 D2
Balcaskie Rd SE1 25 B5
Balchen Rd SE3 34 G5
Balchier Rd SE22 39 G4
Balcombe St NW1 16 G3
Balcorne St E9 12 A4
Balderton St W1 17 A5
Baldock St E3 19 F1
Baldwin Cres SE5 32 B4
Baldwin's Gdns EC1 17 G4
Baldwin Ter N1 18 B1
Bale Rd E1 19 C4
Balfern Gro W4 29 A1
Balfern St SW11 30 F4
Balfe St N1 17 E1
Balfour Pl SW15 36 D2
Balfour Rd N5 11 B1
Balfour St SE17 32 C5
Balham Gro SW12 38 A5
Balham Hill SW12 38 B5
Balham New Rd SW12 38 B5
Balladier Wk E14 19 F4
Ballance Rd E9 12 B3
Ballantine St SW18 37 D2
Ballast Quay SE10 34 A1
Ballater Rd SW2 38 E2
Ballina St SE23 40 B4
Ballingdon Rd SW11 38 A4
Balliol Rd W10 15 E5
Ballogie Av NW10 8 A1
Balls Pond Rd N1 11 C3
Balmer Rd E3 19 D1
Balmes Rd N1 11 C5
Balmoral Gro N7 10 F3

Balmoral Ms W12 22 B3
Balmoral Rd E7 13 F1
Balmoral Rd NW2 8 D3
Balmore CI E14 19 G5
Balmuir Gdns SW15 36 E2
Balnacraig Av NW10 8 A1
Balniel Gate SW1 31 D1
Baltic St E EC1 18 B3
Baltic St W EC1 18 B3
Balvaird Pl SW1 31 D1
Balvernie Gro SW18 37 A5
Bamborough Gdns W12 22 D2
Bamford Rd, Bark. 14 E3
Banbury Ct WC2 6 C2
Banbury Rd E9 12 B4
Banbury St SW11 30 E3
Banchory Rd SE3 34 E3
Bancroft Rd E1 19 A2
Banfield Rd SE15 39 G2
Bangalore St SW15 36 E1
Banim St W6 22 D4
Banister Rd W10 15 F2
Bank End SE1 7 E5
Bankhurst Rd SE6 40 D5
Bank La SW15 36 A5
Bankside SE1 7 D4
Bankside Rd, Ilf. 14 E2
Bank St E14 26 E2
Bankton Rd SW2 38 G2
Bankwell Rd SE13 40 A1
Bannerman Ho SW8 31 F2
Banner St EC1 18 B3
Banning St SE10 34 B1
Bannockburn Rd SE18 28 G5
Banstead St SE15 40 A1
Bantry St SE5 32 C3
Barandon Wk W11 22 F1
Barber's All E13 21 A2
Barbers Rd E15 19 F1
Barbican, The EC2 18 A4
Barb Ms W6 22 E4
Barchard St SW18 37 C3
Barchester St E14 19 G4
Barclay CI SW6 30 B3
Barclay Rd E13 21 B3
Barclay Rd SW6 30 B3
Barden St SE18 35 G3
Bardolph Rd N7 10 E1
Bard Rd W10 22 F1
Bardsley La SE10 33 G2
Barfett St W10 16 A3
Barford St N1 10 G5
Barforth Rd SE15 39 G1
Barge Ho Rd E16 28 D2
Barge Ho St SE1 7 A5
Baring Rd SE12 41 D5
Baring St N1 11 C5
Barker Dr NW1 10 C4
Barker Ms SW4 38 B2
Barker St SW10 30 D2
Barking Rd E6 20 G1
Barking Rd E13 20 G1
Barking Rd E16 20 G1
Bark Pl W2 23 C3
Barkston Gdns SW5 23 C5
Barkworth Rd SE16 32 G1
Barlborough St SE14 33 G2
Barlby Gdns W10 15 F3
Barlby Rd W10 15 F3
Barleycorn Way E14 26 D1
Barlow Dr SE18 35 A4
Barlow Rd NW6 9 A3
Barmouth Rd SW18 37 D4
Barnabas Rd E9 12 B2
Barnaby Pl SW7 23 E5
Barnard CI SE18 28 C5
Barnard Ms SW11 37 F2
Barnard Rd SW11 37 F2
Barnard's Inn EC1 7 A1
Barnby St E15 20 B5
Barnby St NW1 17 C1

Barn Elms Pk SW15 29 E5
Barnes Av SW13 29 C3
Barnes Br SW13 29 A5
Barnes Br W4 29 A5
Barnesbury Ho SW4 38 D3
Barnes CI E12 13 G1
Barnes High St SW13 29 B5
Barnes Rd, Ilf. 14 E2
Barnes St E14 19 C5
Barnes Ter SE8 33 D1
Barnet Gro E2 18 E2
Barney CI SE7 34 F1
Barnfield PI E14 26 E5
Barnfield Rd SE18 35 D2
Barnham St SE1 25 D3
Barnsbury Gro N7 10 F4
Barnsbury Pk N1 10 G4
Barnsbury Rd N1 17 G1
Barnsbury Sq N1 10 G4
Barnsbury St N1 10 G4
Barnsbury Ter N1 10 F4
Barnsdale Av E14 26 E5
Barnsdale Rd W9 16 A3
Barnsley St E1 18 G3
Barnwell Rd SW2 38 G3
Barnwood CI W9 16 C3
Barons Ct Rd W14 29 G1
Barons Keep W14 29 G1
Baronsmead Rd SW13 29 C4
Barons Pl SE1 24 G3
Baron St N1 10 G5
Baron Wk E16 20 C4
Barretts Gro N16 11 D2
Barrett St W1 5 C2
Barriedale SE14 33 C4
Barrier App SE7 27 G4
Barrier Pt Rd E16 27 F2
Barrington CI NW5 10 A2
Barrington Rd E12 14 C1
Barrington Rd SW9 39 A1
Barrington Vil SE18 35 C4
Barrow Hill Rd NW8 16 F1
Barry Rd E6 21 A5
Barry Rd SE22 39 E3
Barset Rd SE15 40 A1
Barter St WC1 17 E4
Bartholomew CI EC1 18 B4
Bartholomew CI SW18 37 D2
Bartholomew La EC2 7 G2
Bartholomew Rd NW5 10 C3
Bartholomew Sq EC1 18 B3
Bartholomew St SE1 25 C4
Bartholomew Vil NW5 10 C3
Barth Rd SE18 28 C5
Bartle Av E6 21 A1
Bartle Rd W11 15 G5
Bartlett CI E14 19 E5
Bartlett Ct EC4 7 A1
Bartletts Pas EC4 7 A1
Barton CI E6 21 B5
Barton Rd W14 29 G1
Bartram Rd SE4 40 C3
Barwick Rd E7 13 E1
Bascombe St SW2 38 G4
Baseing CI E6 28 C1
Basevi Way SE8 33 F2
Basil Av E6 21 A1
Basil St SW3 23 G4
Basing Ct SE15 32 E4
Basingdon Way SE5 39 C2
Basinghall Av EC2 18 C4
Basinghall St EC2 7 F1
Basing St W11 22 G1
Basire St N1 11 B5
Baskerville Rd SW18 37 F5

Basket Gdns SE9 42 A3
Basnett Rd SW11 38 A1
Bassano St SE22 39 E3
Bassein Pk Rd W12 22 B3
Bassett Rd W10 15 F5
Bassett St NW5 10 A3
Bassingham Rd SW18 37 D5
Bastable Av, Bark. 21 G1
Bastwick St EC1 18 A3
Basuto Rd SW6 30 B4
Batavia Rd SE14 33 C3
Batchelor St N1 17 G1
Bateman's Bldgs W1 6 C2
Bateman's Row EC2 18 D3
Bateman St W1 6 C2
Bateson St SE18 28 G5
Bath Rd E7 13 G3
Bath Rd W4 22 A5
Bath St EC1 18 C2
Bath Ter SE1 25 B4
Bathurst Gdns NW10 15 D1
Bathurst St W2 23 E1
Bathway SE18 28 C5
Batman CI W12 22 D2
Batoum Gdns W6 22 E3
Batson St W12 22 C3
Batten St SW11 37 F1
Battersea Br SW3 30 E3
Battersea Br SW11 30 E3
Battersea Br Rd SW11 30 E3
Battersea Ch Rd SW11 30 D4
Battersea High St SW11 30 E4
Battersea Pk SW11 30 G3
Battersea Pk Rd SW8 31 B4
Battersea Pk Rd SW11 30 F5
Battersea Ri SW11 37 F3
Battery Rd SE28 28 G3
Battle Br La SE1 7 H6
Battle Br Rd NW1 17 E1
Battledean Rd N5 11 A2
Batty St E1 18 F5
Baulk, The SW18 37 B5
Bavent Rd SE5 32 B5
Bawdale Rd SE22 39 E3
Bawtree Rd SE14 33 C3
Baxendale St E2 18 F2
Baxter Rd E16 20 F5
Baxter Rd N1 11 C3
Baxter Rd NW10 15 A3
Baxter Rd, Ilf. 14 D2
Bayfield Rd SE9 41 G2
Bayford Rd NW10 15 F2
Bayford St E8 11 G4
Bayham Pl NW1 10 C5
Bayham St NW1 17 D4
Bayley St WC1 17 D4
Baylis Rd SE1 24 G3
Baynes St NW1 10 C4
Bayonne Rd W6 29 G2
Bayswater Rd W2 23 E1
Bayston Rd N16 11 E4
Baythorne St E3 19 D4
Bazely St E14 26 G1
Beacham CI SE7 34 G1
Beachy Rd E3 12 E4
Beacon Gate SE14 40 B1
Beacon Hill N7 10 E2
Beacon Rd SE13 41 A4
Beaconsfield CI SE3 34 D2
Beaconsfield Rd E16 20 C3
Beaconsfield Rd NW10 8 B3
Beaconsfield Rd SE3 34 C3
Beaconsfield Rd SE17 32 C1
Beaconsfield Ter Rd W14 22 G4

Beaconsfield Wk SW6 30 A4
Beadon Rd W6 22 E5
Beak St W1 6 B3
Beale PI E3 19 D1
Beale Rd E3 12 D5
Beanacre CI E9 12 D3
Bear All EC4 7 B1
Bear Gdns SE1 7 D5
Bear La SE1 7 C5
Bearstead Ri SE4 40 D3
Bear St WC2 6 D3
Beaton CI SE15 32 E4
Beatrice PI W8 23 C4
Beatrice Rd SE1 25 F5
Beatson Wk SE16 26 A2
Beatty Rd N16 11 D1
Beatty St NW1 17 C1
Beauchamp PI SW3 23 F4
Beauchamp Rd E7 13 E4
Beauchamp Rd SW11 37 F2
Beauclerc Rd W6 22 D4
Beaufort CI SW15 36 D5
Beaufort Gdns SW3 23 F4
Beaufort St SW3 30 E2
Beaufoy Wk SE11 24 F5
Beaulieu Av E16 27 E2
Beaumont Av W14 29 G1
Beaumont Cres W14 30 A1
Beaumont Gro E1 19 B3
Beaumont PI W1 17 C3
Beaumont Rd E13 19 B3
Beaumont Rd SW19 36 G5
Beaumont Sq E1 13 B3
Beaumont St W1 17 A4
Beaumont Wk NW3 9 G4
Beauval Rd SE22 39 E4
Beavor La W6 22 C5
Bebbington Rd SE18 28 G5
Beccles Dr, Bark. 14 G3
Beccles St E14 26 D1
Beck CI SE13 33 F4
Becket Av E6 21 C2
Becklow Rd W12 22 C3
Beck Rd E8 11 G5
Beckton Retail Pk E6 21 C4
Beckton Rd E16 20 C4
Beckton Triangle Retail Pk E6 21 C3
Beckway St SE17 25 C5
Beckwith Rd SE24 39 C4
Bective Rd E7 13 D1
Bective Rd SW15 37 A1
Bedale St SE1 7 F6
Bedford Av WC1 17 D4
Bedfordbury WC2 6 E3
Bedford CI W4 29 A2
Bedford Ct WC2 6 E4
Bedford Gdns W8 23 B2
Bedford Ho SW4 38 E2
Bedford PI WC1 17 E4
Bedford Rd E6 14 C5
Bedford Rd SW4 38 E1
Bedford Row WC1 17 F4
Bedford Sq WC1 17 D4
Bedford St WC2 6 E3
Bedford Way WC1 17 D3
Bedgebury Rd SE9 41 G2
Beeby Rd E16 20 E4
Beech Av W3 22 A2
Beech CI SW15 36 C5
Beech Ct SE9 42 A4
Beechdale Rd SW2 38 F4
Beechhill Rd SE9 42 B3
Beechmore Rd SW11 30 G4
Beech St EC2 18 B4
Beechwood Rd E8 11 E3
Beecroft Rd SE4 40 C3
Beehive Pas EC3 7 H2
Beehive PI SW9 38 G1

Name	Grid
Beeston Pl SW1	24 B4
Beethoven St W10	15 G2
Begbie Rd SE3	34 F4
Begonia Cl E6	21 A4
Beira St SW12	38 B5
Belfont Wk N7	10 E1
Belford Rd SE18	28 C5
Belfort Rd SE15	33 A5
Belgrade Rd N16	11 D1
Belgrave Gdns NW8	9 C5
Belgrave Ms N SW1	24 A4
Belgrave Ms S SW1	24 A4
Belgrave Ms W SW1	24 A4
Belgrave Pl SW1	24 A4
Belgrave Rd E13	20 F3
Belgrave Rd SW1	24 B5
Belgrave Rd SW13	29 B3
Belgrave Sq SW1	24 A4
Belgrave St E1	19 B5
Belgravia Ho SW4	38 D4
Belgrove St WC1	17 E2
Belinda Rd SW9	39 A1
Belitha Vil N1	10 F4
Bellamy St SW12	38 B5
Bell Dr SW18	36 E5
Bellefields Rd SW9	38 F1
Bellegrave Rd, Well.	35 F5
Bellenden Rd SE15	32 E5
Belleville Rd SW11	37 G3
Bellevue Pl E1	19 A3
Bellevue Rd SW13	29 C5
Bell Inn Yd EC3	7 G2
Bell La E1	18 E4
Bell La E12	27 D2
Bello Cl SE24	39 A5
Bellot St SE10	34 B1
Bells All SW6	30 B5
Bell St NW1	16 F4
Bell St SE18	35 A4
Bell Water Gate	28 C4
Bell Wf La EC4	7 E3
Bellwood Rd SE15	40 B2
Belmont Gro SE13	33 F5
Belmont Hall Ct SE13	33 F5
Belmont Ms, Well.	42 G1
Belmont Cl SW4	38 C1
Belmont Gro SE13	41 A1
Belmont Hill SE13	41 A1
Belmont Pk SE13	41 A2
Belmont Rd SW4	38 C1
Belmont St NW1	10 A4
Belmore La N7	10 D2
Belmore St SW8	31 D4
Beloe Cl SW15	36 C1
Belsham St E9	12 A3
Belsize Av NW3	9 E3
Belsize Cres NW3	9 E2
Belsize Gro NW3	9 F3
Belsize La NW3	9 E3
Belsize Pk NW3	9 E3
Belsize Pk Gdns NW3	9 F3
Belsize Rd NW6	9 C5
Belsize Sq NW3	9 E3
Belsize Ter NW3	9 E3
Belson Rd SE18	28 B5
Belthorn Cres SW12	38 C5
Belton Rd E7	13 E4
Belton Rd E11	13 B1
Belton Rd NW2	8 C3
Belton Way E3	19 E4
Beltran Rd SW6	30 C5
Belvedere Ms SE15	39 G1
Belvedere Pl SE1	25 A3
Belvedere Rd SE1	24 F2
Belvedere Twr, The SW10	30 D4
Belvoir Rd SE22	39 F5
Bembridge Cl NW6	8 G4
Bemerton Est N1	10 F4
Bemerton St N1	10 F5
Bemish Rd SW15	36 F1
Benbow Rd W6	22 D4
Benbow St SE8	33 E2
Bendemeer Rd SW15	36 F1
Bendish Rd E6	14 A4
Bendon Valley SW18	37 C5
Benedict Rd SW9	38 F1
Bengal Rd, Ilf.	14 D1
Bengeworth Rd SE5	39 B1
Benham Cl SW11	37 E1
Benhill Rd SE5	32 C3
Benin St SE13	41 A5
Benjamin Cl E8	11 F5
Benjamin St EC1	18 A4
Ben Jonson Rd E1	19 B4
Benledi St E14	20 A5
Bennelong Cl W12	22 D1
Bennerley Rd SW11	37 F3
Bennet's Hill EC4	7 C3
Bennett Gro SE13	33 F4
Bennett Pk SE3	41 C1
Bennett Rd E13	20 F3
Bennett Rd N16	11 D1
Bennett St SW1	**6 A5**
Bennett St W4	29 A2
Benn St E9	12 C3
Bensbury Cl SW15	36 D5
Benson Av E6	20 F1
Bentham Rd E9	12 B3
Bentinck St W1	17 A5
Bentworth Rd W12	15 D5
Benwell Rd N7	10 G1
Benworth St E3	19 D2
Berber Rd SW11	37 G3
Berens Rd NW10	15 F2
Beresford Rd N5	11 B2
Beresford Rd SE18	28 D5
Beresford St SE18	28 D4
Beresford Ter N5	11 B2
Berestede Rd W6	29 B1
Berger Rd E9	12 B3
Bering Wk E16	20 G5
Berkeley Ho E3	19 E3
Berkeley Rd E12	14 A2
Berkeley Rd SW13	29 C4
Berkeley Sq W1	24 B1
Berkeley St W1	24 B1
Berkley Rd NW1	9 G4
Berkshire Rd E9	12 D3
Bermans Way NW10	8 A1
Bermondsey Wall E SE16	25 F3
Bermondsey Wall W SE16	25 F3
Bernard Ashley Dr SE7	34 E1
Bernard Cassidy St E16	20 C4
Bernard St WC1	17 E3
Bernays Gro SW9	38 F2
Berners Ms W1	17 C4
Berners Pl W1	**6 B1**
Berners Rd N1	10 G5
Berners St W1	17 C4
Bernhardt Cres NW8	16 F3
Berry Cl NW10	8 A3
Berryfield Rd SE17	32 A1
Berryhill SE9	42 D2
Berryhill Gdns SE9	42 D2
Berry St EC1	18 A3
Berthon St SE8	33 E3
Bertie Rd NW10	8 C3
Bertrand St SE13	40 F1
Berwick Cres, Sid.	42 G4
Berwick Rd E16	20 E5
Berwick St W1	**6 B1**
Beryl Av E6	21 A4
Beryl Rd W6	29 F1
Besant Rd NW2	8 G1
Bessborough Gdns SW1	31 D1
Bessborough Pl SW1	31 D1
Bessborough St SW1	31 D1
Bessemer Rd SE5	32 B5
Bessie Lansbury Cl E6	21 C6
Besson St SE14	33 A4
Bestwood St SE8	26 B5
Bethell Av E16	20 C3
Bethnal Grn Est E2	19 A2
Bethnal Grn Rd E1	18 E3
Bethnal Grn Rd E2	18 E3
Bethwin Rd SE5	32 A3
Betterton St WC2	6 E2
Bettons Pk E15	13 B5
Bettridge Rd SW6	30 A5
Bevan St N1	11 B5
Bevenden St N1	18 C2
Beverley Cl SW13	29 B5
Beverley Ct SE4	40 D1
Beverley Gdns SW13	36 B1
Beverley Path SW13	29 B5
Beverley Rd E6	20 G2
Beverley Rd SW13	36 B1
Beverley Rd W4	29 B1
Beverstone Rd SW2	38 F3
Bevington Rd W10	15 G4
Bevington St SE16	25 F3
Bevis Marks EC3	7 J1
Bewdley St N1	10 G4
Bewick Ms SE15	33 A3
Bewick St SW8	31 B5
Bexhill Rd SE4	40 D5
Bexley Rd SE9	42 D3
Bianca Rd SE15	32 D2
Bibury Cl SE15	32 D2
Bickenhall St W1	16 G4
Bicknell Rd SE5	39 B1
Bidborough St WC1	17 D2
Bidder St E16	20 B4
Biddestone Rd N7	10 F1
Biddulph Rd W9	16 C2
Bidwell St SE15	32 G4
Biggerstaff Rd E15	12 G5
Bigland St E1	18 G5
Bignell Rd SE18	35 D1
Bignold Rd E7	13 C5
Billingford Cl SE4	40 B2
Billing Pl SW10	30 C3
Billing Rd SW10	30 C3
Billing St SW10	30 C3
Billington Rd SE14	33 B3
Billiter Sq EC3	7 J3
Billiter St EC3	7 J2
Billson St E14	26 G5
Bina Gdns SW5	23 D5
Binden Rd W12	22 B4
Binfield Rd SW4	31 E4
Bingfield St N1	10 E5
Bingham St N1	11 C3
Bingley Rd E16	20 F5
Binney St W1	17 A5
Binns Rd W4	29 A1
Birch Cl E16	20 B4
Birchdale Rd E7	13 F2
Birches, The SE7	34 F2
Birchfield St E14	26 E1
Birch Gro SE12	41 C5
Birchington Rd NW6	9 B5
Birchin La EC3	**7 G2**
Birchlands Av SW12	37 G5
Birchmere Row SE3	34 C5
Birdbrook Rd SE3	41 F1
Birdcage Wk SW1	24 C3
Birdhurst Rd SW18	37 D2
Bird in Bush Rd SE15	32 F3
Birdsfield La E3	12 D5
Birkbeck Rd E8	11 E2
Birkbeck St E2	18 G2
Birkenhead St WC1	17 E2
Birkwood Cl SW12	38 D5
Birley St SW11	31 A5
Birse Cres NW10	8 A1
Biscay Rd W6	29 F1
Biscoe Way SE13	41 A1
Bishop Kings Rd W14	22 G5
Bishop's Av E13	13 E5
Bishop's Av NW6	29 F5
Bishops Br Rd W2	16 D5
Bishops Br Rd W2	16 D5
Bishop's Ct EC4	**7 B1**
Bishop's Ct WC2	**6 J1**
Bishopsgate EC2	**7 H2**
Bishopsgate Chyd EC2	**7 H1**
Bishop's Pk SW6	29 F5
Bishop's Pk Rd SW6	29 F5
Bishops Rd SW6	30 A4
Bishops Rd SW11	30 F3
Bishops Ter SE11	24 G5
Bishop St N1	11 B5
Bishops Way E2	18 G1
Bishop Way NW10	8 A4
Bisson Rd E15	19 G1
Blackburne's Ms W1	24 A1
Blackburn Rd NW6	9 C3
Blackett St SW15	36 F1
Blackfen Rd, Sid.	42 G3
Blackfriars Br EC4	**7 B3**
Blackfriars Br SE1	**7 B3**
Blackfriars Ct EC4	**7 B3**
Black Friars La EC4	**7 B3**
Blackfriars Pas EC4	**7 B3**
Blackfriars Rd SE1	25 A2
Blackheath Av SE10	34 C5
Blackheath Gro SE3	34 C5
Blackheath Hill SE10	33 G4
Blackheath Pk SE3	41 C1
Blackheath Ri SE13	33 G5
Blackheath Rd SE10	33 F4
Blackheath Vale SE3	34 B5
Blackheath Village SE3	34 C5
Blackhorse Rd SE8	33 C1
Blacklands Ter SW3	23 G5
Black Lion La W6	22 C5
Blackpool Rd SE15	32 G5
Black Prince Rd SE1	24 F5
Black Prince Rd SE11	24 F5
Blackstone Est E8	11 G4
Blackstone Rd NW2	8 E2
Blackthorn St E3	19 E3
Blacktree Ms SW9	38 G1
Blackwall La SE10	34 B1
Blackwall Pier E14	27 B1
Blackwall Tnl East E14	20 A4
Blackwall Tunnel E14	27 B2
Blackwall Tunnel App SE10	27 B3
Blackwall Tunnel Northern App E3	19 E1
Blackwall Tunnel Northern App E14	19 E1
Blackwall Way E14	26 G1
Blackwater Cl E7	13 C1
Blackwater St SE22	39 E3
Blackwell Cl E5	12 B1
Blackwood St SE17	32 C1
Blagdon Rd SE13	40 F4
Blagrove Rd W10	15 G4
Blair Cl N1	11 B3
Blair Cl, Sid.	42 G3
Blair St E14	20 A5
Blake Av, Bark.	14 G5
Blake Cl W10	15 E4
Blake Cl, Well.	35 G4
Blake Gdns SW6	30 C4
Blake Rd E16	20 C3
Blaker Rd E15	12 G5
Blake Rd SE15	32 D3
Blanchard Way E8	11 F3
Blanchedowne SE5	39 C2
Blanche St E16	20 C3
Blandfield Rd SW12	38 A4
Blandford Rd W4	22 A4
Blandford Sq NW1	16 F3

Name	District	Ref
Blandford St W1	17	A4
Bland St SE9	41	G2
Blaney Cres E6	21	D2
Blann Cl SE9	41	H3
Blantyre St SW10	30	E3
Blashford NW3	9	H2
Blashford St SE13	41	A5
Blasker Wk E14	33	E1
Blendon Ter SE18	35	E1
Blenheim Cres W11	15	G5
Blenheim Gdns NW2	8	E2
Blenheim Gdns SW2	38	F4
Blenheim Gro SE15	32	F5
Blenheim Rd E6	20	G2
Blenheim Rd E15	13	H3
Blenheim Rd NW8	16	D1
Blenheim Rd W4	28	B2
Blenheim Ter NW8	16	D1
Blenkarne Rd SW11	37	G4
Blessington Cl SE13	41	A1
Blessington Rd SE13	41	A1
Bletchley Ct N1	18	C1
Bletchley St N1	18	B1
Bliss Cres SE13	33	F5
Blissett St SE10	33	G4
Blithfield St W8	23	C4
Bloemfontein Av W12	22	D2
Bloemfontein Rd W12	22	D1
Blomfield Rd W9	16	D4
Blomfield St EC2	18	C4
Blomfield Vil W2	16	C4
Blondel St E3	31	A5
Blondin St E3	12	D4
Bloomfield Pl W1	24	B1
Bloomfield Rd SE18	35	D1
Bloomfield Ter SW1	31	A1
Bloom Pk Rd SW6	30	A3
Bloomsbury Ho SW4	38	D4
Bloomsbury Pl WC1	17	E4
Bloomsbury Sq WC1	17	E4
Bloomsbury St WC1	17	E4
Bloomsbury Way WC1	6	E1
Blore Ct W1	6	C2
Blossom St E1	18	D3
Blount St E14	19	C5
Bloxam Gdns SE9	42	A3
Blucher Rd SE5	32	B3
Blue Anchor La SE16	25	F5
Blue Anchor Yd E1	25	F1
Blue Ball Yd SW1	6	A6
Bluebell Av E12	13	G2
Bluebell Way, Ilf.	14	D3
Bluebird Way SE28	28	F3
Blundell St N7	10	E4
Blunts Rd SE9	42	C3
Blurton Rd E5	12	A1
Blythe Cl SE6	40	D5
Blythe Hill SE6	40	D5
Blythe Hill La SE6	40	D5
Blythe Rd W14	22	D2
Blythe St E2	18	G2
Boathouse Wk SE15	32	E3
Bobbin Cl SW4	38	C2
Bocking St E8	11	G5
Bodney Rd E8	11	G2
Bohemia Pl E8	11	G3
Bohn Rd E1	19	C4
Boileau Rd SW13	29	C3
Bolden St SE8	33	F5
Boleyn Rd E6	20	G1
Boleyn Rd E7	13	D4
Boleyn Rd N16	11	D2
Bolina Rd SE16	33	A1
Bolingbroke Gro SW11	37	F2
Bolingbroke Rd W14	22	F4
Bolingbroke Wk SW11	30	E3
Bolney St SW8	31	F3
Bolsover St W1	17	A3
Bolt Ct EC4	7	A2
Bolton Cres SE5	32	A2
Bolton Gdns NW10	15	F1
Bolton Gdns SW5	30	C1
Bolton Gdns Ms SW10	30	C1
Bolton Rd E15	13	C3
Bolton Rd NW8	9	C5
Bolton Rd NW10	8	A5
Boltons, The SW10	30	D1
Boltons Pl SW5	30	D1
Bolton St W1	24	B2
Bomore Rd W11	22	F1
Bonar Rd SE15	32	F3
Bonchurch Rd W10	15	G4
Bond Ct EC4	7	F2
Bond St E15	13	B2
Bond St W4	22	A5
Bondway SW8	31	E2
Boneta Rd E18	28	B4
Bonfield Rd SE13	40	G2
Bonham Rd SW2	38	F3
Bonhill St EC2	18	C3
Bonita Ms SE4	40	B1
Bonner Rd E2	19	A1
Bonner St E2	19	A1
Bonneville Gdns SW4	38	C4
Bonnington Sq SW8	31	F2
Bonny St NW1	10	C4
Bonsor St SE5	32	D3
Book Ms WC2	6	D2
Boones Rd SE13	41	B2
Boone St SE13	41	B2
Boord St SE10	27	B4
Bordon Wk SW15	36	C5
Boreham Av E16	20	D5
Borgard Rd SE18	28	B5
Borland Rd SE15	40	A2
Borneo St SW15	36	E1
Borough High St SE1	25	B3
Borough Rd SE1	25	A4
Borrodaile Rd SW18	37	C4
Borthwick Rd E15	13	B1
Borthwick St SE8	33	E1
Boscobel Pl SW1	24	A5
Boscobel St NW8	16	E3
Boscombe Cl E5	12	C2
Boscombe Gdns SW4	38	C4
Boscombe Rd W12	22	C3
Boston Gdns W4	29	A2
Boston Pl NW1	16	G3
Boston Rd E6	21	A2
Boswell Rd WC1	17	E4
Boswell St WC1	17	E4
Bosworth Rd W10	15	G3
Botha Rd E13	20	E4
Bothwell Cl E16	20	C4
Botolph All EC3	7	H3
Botolph La EC3	7	H3
Boughton Rd SE28	28	G4
Boulcott St E1	19	B5
Boulevard, The SW6	30	D4
Boultwood Rd E6	21	A5
Boundary La E11	13	H1
Boundary La SE17	32	B2
Boundary Rd E13	20	F1
Boundary Rd NW8	9	C5
Boundary Rd, Bark.	21	E1
Boundary Rd, Sid.	42	G3
Boundary St E2	18	E3
Bourchier St W1	6	C2
Bourdon St W1	24	B1
Bourke Cl SW4	38	E4
Bournbrook Rd SE3	41	G1
Bourne Est EC1	17	G4
Bournemouth Cl SE15	32	F5
Bournemouth Rd SE15	32	F5
Bourne St SW1	24	A5
Bourne Ter W2	16	C4
Bournville Rd SE6	40	E5
Bousfield Rd SE14	33	B5
Boutflower Rd SW11	37	F2
Bouverie Pl W2	16	E5
Bouverie St EC4	7	A2
Boveney Rd SE23	40	B5
Bovill Rd SE23	40	B5
Bovingdon Rd SW6	30	C4
Bowater Cl SW2	38	E4
Bowater Pl SE3	34	E3
Bowater Rd SE18	27	G4
Bow Back Rivers Wk E15	12	F4
Bow Br Est E3	19	F2
Bow Chyd EC4	7	E2
Bow Common La E3	19	D3
Bowden St SE11	31	G1
Bowditch SE8	33	D1
Bowen St E14	19	F5
Bower Av SE10	34	B4
Bowerdean St SW6	30	C4
Bowerman Av SE14	33	C2
Bower St E1	19	B5
Bowers Wk E6	21	A5
Bowes Rd W3	22	A1
Bowfell Rd W6	29	E2
Bowhill Cl SW9	31	G3
Bowie Cl SW4	38	D5
Bow Ind Pk E15	12	E4
Bowland Rd SW4	38	D2
Bow La EC4	7	E2
Bowl Ct EC2	18	D3
Bowling Grn Cl SW15	36	D5
Bowling Grn La EC1	17	G3
Bowling Grn Pl SE1	25	C3
Bowling Grn St SE11	31	G2
Bowman Av E16	27	C1
Bowmans Lea SE23	40	A5
Bowness Rd SE6	40	F5
Bowood Rd SW11	38	A2
Bow Rd E3	19	D2
Bowsprit Pt E14	26	E4
Bow St E15	13	B2
Bow St WC2	6	F2
Bowyer Cl E6	21	B4
Bowyer Pl SE5	32	B3
Bowyer St SE5	32	B3
Boxall Rd SE21	39	D4
Boxley St E16	27	E2
Boyard Rd SE18	35	D1
Boyce St SE1	6	H6
Boyce Way E13	20	D3
Boydell Ct NW8	9	D2
Boyfield St SE1	25	A3
Boyle St W1	6	A3
Boyne Rd SE13	40	G1
Boyne Ter Ms W11	23	A2
Boyson Rd SE17	32	C2
Brabant Ct EC3	7	H3
Brabazon St E14	19	F5
Braburn Gro SE15	33	A5
Bracewell Rd W10	15	E4
Bracken Av SW12	38	A4
Brackenbury Gdns W6	22	D4
Brackenbury Rd W6	22	D4
Bracken Cl E6	21	B4
Bracken Gdns SW13	29	C5
Brackley Rd W4	29	A1
Brackley Ter W4	29	A1
Bracklyn St N1	18	C1
Bracknell Gdns NW3	9	C1
Bracknell Gate NW3	9	C2
Bracknell Way NW3	9	C1
Bradbourne St SW6	30	B5
Bradbury St N16	11	D2
Braddyll St SE10	34	B1
Bradenham Cl SE17	32	C2
Bradfield Rd E16	27	D3
Bradgate Rd SE6	40	E4
Brading Rd SW2	38	F5
Brading Ter W12	22	C4
Bradiston Rd W9	16	A3
Bradley Stone Rd E6	21	B4
Bradmead SW8	31	B4
Bradmore Pk Rd W6	22	D4
Bradstock Rd E9	12	B3
Brad St SE1	7	A6
Bradwell St E1	19	B2
Bradymead E6	21	C5
Brady St E1	18	G3
Braemar Rd E13	20	C3
Braes St N1	11	A4
Braganza St SE17	32	A1
Braham St E1	18	E5
Braid Av W3	15	A5
Braidwood St SE1	7	H6
Brailsford Rd SW2	38	G3
Braintree St E2	19	A2
Braithwaite Twr W2	16	E4
Bramah Grn SW9	31	G4
Bramber Rd W14	30	A2
Bramblebury Rd SE18	35	E1
Bramcote Gro SE16	33	A1
Bramcote Rd SW15	36	D2
Bramerton St SW3	30	F2
Bramfield Rd SW11	37	F4
Bramford Rd SW18	37	D2
Bramham Gdns SW5	30	C1
Bramhope La SE7	34	E2
Bramlands Cl SW11	37	F1
Bramley Rd W10	22	F1
Brampton Rd E6	20	G2
Bramshaw Rd E9	12	B3
Bramshill Rd NW10	15	B1
Bramshot Av SE7	34	B2
Bramston Rd NW10	15	C1
Bramwell Ms N1	10	F5
Brancaster Rd E12	14	B1
Branch Pl N1	11	C5
Branch Rd E14	26	C1
Branch St SE15	32	D3
Brandlehow Rd SW15	37	A2
Brandon Est SE17	32	A2
Brandon Rd N7	10	E4
Brandram Rd SE13	41	B1
Brandreth Rd E6	21	B5
Brand St SE10	33	G3
Brangton Rd SE11	31	F1
Branksea St SW6	29	G3
Branksome Rd SW2	38	E3
Branscombe St SE13	40	F1
Brantwood Rd SE24	39	B3
Brasenose Dr SW13	29	E2
Brassett Pl E15	13	B5
Brassey Rd NW6	9	A3
Brassey Sq SW11	38	A1
Brassie Av W3	15	A5
Brathway Rd SW18	37	B5
Bravington Rd W9	16	A4
Braxfield Rd SE4	40	C2
Bray NW3	9	F4
Brayards Rd SE15	32	G5
Braybrook St W12	15	B4
Brayburne Av SW4	31	C5
Bray Dr E16	27	C1
Bray Pas E16	27	D1
Bray Pl SW3	23	G5
Braywood Rd SE9	42	F2
Bread St EC4	7	E2
Breakspears Rd SE4	40	D1
Bream Gdns E12	21	C2
Bream's Bldgs EC4	6	J1
Bream St E3	12	E2
Breasley Cl SW15	36	D2
Brecknock Rd N7	10	C1
Brecknock Rd N19	10	C1
Brecknock Rd Est N7	10	C1
Brecon W6	29	G2
Brede Cl E6	21	C2
Bredgar SE13	40	G2
Breer St SW6	37	C1
Bremer Rd SW7	23	D3

Brenchley Gdns SE23	40	A4
Brendon Av NW10	8	A1
Brendon St W1	16	F5
Brenley Gdns SE9	41	G2
Brenthouse Rd E9	11	G4
Brenthurst Rd NW10	8	B3
Brenton St E14	19	C5
Brent Rd E16	20	D4
Brent Rd SE18	35	D3
Bressenden Pl SW1	24	C4
Brett Rd E8	11	G2
Brewer St W1	**6**	**B3**
Brewery Rd N7	10	E4
Brewery Rd SE18	36	C2
Brewhouse La E1	25	G2
Brewhouse La SW15	36	G1
Brewhouse Rd SE18	28	B5
Brewster Gdns W10	15	E4
Brewster Ho E14	26	D1
Briant St SE14	33	B4
Briar Rd NW2	8	E1
Briar Wk SW15	36	D2
Briarwood Rd SE3	38	D3
Brick Ct EC4	**6**	**J2**
Brick La E1	18	E4
Brick La E2	18	E2
Bricklayer's Arms Distribution Cen SE1	25	D5
Brick St W1	24	B2
Bride Ct EC4	**7**	**B2**
Bride La EC4	**7**	**B2**
Bride St N7	10	F3
Bridewain St SE1	25	E4
Bridewell Pl EC4	**7**	**B2**
Bridge App NW1	10	A4
Bridge Av W6	29	E1
Bridgefoot SE1	31	E1
Bridgeland Rd E16	27	D1
Bridge La SW11	30	F4
Bridgeman Rd N1	10	F1
Bridgeman St NW8	16	F1
Bridge Meadows SE14	33	B2
Bridgend Rd SW18	37	D2
Bridge Pk SW18	37	B3
Bridge Pl SW1	24	B5
Bridge Rd E6	14	B4
Bridge Rd E15	13	A4
Bridge Rd NW10	8	A3
Bridges Ct SW11	37	E1
Bridges Pl SW6	30	A4
Bridge St SW1	24	E3
Bridge Vw W6	29	E1
Bridgeway St NW1	17	C1
Bridge Yd SE1	**7**	**G5**
Bridgwater Rd E15	12	G5
Bridle La W1	**6**	**B3**
Bridport Pl N1	18	C1
Brief St SE5	32	A4
Brierley Rd E11	13	A1
Brightfield Rd SE12	41	C3
Brightling Rd SE4	40	D4
Brightlingsea Pl E14	26	D1
Brighton Rd E6	21	C2
Brighton Rd N16	11	D1
Brighton Rd SW9	38	F2
Brightside Rd SE13	41	A4
Bright St E14	19	F5
Brill Pl NW1	17	D1
Brindley St SE14	33	D4
Brindley Clos SE18	35	D3
Brinklow Ho W2	16	C4
Brinkworth Way E9	12	D3
Brinton Wk SE1	**7**	**B6**
Brion Pl E14	19	G4
Brisbane St SE5	32	C3
Briset Rd SE9	41	G1
Bristol Gdns W9	16	E2
Bristol Rd E7	13	F3
Britannia Gate E16	27	D2
Britannia Rd E14	26	E5
Britannia Rd SW6	30	C3
Britannia Row N1	11	A5
Britannia Wk N1	17	F2
British Gro W4	29	B1
British Gro Pas W4	29	B1
British St E3	19	D2
Britten St SW3	30	F1
Britton St EC1	18	A3
Brixham Gdns, Ilf.	14	G2
Brixham St E16	28	B2
Brixton Hill SW2	38	E5
Brixton Oval SW2	38	G2
Brixton Rd SW9	31	G5
Brixton Sta Rd SW9	38	G2
Brixton Water La SW2	38	F3
Broadbridge Cl SE3	34	D3
Broad Ct WC2	**6**	**F2**
Broadfield La NW1	10	E4
Broadfield Rd SE6	41	B5
Broadfields Way NW10	8	B2
Broadgate E13	20	F1
Broadgate E16	20	G5
Broadhinton Rd SW4	38	B1
Broadhurst Gdns NW6	9	C3
Broad La EC2	18	D4
Broadley St NW8	16	F3
Broadley Ter NW1	16	F3
Broad Sanctuary SW1	24	D3
Broad Wk NW1	17	B2
Broad Wk SE3	41	F1
Broad Wk W1	24	A2
Broad Wk, The W8	23	C2
Broadwalk E15	13	A4
Broadwalk Pl E14	26	G2
Broadwall SE1	**7**	**A5**
Broadwater Rd SE28	28	F4
Broadway E15	13	A4
Broadway SW1	24	D4
Broadway, Bark.	14	E4
Broadway, The E13	20	E1
Broadway Mkt E8	11	G5
Broadwick St W1	**6**	**A3**
Brockenhurst Gdns, Ilf.	14	E2
Brockham St SE1	25	B4
Brockill Cres SE4	40	C2
Brocklebank Rd SE7	27	E5
Brocklebank Rd SW18	37	D5
Brocklehurst St SE14	33	B3
Brockley Footpath SE15	40	A2
Brockley Gdns SE4	33	B5
Brockley Gro SE4	40	D3
Brockley Hall Rd SE4	40	C4
Brockley Ms SE4	40	C3
Brockley Pk SE23	40	C4
Brockley Ri SE23	40	C4
Brockley Rd SE4	40	D1
Brockley Vw SE23	40	D5
Brockley Way SE4	40	B3
Brock Pl E3	19	F3
Brock Rd E13	20	E4
Brockwell Pk Gdns SE24	38	G5
Brockwell Pk Row SW2	38	G4
Brodlove La E1	26	B1
Broken Wf EC4	**7**	**D3**
Brokesley St E3	19	D3
Broke Wk E8	11	F5
Bromar Rd SE5	39	D1
Bromehead Rd E1	19	F5
Bromell's Rd SW4	38	C2
Brome Rd SE9	42	B1
Bromfelde Rd SW4	31	D5
Bromfelde Wk SW4	31	D5
Bromfield St N1	17	G1
Bromley Hall Rd E14	19	G4
Bromley High St E3	19	F2
Bromley St E1	19	B4
Brompton Pk Cres SW6	30	C2
Brompton Pl SW3	23	F4
Brompton Rd SW1	23	F4
Brompton Rd SW3	23	F4
Brompton Rd SW7	23	F4
Brompton Sq SW3	23	F4
Bromyard Av W3	22	A2
Bromyard Ho SE15	32	G3
Brondesbury Ct NW2	8	E3
Brondesbury Pk NW2	8	D3
Brondesbury Pk NW2	8	D3
Brondesbury Rd NW6	16	A1
Brondesbury Vil NW6	16	A1
Bronsart Rd SW6	29	G3
Bronte Ho NW6	16	B2
Bronti Cl SE17	32	B1
Bronze St SE8	33	E3
Brookbank Rd SE13	40	E1
Brookdale Rd SE6	40	F4
Brook Dr SE11	24	G5
Brooke Av E6	21	B3
Brooke St EC1	17	G4
Brookfield Rd E9	12	C3
Brook Gdns SW13	36	B1
Brook Grn W6	22	F5
Brookhill Cl SE18	35	D1
Brookhill Rd SE18	35	D1
Brooking Rd E7	13	D2
Brooklands Pk SE3	41	D1
Brooklands Rd SW4	38	D1
Brook La SE3	34	E1
Brookmill Rd SE8	33	E4
Brook Av E6	21	B3
Brooksbank St E9	12	B3
Brooksby St N1	10	G4
Brooksby's Wk E9	12	B2
Brook's Ms W1	24	B1
Brook Rd E13	13	D5
Brook St W1	17	B5
Brook St W2	23	E1
Brooksville Av NW6	8	G5
Brookville Rd SW6	30	A3
Brookway SE3	41	D1
Brookwood Av SW13	29	B5
Brookwood Rd SW18	37	B3
Broome Way SE5	32	B3
Broomfield St E14	19	E4
Broomgrove Rd SW9	31	F5
Broomhill Rd SW18	37	B3
Broomhouse La SW6	30	B5
Broomhouse Rd SW6	30	B5
Broomsleigh St NW6	9	A2
Broomwood Rd SW11	37	G4
Brougham Rd E8	11	F5
Brougham St SW11	30	G5
Broughton Dr SW9	39	A2
Broughton Rd SW6	30	D4
Broughton St SW8	31	A5
Brownfield St E14	19	F5
Brown Hart Gdns W1	24	A1
Brownhill Rd SE6	40	F5
Browning Cl, Well.	35	G4
Browning Rd E12	14	B3
Browning St SE17	32	B1
Brownlow Ms WC1	17	F3
Brownlow Rd E8	11	E5
Brownlow Rd NW10	8	A4
Brown's Bldgs EC3	**7**	**J2**
Browns La NW5	10	B2
Brown St W1	16	G5
Broxash Rd SW11	38	A4
Broxwood Way NW8	9	F5
Bruce Rd E3	19	F2
Bruckner St W10	16	A2
Brunel Est W2	16	B4
Brunel Rd SE16	26	A3
Brunel Rd W3	15	A4
Brune St E1	18	E3
Brunswick Ct SE1	25	D3
Brunswick Gdns W8	23	B2
Brunswick Pk SE5	32	C4
Brunswick Pl N1	18	C2
Brunswick Pl NW1	17	A3
Brunswick Quay SE16	26	B4
Brunswick Sq WC1	17	E3
Brunswick Vil SE5	32	D4
Brunton Pl E14	19	C5
Brushfield St E1	18	D4
Brussels Rd SW11	37	E2
Bruton La W1	24	B1
Bruton Pl W1	24	B1
Bruton St W1	24	B1
Bryan Av NW10	8	D4
Bryan Rd SE16	26	D3
Bryanston Pl W1	16	G4
Bryanston Sq W1	16	G4
Bryanston St W1	16	G5
Bryant Cl E2	18	E1
Bryant St E15	13	A4
Bryantwood Rd N7	10	G2
Brydges Pl WC2	**6**	**E4**
Brydges Rd E15	13	A2
Brymay Cl E3	19	E1
Brynmaer Rd SW11	30	G4
Bryony Rd W12	22	C1
Buchanan Gdns NW10	15	D1
Buchan Rd SE15	40	A1
Bucharest Rd SW18	37	D5
Buckfast St E2	18	F2
Buckhold Rd SW18	37	B4
Buckhurst St E1	18	G3
Buckingham Arc WC2	**6**	**F4**
Buckingham Av, Well.	42	G2
Buckingham Gate SW1	24	C4
Buckingham La SE23	40	C5
Buckingham Palace Rd SW1	24	B5
Buckingham Rd E15	13	C2
Buckingham Rd N1	18	D1
Buckingham Rd NW10	15	B1
Buckingham St WC2	**6**	**F4**
Buckland Cres NW3	9	E4
Buckland St N1	18	C1
Bucklers All SW6	30	A2
Bucklersbury EC4	**7**	**F2**
Bucklersbury Pas EC4	**7**	**F2**
Buckley Cl SE23	39	G5
Buckley Rd NW6	9	A4
Buckmaster Rd SW11	37	F2
Bucknall St WC2	**6**	**D1**
Bucknell Cl SW2	38	F2
Bucknall Rd SW2	38	F2
Buckstone Cl SE23	40	A4
Buck St NW1	10	B4
Buckters Rents SE16	26	C2
Budge Row EC4	**7**	**F3**
Budge's Wk W2	23	D1
Buer Rd SW6	29	G5
Bugsby's Way SE7	27	D5
Bugsby's Way SE10	27	D5
Bulinga St SW1	24	D5
Bullace Row SE5	32	C2
Bullards Pl E2	19	B2
Bullen St SW11	30	F5
Buller Cl SE15	32	F3

Street	Ref.
Buller Rd, Bark.	14 G4
Bull Inn Ct WC2	**6 F4**
Bullivant St E14	26 G1
Bull Rd E15	20 C1
Bull's Head Pas EC3	**7 H2**
Bulmer Pl W11	23 B2
Bulstrode St W1	17 A5
Bulwer St W12	23 G1
Bunhill Row EC1	18 C3
Bunhouse Pl SW1	31 A1
Bunning Way N7	10 E4
Bunton St SE18	28 C4
Burbage Cl SE1	25 A4
Burbage Rd SE21	39 A4
Burbage Rd SE24	39 B4
Burcham St E14	19 F5
Burchell Rd SE15	32 G4
Burder Cl N1	11 D3
Burdett Rd E3	19 D3
Burdett Rd E14	19 D3
Burford Rd E6	21 A4
Burford Rd E15	13 A4
Burges Ct E6	14 C4
Burges Gro SW13	29 C2
Burges Rd E6	14 A4
Burgess Hill NW2	9 B1
Burgess Rd E15	13 B1
Burge St SE1	25 C4
Burghley Hall Cl SW19	36 G5
Burghley Rd NW5	10 B2
Burghley Twr W3	22 B1
Burgh St N1	18 A1
Burgon St EC4	**7 C2**
Burgos Gro SE10	33 G3
Burgoyne Rd SW9	38 F1
Burke Cl SW15	36 A2
Burke St E16	20 C5
Burland Rd SW11	37 G3
Burleigh Pl SW15	36 F3
Burleigh St WC2	**6 G3**
Burley Rd E16	20 F5
Burlington Arc W1	**6 A4**
Burlington Cl W9	16 C5
Burlington Gdns W1	**6 A4**
Burlington La W4	29 A3
Burlington Ms SW15	37 A3
Burlington Rd SW6	30 D5
Burma Rd N16	11 C1
Burnaby St SW10	30 D3
Burne Jones Ho W14	23 A5
Burnels Av E6	21 C2
Burnet St NW1	16 F4
Burnett Cl E9	12 A2
Burney St SE10	33 G3
Burnfoot Av SW6	29 G4
Burnham NW3	9 F4
Burnham St E2	19 A2
Burnley Rd NW10	8 C2
Burnley Rd SW9	31 F5
Burnsall St SW3	30 G1
Burnside Cl SE16	26 B2
Burns Rd NW10	8 B5
Burns Rd SW11	30 G5
Burnt Ash Hill SE12	41 A3
Burnt Ash Rd SE12	41 C3
Burnthwaite Rd SW6	30 A4
Burrage Gro SE18	28 E5
Burrage Pl SE18	35 D1
Burrage Rd SE18	35 E2
Burrard Rd E16	20 E5
Burrard Rd NW6	9 B2
Burr Cl E1	25 F2
Burrell St SE1	**7 B5**
Burrells Wf Sq E14	33 F1
Burrow Rd SE22	39 F2
Burrows Rd NW10	15 E2
Burslem St E1	18 F5
Burstock Rd SW15	36 G2
Burston Rd SW15	36 F3
Burton La SW9	31 G5
Burton Rd NW6	9 A4
Burton Rd SW9	32 A5
Burton St WC1	17 D2
Burt Rd E16	27 F2
Burwash Rd SE18	35 F1
Burwell Wk E3	19 E3
Burwood Pl W2	16 F5
Bury Cl WC1	**7 J1**
Bury Pl WC1	**6 E1**
Bury St EC3	**7 J2**
Bury St SW1	**6 A5**
Bury Wk SW3	30 F1
Busby Pl NW5	10 D3
Bushberry Rd E9	12 C3
Bushby Hill Rd SE5	32 D4
Bushey Rd E13	20 F1
Bush La EC4	**7 F3**
Bushmoor Cres SE18	35 E3
Bush Rd E8	11 G5
Bush Rd SE8	26 E5
Bushwood Dr SE1	25 E5
Butcher Row E1	26 B1
Butcher Row E14	26 B1
Butchers Rd E16	20 D5
Bute Gdns W6	22 F5
Bute St SW7	23 E5
Butlers Wf SE1	25 E2
Butterfly La SE9	42 D4
Buttermere Dr SW15	36 G3
Buttermere Wk E8	11 E3
Butterwick W6	22 E5
Buttesland St N1	18 C2
Buttmarsh Cl SE18	35 D1
Buttsbury Rd, Ilf.	14 E2
Buxhall Cres E9	12 D5
Buxted Rd E8	11 E4
Buxted Rd SE22	39 D2
Buxton Rd E6	21 A2
Buxton Rd E15	13 B2
Buxton Rd N19	8 D3
Buxton Rd NW2	8 D3
Buxton Rd SW14	36 A1
Buxton St E1	18 E3
Byam St SW6	30 D5
Bye, The W3	22 A1
Byfeld Gdns SW13	29 C4
Byfield Cl SE16	26 C3
Byford Cl E15	13 B4
Bygrove St E14	19 F5
Byng Pl WC1	17 D3
Byng St E14	26 E3
Byron Av E12	14 A3
Byron Cl E8	11 F5
Byron Ms NW3	9 F2
Bythorn St SW9	38 F1
Byward St EC3	**7 J4**
Bywater Pl SE16	26 C2
Bywater St SW3	30 G1

C

Street	Ref.
Cabbell St NW1	16 F4
Cable St E1	25 F1
Cable Trade Pk SE7	27 F5
Cabot Pl E14	26 E2
Cabot Sq E14	26 E2
Cabul Rd SW11	30 F5
Cade Rd SE10	34 A4
Cader Rd SW18	37 D4
Cadet Dr SE1	25 F5
Cadet Pl SE10	34 B1
Cadiz St SE17	32 B1
Cadogan Gdns SW3	23 G5
Cadogan Gate SW1	23 G5
Cadogan La SW1	24 A4
Cadogan Pl SW1	23 G4
Cadogan Pl SE18	28 D4
Cadogan Sq SW1	23 G4
Cadogan Sq SW3	23 G5
Cadogan Ter E9	12 D3
Caedmon Rd N7	10 F1
Cahir St E14	26 F5
Caird St W10	15 G2
Cairns Rd SW11	37 F3
Caistor Pk Rd E15	13 C5
Caistor Rd SW12	38 B5
Caithness Rd W14	22 F5
Calabria Rd N5	11 A3
Calais St SE5	32 A4
Calbourne Rd SW12	37 G5
Caldecot Rd SE5	32 B5
Calderon Rd E11	12 G1
Caldervale Rd SW4	38 D3
Calderwood St SE18	28 C5
Caldwell St SW9	31 F3
Caledonian Rd N1	17 F1
Caledonian Rd N7	10 F2
Caledonian Wf E14	27 A5
Caledonia St N1	17 E1
Caledon Rd E6	14 A5
Cale St SW3	30 G1
Caletock Way SE10	34 C1
Callcott Rd NW6	9 A4
Callendar Rd SW7	23 E4
Callow St SW3	30 E2
Calshot St N1	17 F1
Calthorpe St WC1	17 F3
Calton Av SE21	39 D3
Calvert Av E2	18 D2
Calverton Rd E6	14 C5
Calverton SE10	34 C1
Calvert Rd SE10	34 C1
Calvert's Bldgs SE1	**7 F6**
Calvin St E1	18 E3
Calydon Rd SE7	34 E1
Calypso Way SE16	26 D4
Cambalt Rd SW15	36 D3
Cambert Way SE3	41 E2
Camberwell Ch St SE5	32 C4
Camberwell Glebe SE5	32 C4
Camberwell Grn SE5	32 C4
Camberwell Gro SE5	32 C4
Camberwell New Rd SE5	31 G3
Camberwell Rd SE5	32 B2
Camberwell Sta Rd SE5	32 B4
Camborne Rd SW18	37 B5
Cambria Rd SE5	39 B1
Cambria St SW6	30 C3
Cambridge Av NW6	16 B1
Cambridge Barracks Rd SE18	28 B5
Cambridge Circ WC2	**6 D2**
Cambridge Cres E2	18 G1
Cambridge Dr SE12	41 D3
Cambridge Gdns NW6	16 B1
Cambridge Gdns W10	15 G5
Cambridge Gro W6	22 D5
Cambridge Heath Rd E1	18 G1
Cambridge Heath Rd E2	18 G1
Cambridge Pl W8	23 C3
Cambridge Rd NW6	16 B2
Cambridge Rd SW11	30 G4
Cambridge Rd SW13	29 B5
Cambridge Rd, Bark.	14 E4
Cambridge Row SE18	35 D1
Cambridge Sq W2	16 F5
Cambridge St SW1	31 B1
Cambus Rd E16	20 D4
Camden High St NW1	10 B5
Camdenhurst St E14	19 C5
Camden Lock Mkt NW1	10 D3
Camden Pk Rd NW1	10 D3
Camden Pas N1	11 A5
Camden Rd N7	10 D2
Camden Rd N7	10 C4
Camden Row SE3	34 B5
Camden Sq NW1	10 D3
Camden St NW1	10 C4
Camden Wk N1	11 A5
Camellia St SW8	31 E3
Camelot Cl SE28	28 F3
Camel Rd E16	27 G2
Camera Pl SW10	30 E2
Camilla Rd SE16	25 G5
Camlet St E2	18 E3
Camley St NW1	10 D4
Camomile St EC3	**7 H1**
Campana Rd SW6	30 B4
Campbell Gordon Way NW2	8 D1
Campbell Rd E3	19 E2
Campbell Rd E6	14 A5
Campden Gro W8	23 B3
Campden Hill Gdns W8	23 B2
Campden Hill Rd W8	23 B2
Campden Hill Sq W8	23 A2
Campden St W8	23 B2
Campfield Rd SE9	41 G5
Campion Cl E6	28 B1
Campion Rd SW15	36 E2
Camplin St SE14	33 B3
Campshill Rd SE13	40 G3
Cam Rd E15	13 A5
Canada Est SE16	26 A4
Canada Gdns SE13	40 G3
Canada Sq E14	26 F2
Canada St SE16	26 B3
Canada Way W12	22 D1
Canal Cl E1	19 C3
Canal Cl W10	15 F3
Canal Gro SE15	32 F2
Canal Path E2	11 E5
Canal St SE5	32 C2
Canal Wk N1	11 C5
Canal Way NW10	15 B3
Canal Way W10	15 F3
Canal Way Wk W10	15 F3
Canberra Rd SE7	34 F2
Cancell Rd SW9	31 G4
Candahar Rd SW11	30 F5
Candle Gro SE15	39 G1
Candy St E3	12 D5
Canfield Gdns NW6	9 D4
Canford Rd SW11	38 A3
Canham Rd W3	22 A3
Cann Hall Rd E11	13 B1
Canning Cross SE5	32 D5
Canning Pas W8	23 D4
Canning Pl W8	23 D4
Cannon Dr E14	26 E1
Cannon Hill NW6	9 B2
Cannon Pl SE7	35 A1
Cannon St EC4	**7 D2**
Cannon St Rd E1	18 G5
Cannon Wf Business Centre SE8	26 C5
Canon Beck Rd SE16	26 A3
Canonbie Rd SE23	40 A5
Canonbury Cres N1	11 B4
Canonbury Gro N1	11 B4
Canonbury La N1	11 A4
Canonbury Pk N N1	11 B3
Canonbury Pk S N1	11 B3
Canonbury Pl N1	11 A3
Canonbury Rd N1	11 A3
Canonbury Sq N1	11 A4
Canonbury St N1	11 B4
Canonbury Vil N1	11 A4
Canon Row SW1	24 E3
Canon St N1	11 B5
Canrobert St E2	18 G2
Cantelowes Rd NW1	10 D3

Canterbury Cres
SW9   38 G1
Canterbury Pl SE17   25 A5
Canterbury Rd NW6   16 B1
Canterbury Ter NW6   16 B1
Cantium Retail Pk
SE1   32 F2
Canton St E14   19 E5
Cantrell Rd E3   19 D3
Cantwell Rd SE18   35 D3
Canute Gdns SE18   26 B5
Canvey St SE1   **7 C5**
Capel Ct EC2   **7 G2**
Capel Pt E7   13 E1
Capel Rd E7   13 E1
Capel Rd E12   13 F1
Capland St NW8   16 E3
Caple Rd NW10   15 B1
Capper St WC1   17 C3
Capstan Rd SE8   26 D5
Capstan Sq E14   26 G3
Capstan Way SE16   26 G2
Caradoc Cl W2   16 B5
Caradoc St SE10   34 B1
Caraway Cl E13   20 E4
Carbis Rd E14   19 D5
Carburton St W1   17 B4
Carden Rd SE15   39 G1
Cardiff St SE18   35 G3
Cardigan Rd E3   19 D1
Cardigan Rd SW13   29 C5
Cardigan St SE11   31 G1
Cardinal Bourne St
SE1   25 C4
Cardinal Hinsley Cl
NW10   15 C1
Cardinal Pl SW15   36 F2
Cardine Ms SE15   32 G3
Cardington St NW1   17 C2
Cardozo Rd N7   10 E2
Cardross St W6   22 D4
Cardwell Rd N7   10 E1
Carew St SE5   32 B5
Carey Gdns SW8   31 C4
Carey La EC2   **7 D1**
Carey St WC2   **6 H2**
Carker's La NW5   10 B2
Carleton Rd N7   10 D2
Carlile Cl E3   19 D3
Carlingford Rd NW3   9 E1
Carlisle Av EC3   **7 J2**
Carlisle Av W3   15 A5
Carlisle La SE1   24 F4
Carlisle Ms NW8   16 E4
Carlisle Pl SW1   24 C4
Carlisle Rd NW6   8 G5
Carlisle St W1   **6 C2**
Carlos Pl W1   24 A1
Carlton Cl SW9   32 A4
Carlton Dr SW15   36 G3
Carlton Gdns SW1 **6 C6**
Carlton Gro SE15   32 G4
Carlton Hill NW8   16 C1
Carlton Ho Ter SW1 **6 C6**
Carlton Rd E12   13 G1
Carlton St SW1   **6 C4**
Carlton Twr Pl SW1   23 G4
Carlton Vale NW6   16 C1
Carlyle Pl SW15   36 F2
Carlyle Rd E12   14 A1
Carlyle Sq SW3   30 E1
Carmalt Gdns SW15 36 F2
Carmelite St EC4   **7 A3**
Carmen St E14   19 F5
Carmichael Ms
SW18   37 E5
Carnaby St W1   **6 A2**
Carnarvon Rd E15   13 C3
Carnbrook Rd SE3   41 G1
Carnecke Gdns SE9   42 A3
Carnegie St N1   10 F5
Carnoustie Dr N1   10 F4
Carnwath Rd SW6   37 B1
Carolina Cl E15   13 B2
Caroline Gdns SE2   32 G3
Caroline Pl SW11   31 A5

Caroline Pl W2   23 C1
Caroline St E1   19 B5
Caroline Ter SW1   24 A5
Caroline Wk W6   29 G2
Carol St NW1   10 C5
Carpenters Pl SW4   38 D2
Carpenters Rd E15   12 F3
Carrara Cl SW9   39 A2
Carrara Rd E8   11 F2
Carrara Wf SW6   36 G1
Carr Gro SE18   26 A5
Carriage Dr E SW11   31 A3
Carriage Dr N SW11   31 A2
Carriage Dr S SW11   30 G4
Carriage Dr W SW11 30 G3
Carriage Dr SE18   30 G4
Carrol Cl NW5   10 B1
Carroll Cl E15   13 C2
Carronade Pl SE28   28 D4
Carron Cl E14   19 F5
Carroun Rd SW8   31 F3
Carr St E14   19 C4
Carslake Rd SW15   36 E4
Carson Rd E16   20 D3
Carston Cl SE12   41 C3
Carswell Rd SE6   40 G5
Carteret St SW1   24 D3
Carteret Way SE8   26 C5
Carter La EC4   **7 C2**
Carter Pl SE17   32 B1
Carter Rd E13   13 E5
Carter St SE17   32 B2
Carthew Rd W6   22 D4
Carthew Vil W6   22 D4
Cartier Circle E14   26 F2
Cartier Circle E14   **6 F4**
Cartridge Pl SE18   28 D4
Cartwright Gdns
WC1   17 E2
Cartwright St E1   25 E1
Cartwright Way
SW13   29 B4
Carver Rd SE24   39 B4
Cary Rd E11   13 B1
Casella Rd SE14   33 B3
Casey Cl NW8   16 F2
Casino Av SE24   39 B3
Caspian Gdns SE5   32 C3
Caspian Wk E16   20 G5
Cassidy Rd SW6   30 B3
Cassland Rd E9   12 A4
Casslee Rd SE6   40 D5
Casson St E1   18 F4
Castellain Rd W9   16 C3
Castello Av SW15   36 E3
Castelnau SW13   29 D2
Casterbridge NW6   9 C5
Casterbridge Rd
SE3   41 D1
Castile Rd SE18   28 C5
**Castle Baynard St
EC4**   **7 C3**
Castlebrook Cl SE11 25 A5
Castlecombe Dr
SW19   36 F5
Castle Ct EC3   **7 G2**
Castlehaven Rd
NW1   10 B4
Castle La SW1   24 C4
Castlemaine Twr
SW11   30 G4
Castle Pl NW1   10 B3
Castle Pt E13   20 F1
Castle Rd NW1   10 B3
Castletown Rd W14   29 G1
Castlewood Dr SE9   35 F5
Castle Yd SE1   **7 C5**
Castor La E14   19 F1
Caterham Rd SE13   40 G1
Catesby St SE17   25 C5
Catford Bdy SE6   40 E5
Catford Hill SE6   40 E5
Cathay St SE16   25 G3
Cathcart Rd SW10   30 D2
Cathcart St NW5   10 B3

Cathedral St SE1   **7 F5**
Catherine Gro SE10   33 F4
Cathcart Rd SW12   22 D3
Cathnor Rd W12   22 D3
Catlin St SE16   25 G5
Cato Rd SW4   38 D1
Cato St W1   16 F4
Catton St WC1   17 F4
Caulfield Rd E6   14 B4
Caulfield Rd SE15   32 G5
Causeway, The
SW18   37 C2
Causton St SW1   24 D5
Cautley Av SW4   38 C3
Cavalry Gdns SW15   36 G3
Cavell St E1   18 G4
Cavendish Av NW8   16 F2
Cavendish Cl NW8   16 E2
Cavendish Ct EC3 **7 J1**
Cavendish Gdns,
Bark.   14 G2
Cavendish Pl W1   17 B5
Cavendish Rd NW6   8 B4
Cavendish Rd SW12 38 B4
Cavendish Sq W1   17 B5
Cavendish St N1   18 C1
Cave Rd E13   20 E1
Caversham Rd NW5   10 C3
Caversham St SW3   30 G2
Caverswall St SW12 15 E5
Caxton Gro E3   19 E2
Caxton Rd W12   22 F3
Caxton St SW1   24 C4
Cearns Ho E6   13 G5
Cecil Av, Bark.   14 F4
Cecil Ct WC2   **6 D4**
Cecilia Rd E8   11 F2
Cecil Rd E13   13 D5
Cecil Rd NW10   8 A5
Cecil Rd, Ilf.   14 D1
Cedar Cl E3   12 D5
Cedar Cl SE9   42 A4
Cedarhurst Dr SE9   43 F3
Cedarne Rd SW6   30 C3
Cedar Rd NW2   8 E1
Cedars Cl SE13   41 A1
Cedars Rd E15   13 B3
Cedars Rd SW13   29 B5
Cedar Way NW1   10 D4
Celandine Cl E14   19 E4
Celandine Dr E8   11 E4
Celandine Dr E8   11 E4
Celestial Gdns SE13 41 A2
Celia Rd N19   10 D1
Celtic St E14   19 F4
Cemetery La SE7   35 A2
Cemetery Rd E7   13 C1
Centaur St SE1   24 F4
Central Av SW11   30 G3
Central Mkts EC1   18 A4
Central Pk Rd E6   20 G1
Central St EC1   18 B2
**Centre at the Circ
W1**
Centre St E2   18 F1
Centurion Cl N7   10 F4
Cephas Av E1   19 A3
Cephas St E1   19 A3
Cerise Rd SE15   32 F4
Ceylon Rd W14   22 F4
Chadbourn St E14   19 F4
Chadd Grn E13   13 D5
Chadwell Rd E7   12 D5
Chadwell St EC1   17 G2
Chadwick Cl SW15   36 B5
Chadwick Rd NW10   8 B5
Chadwick Rd SE15   32 E5
Chadwick St SW1   24 D4
Chadwin Rd E13   20 E2
Chagford St NW1   16 G3

Chalbury Wk N1   17 F1
Chalcot Cres NW1   9 G5
Chalcot Gdns NW3 **9 G3**
Chalcot Rd NW1   10 A4
Chalcot Sq NW1   10 A4
Chalcroft Rd SE13   41 B3
Chaldon Rd SW6   29 G3
Chale Rd SW2   38 E4
Chalk Farm Rd NW1   10 A3
Chalk Rd E13   20 E4
Challoner St W14   30 A1
Chalsey Rd SE4   40 D2
Chalton St NW1   17 D1
Chamberlayne Rd
NW10   15 F2
Chambers La NW10   8 D4
Chambers St N7   10 E1
Chambers St SE16   25 F3
Chambers St E1   25 E1
Chambord St E2   18 E2
Champion Gro SE5   39 C1
Champion Hill SE5   39 C1
Champion Hill Est
SE5   39 D1
Champion Pk SE5   32 C5
Chancellors Rd W6   29 F1
Chancellors St W6   29 F1
Chancel St SE1   **7 B5**
Chancery La WC2 **6 H1**
Chance St E1   18 E3
Chance St E2   18 E3
Chandler Av E16   20 D4
Chandlers Ms E14   26 E3
Chandlers Way SW2 38 G5
Chandos Pl WC2   **6 E4**
Chandos Rd E15   13 A2
Chandos Rd NW2   8 E2
Chandos Rd NW10   15 A3
Chandos St W1   17 B4
Change All EC3   **7 G2**
Channelsea Rd E15   13 A5
Chantrey Rd SW9   38 F1
Chant Rd E15   11 A5
Chant Sq E15   13 A4
Chant St E15   13 A4
Chapel Ho St E14   33 F1
Chapel Mkt N1   17 G1
Chapel Pl W1   17 B5
Chapel Side W2   23 C1
Chapel St NW1   16 F4
Chapel St SW1   24 A4
Chaplin Cl SE1   24 G3
Chaplin Rd E15   20 B1
Chaplin Rd E9   8 C3
Chapman Pk Ind Est
NW10   8 B3
Chapman Rd E9   12 D3
Chapman St E1   25 G1
Chapone Pl W1   **6 C2**
Chapter Ho EC4   **7 D2**
Chapter Rd NW2   8 C4
Chapter Rd SE17   32 A1
Chapter St SW1   24 D5
Charecroft Way
W12   22 F3
Charford Rd E16   20 D4
Chargeable La E13   20 C3
Chargeable St E16   20 C3
Charing Cross SW1 **6 E5**
**Charing Cross Rd
WC2**   **6 D1**
Charlbert St NW8   16 F1
Charlemont Rd E6   21 B2
Charles Barry Cl
SW4   38 C1
Charles Coveney Rd
SE15   32 E4
Charles Dickens Ho
E2   18 G2
Charles Grinling Wk
SE18   28 C5
Charles II St SW1 **6 C5**
Charles Sq N1   18 D2
Charles St E16   27 G2
Charles St SW13   29 A5

Charles St W1 24 B2
Charleston St SE17 25 B5
Charles Whincup Rd E16 27 E2
Charleville Rd W14 29 C2
Charlotte Despard Av SW11 31 A4
Charlotte Ms W10 15 F5
Charlotte Rd EC2 18 D3
Charlotte Row SW4 38 C1
Charlotte St W1 17 C4
Charlotte Ter N1 10 F5
Charlton On La SE7 34 F1
Charlton Dene SE7 34 F1
Charlton Kings Rd NW5 10 D2
Charlton La SE7 34 G3
Charlton Pk La SE7 34 G3
Charlton Pk Rd SE7 34 G3
Charlton Pl N1 10 F3
Charlton Rd NW10 8 A5
Charlton Rd SE3 34 D3
Charlton Rd SE7 34 E3
Charlton Way SE3 34 B4
Charlwood Pl SW1 24 C5
Charlwood Rd SW15 36 F1
Charlwood St SW1 31 C1
Charnwood Gdns E14 26 E5
Charrington St NW1 17 D1
Charterhouse Rd E8 11 F1
Charterhouse Sq EC1 18 A4
Charterhouse St EC1 18 A4
Charteris Rd NW6 9 A5
Chartfield Av SW15 36 D3
Chartfield Sq SW15 36 F3
Chart St N1 13 G1
Chase, The E12 13 G1
Chase, The SW4 38 B1
Chaseley St E14 19 C5
Chatfield Rd SW11 37 D1
Chatham Pl E9 12 A3
Chatham Rd SW11 37 G4
Chatham St SE17 25 C5
Chatsworth Ct W8 23 B5
Chatsworth Rd E15 13 C2
Chatsworth Rd NW2 8 F3
Chatto Rd SW11 37 G3
Chaucer Ct N16 11 D1
Chaucer Dr SE1 25 E5
Chaucer Rd E7 13 D3
Chaucer Rd SE24 39 B3
Chaucer Rd, Well. 35 G4
Chaundrye Cl SE9 42 A4
Chauntler Cl E16 20 E5
Cheapside EC2 7 E2
Cheesemans Ter W14 30 A1
Chelmer Rd E9 12 B2
Chelmsford Cl W6 29 F2
Chelmsford Sq NW10 8 E5
Chelsea Br SW1 31 B2
Chelsea Br SW8 31 B2
Chelsea Br Rd SW1 31 A1
Chelsea Embk SW3 30 F2
Chelsea Harbour SW10 30 D4
Chelsea Harbour Dr SW10 30 D4
Chelsea Manor Gdns SW3 30 F2
Chelsea Manor St SW3 30 F1
Chelsea Pk Gdns SW3 30 E2
Chelsea Sq SW3 30 E1
Chelsea Wf SW10 30 E3
Chelsham Rd SW4 38 D1
Chelsworth Dr SE18 35 F2
Cheltenham Gdns E6 21 A1

Cheltenham Rd SE15 40 A2
Cheltenham Ter SW3 30 G1
Chelverton Rd SW15 36 F2
Chelwood Wk SE4 40 C2
Chenappa Cl E13 20 D2
Chenies Pl NW1 17 D1
Chenies St WC1 17 D4
Cheniston Gdns W8 23 C4
Chepstow Cres W11 23 B1
Chepstow Pl W2 16 B5
Chepstow Rd W2 16 B5
Chepstow Vil W11 23 A1
Chepstow Way SE15 32 E3
Cherbury St N1 18 C1
Cheriton Dr SE18 35 F3
Cherry Gdn St SE16 25 G3
Cherrywood Cl E3 19 C2
Cherrywood Dr SW15 36 F2
Chertsey Rd, Ilf. 14 F1
Cheryls Cl SW6 30 C2
Chesham Ms SW1 24 A4
Chesham Pl SW1 24 A4
Chesham St SW1 24 A4
Cheshire Ct EC4 7 A2
Cheshire St E2 18 E3
Chesholm Rd N16 11 D1
Cheshunt Rd E7 13 E3
Chesil Ct E2 19 A1
Chesilton Rd SW6 30 A4
Chesley Gdns E6 21 A1
Chesney St SW11 31 A4
Chesson Rd W14 30 A2
Chester Cl SW1 24 A3
Chester Cl SW13 36 D1
Chester Cl SE5 32 C3
Chesterfield Gdns W1 24 B2
Chesterfield Gro SE22 39 E4
Chesterfield Hill W1 24 B1
Chesterfield St W1 24 B2
Chesterfield Wk SE10 34 A4
Chesterfield Way SE15 33 A3
Chesterford Gdns NW3 9 C1
Chester Gate NW1 17 B2
Chester Ms SW1 24 B4
Chester Rd E13 13 G4
Chester Rd E16 20 B3
Chester Rd NW1 17 A2
Chester Rd, Sid. 42 G3
Chester Row SW1 24 A5
Chester Sq SW1 24 B4
Chester St E2 18 E2
Chester St SW1 24 B4
Chesterton Rd E13 20 D2
Chesterton Rd W10 15 F4
Chesterton Ter E13 20 D2
Chester Way SE11 24 G5
Chestnut Av E7 13 E1
Chestnut Cl SE14 33 D4
Chestnut Gro SW12 38 A5
Chestnut Ri SE18 35 F2
Chetwood Wk E6 21 A5
Chetwynd Rd NW5 10 B1
Cheval Pl SW7 23 F4
Cheval St E14 26 E4
Chevening Rd NW6 16 B1
Chevening Rd SE10 34 C1
Chevron Cl E16 20 D5
Cheyne Gdns SW3 30 F2
Cheyne Ms SW3 30 F2
Cheyne Pl SW3 30 G2
Cheyne Row SW3 30 F2
Cheyne Wk SW3 30 F2
Cheyne Wk SW10 30 E3
Chichele Rd NW2 8 F2
Chicheley St SE1 24 F3

Chichester Cl E6 21 A5
Chichester Cl SE3 34 F4
Chichester Rents WC2 6 J1
Chichester Rd NW6 16 B1
Chichester Rd W2 16 B4
Chichester Rd SW1 31 C1
Chichester Way E14 33 H1
Chicksand St E1 18 E4
Chiddingstone St SW6 30 B5
Childeric Rd SE14 33 C3
Childers St SE8 33 B2
Child La SE10 27 C4
Child's Pl SW5 23 B5
Child's St SW5 23 B5
Chillingworth Rd N7 10 F2
Chiltern Rd E3 19 E3
Chiltern St W1 17 A4
Chilton Gro SE8 26 B5
Chiltonian Ind Est SE12 41 C4
Chilton St E2 18 E3
Chilver St SE10 34 C1
Chilworth Ms W2 16 D5
Chilworth St W2 16 D5
Ching Ct WC2 6 E2
Chipka St E14 26 G3
Chipley St SE14 33 C2
Chippenham Gdns NW6 16 B2
Chippenham Ms W9 16 B3
Chippenham Rd W9 16 B3
Chipstead St SW6 30 B5
Chip St SW4 38 D1
Chisenhale Rd E3 19 C1
Chisledon Wk E9 12 D3
Chiswell St EC1 18 B4
Chiswick La W4 29 A1
Chiswick La S W4 29 B1
Chiswick Mall W4 29 B2
Chiswick Mall W6 29 B2
Chiswick Wf W4 29 B2
Chitty St W1 17 C4
Chivalry Rd SW11 37 F3
Chobham Rd E15 13 A2
Cholmeley Av NW10 15 C1
Choumert Gro SE15 32 F5
Choumert Ms SE15 32 F5
Choumert Rd SE15 32 E5
Choumert Sq SE15 32 F5
Chrisp St E14 19 F4
Christchurch Av NW6 8 G4
Christchurch Ct NW6 8 G4
Christ Ch Pas EC1 7 C1
Christchurch St SW3 30 G2
Christchurch Way SE10 27 B5
Christian Ct SE16 26 D2
Christian St E1 18 F5
Christie Rd E9 12 C3
Christopher Cl SE16 26 B3
Christopher St EC2 18 C3
Chryssell Rd SW9 31 G3
Chubworthy St SE14 33 C2
Chudleigh Cres, Ilf. 14 F2
Chudleigh Rd NW6 8 F4
Chudleigh Rd SE4 40 D3
Chudleigh St E1 19 B5
Chumleigh St SE5 32 D2
Churchbury Rd SE9 41 G5
Church Cres E9 12 B4
Church Entry EC4 7 C2
Church Gate SW6 36 G1
Church Gro SE13 40 E3
Church Hill SE18 28 B4
Churchill Gdns SW1 31 C1
Churchill Gdns Rd SW1 31 B1
Churchill Pl E14 26 F2
Churchill Rd E16 20 F5
Churchill Rd NW2 8 D3
Churchill Rd NW5 10 B1

Churchill Wk E9 12 A2
Churchmead Rd NW10 8 C3
Church Path N5 11 A2
Church Path NW10 8 A4
Church Pl SW1 6 B4
Church Rd E12 14 B2
Church Rd N1 11 B3
Church Rd NW10 8 A5
Church Rd SW13 29 B5
Church Rd, Bark. 14 E3
Church Row NW3 9 D1
Church St E15 13 B5
Church St E16 28 D2
Church St NW8 16 E3
Church St W2 16 E4
Church St W4 29 A2
Church St East N18 16 E3
Church St N E15 13 B5
Church Ter SE13 41 B1
Church Ter SW8 31 D5
Church Wk N16 11 C1
Church Wk SW13 29 C4
Church Wk SW15 36 D3
Churchway NW1 17 D2
Churchwell Path E9 12 A2
Churston Av E13 13 E5
Churton Pl SW1 24 C5
Churton St SW1 24 C5
Cicada Rd SW18 37 D3
Cicely Rd SE15 32 F4
Cinnabar Wf E1 25 F2
Cinnamon Row SW11 37 D1
Cinnamon St E1 25 G2
Circular Way SE18 35 B2
Circus Rd NW8 16 E2
Circus St SE10 33 G3
Cirencester St W2 16 C4
Citizen Rd N7 10 G1
City Gdn Row N1 18 A1
City Mill River Towpath E15 12 F4
City Rd EC1 18 A1
Clabon Ms SW1 23 G4
Clack St SE16 26 A3
Clacton Rd E6 20 G2
Claire Pl E14 26 E4
Clancarty Rd SW6 30 B5
Clandon St SE8 33 E5
Clanricarde Gdns W2 23 B1
Clapham Common N Side SW4 38 B2
Clapham Common S Side SW4 38 B3
Clapham Common W Side SW4 38 A2
Clapham Cres SW4 38 D2
Clapham Est SW11 37 F2
Clapham High St SW4 38 D2
Clapham Manor St SW4 38 C1
Clapham Pk Est SW4 38 D4
Clapham Pk Rd SW4 38 D2
Clapham Rd SW9 38 E1
Clapham Rd Est SW4 38 D1
Claps Gate La E6 21 D3
Clapton Pas E5 12 A2
Clapton Sq E5 12 A2
Clapton Way E5 11 F1
Clara Pl SE18 28 C5
Clare Cor SE9 42 D5
Claredale St E2 18 F1
Clare Gdns E7 13 D1
Clare Ho E3 12 D5
Clare La N1 11 B4
Clare Mkt WC2 6 G2
Claremont Cl E16 28 C2
Claremont Cl N1 17 G1
Claremont Rd E7 13 E2
Claremont Rd W9 15 G1

Claremont Sq N1 17 G1
Claremont St E16 28 C2
Claremont St SE10 18 F3
Clarence Av SW4 38 D4
Clarence Cres SW4 38 D4
Clarence Gdns NW1 17 B2
Clarence La SW15 36 A4
Clarence Ms E5 11 G2
Clarence Ms SE16 26 B2
Clarence Ms SW12 38 B5
Clarence Pl E5 11 G2
Clarence Rd E5 11 G1
Clarence Rd E12 13 A2
Clarence Rd E16 20 B3
Clarence Rd NW6 9 A4
Clarence Rd SE8 33 F2
Clarence Wk SW4 31 E5
Clarence Way NW1 10 B4
Clarence Way Est NW1 10 B4
Clarendon Cl E9 12 A4
Clarendon Dr SW15 36 E2
Clarendon Gdns W9 16 D3
Clarendon Pl W2 23 F1
Clarendon Ri SE13 40 G1
Clarendon Rd W11 22 G1
Clarendon St SW1 31 B1
Clarendon Wk W11 15 G5
Clare Rd NW6 8 C4
Clare Rd SE14 33 F3
Clare St E2 18 G1
Clareville Gro SW7 23 D5
Clareville St SW7 23 D5
Clarewood Wk SW9 38 G2
Clarges Ms W1 24 B2
Clarges St W1 24 B2
Claribel Rd SW9 32 A5
Clarissa St E8 11 E5
Clarkson Rd E16 20 C5
Clarkson Row NW1 17 B1
Clarksons, The, Bark. 21 E1
Clarkson St E2 18 G2
Clarks Pl EC2 7 H1
Clark St E1 18 G4
Claude Rd E13 13 E5
Claude St E14 32 G5
Claude St E14 26 E5
Claudia Jones Way SW2 38 E4
Claughton Rd E13 20 F1
Clavell St SE10 33 G2
Claverdale Rd SW2 38 F5
Clavering Av SW13 39 D2
Claverton St SW1 31 C1
Claxton Gro W6 29 F1
Claybrook Rd W6 29 F2
Claylands Pl SW8 31 F4
Claylands Rd SW8 31 F3
Claymill Ho SE18 35 E1
Claypole Rd E15 19 G1
Clays La E15 12 F2
Clays La E15 12 F2
Clayton Cres N1 10 E5
Clayton Ms SE10 34 A4
Clayton Rd SE15 32 F4
Clayton St SE11 31 G2
Cleanthus Rd SE18 35 D4
Clearwell Dr W9 16 C3
Cleaver Sq SE11 31 G1
Cleaver St SE11 31 G1
Clegg St E13 20 D1
Clematis St W12 22 B1
Clem Attlee Ct SW6 30 A2
Clemence St E14 19 D4
Clement Av SW4 38 D2
Clement Cl NW6 8 C5
Clements Av E16 27 D1
Clement's Inn WC2 6 H2
Clement's Inn Pas WC2 6 H2
Clements La EC4 7 G3
Clements Rd E6 14 B4
Clements Rd SE16 25 F4
Clephane Rd N1 11 B3
Clerkenwell Cl EC1 17 G3
Clerkenwell Grn EC1 18 A3

Clerkenwell Rd EC1 17 G3
Clermont Rd E9 12 A5
Cleveland Av W4 22 B5
Cleveland Gdns SW13 29 B5
Cleveland Pl SW1 6 B5
Cleveland Rd N1 11 C4
Cleveland Rd SW13 29 B5
Cleveland Row SW1 6 A6
Cleveland Sq W2 16 D5
Cleveland St W1 17 B3
Cleveland Ter W2 16 D5
Cleveland Way E1 19 A3
Cleveley Cl SE7 27 G5
Cleverly Est W12 22 C2
Cleve Rd NW6 9 B4
Cleves Rd E6 13 G5
Clewer Cres E4 19 A4
Clifden Rd E5 12 A2
Clifford Dr SW9 39 A2
Clifford Gdns NW10 15 E1
Clifford Rd E16 20 B4
Clifford's Inn Pas EC4 6 J2
Clifford St W1 6 A4
Clifford Way NW10 8 B1
Cliff Rd NW1 10 D3
Cliff Ter SE8 33 E5
Cliffview Rd SE13 40 D1
Cliff Vil NW1 10 D3
Clifton Av W12 22 B2
Clifton Cres SE15 32 G3
Clifton Gdns SW9 16 D3
Clifton Hill NW8 16 C1
Clifton Pl W2 23 E1
Clifton Ri SE14 33 C3
Clifton Rd E7 13 G3
Clifton Rd E16 20 B4
Clifton Rd N1 11 B3
Clifton Rd NW10 16 A1
Clifton Rd W9 16 D4
Clifton St EC2 18 D3
Clifton Vil W9 16 C4
Clifton Wk E6 21 A5
Clifton Way SE15 32 G3
Clinch Ct E16 20 D4
Clink St SE1 7 E5
Clinton Rd E3 19 C2
Clinton Rd E7 13 D1
Clipper Way SE13 40 G2
Clipstone Ms W1 17 C3
Clipstone St W1 17 C4
Clitheroe Rd SW9 31 E5
Cliveden Pl SW1 24 A5
Cloak La EC4 7 E3
Clockhouse Av, Bark. 14 E5
Clockhouse Pl SW15 36 G3
Clock Twr Pl N7 10 E3
Clonbrock Rd N16 11 D1
Cloncurry St SW6 29 F5
Clonmel Rd SW6 30 A3
Cloth Fair EC1 18 A4
Clothier St E1 7 J1
Clothworkers Rd SE18 35 F3
Cloudesley Pl N1 10 G5
Cloudesley Rd N1 10 G5
Cloudesley Sq N1 10 G5
Cloudesley St N1 10 G5
Clova Rd E7 13 C3
Clove Cres E14 27 A1
Clove Hitch Quay SW11 37 D1
Cloysters Grn E1 25 F2
Club Row E1 18 E3
Club Row E2 18 E3
Clumy Ms SW5 23 B5
Cluse St N1 11 B5
Clutton St E14 19 F4
Clydesdale Rd W11 16 A5
Clyde St SE8 33 D2
Clyston St SW8 31 C5
Coach Ho Ms SE23 40 B4
Coalecroft Rd SW15 36 E2
Coates Av SW18 38 F4

Coate St E2 18 F1
Cobbett Rd SE9 42 A1
Cobbett St SW8 31 F3
Cobble La N1 10 G4
Cobbold Est NW10 8 B3
Cobbold Rd NW10 8 B3
Cobbold Rd W12 22 A3
Cobb St E1 18 E4
Cobham Cl SW11 37 F4
Coborn Rd E3 19 D2
Coborn St E3 19 D2
Cobourg Rd SE5 32 E2
Cobourg St NW1 17 C2
Cochrane St NW8 16 E1
Cockayne Way SE8 33 C1
Cock La EC1 18 A4
Cockspur Ct SW1 6 D5
Cockspur St SW1 6 D5
Coda Cen, The SW6 29 G3
Code St E1 18 E3
Codling Cl E1 25 F2
Codrington Hill SE23 40 C5
Cody Rd E16 20 A3
Cody Rd Business Cen SE16 20 A3
Coin St SE1 6 J5
Coity Rd NW5 10 A3
Coke St E1 18 F5
Colbeck Ms SW7 23 C5
Coldbath St SE13 33 F4
Cold Blow La SE14 33 B3
Cold Harbour E14 26 G3
Coldharbour La SE5 38 G2
Coldharbour La SW9 38 G2
Coldstream Gdns SW18 37 A4
Colebeck Ms N1 11 A3
Colebert Av E1 19 A3
Colebrooke Row N1 18 A1
Coleford Rd SW18 37 D3
Colegrave Rd E15 13 A2
Colegrove Rd SE15 32 E3
Coleherne Ct SW5 30 C1
Coleherne Ms SW10 30 C1
Coleherne Rd SW10 30 C1
Colehill La SW6 29 G4
Coleman Flds N1 11 B5
Coleman Rd SE5 32 D3
Coleman St EC2 7 F1
Colenso Rd E5 12 A1
Colepits Wd Rd SE9 42 E3
Coleraine Rd SE3 34 C2
Coleridge Av E12 14 A3
Coleridge Cl SW8 31 B5
Coleridge Gdns SW10 30 D3
Coleridge Sq SW10 30 D3
Colestown St SW11 30 F5
Cole St SE1 25 B3
Colet Gdns W14 22 F5
Coley St WC1 17 F3
Colinette Rd SW15 36 E2
Colin Rd NW10 8 C3
Coliston Rd SW18 37 B5
College App SE10 33 G2
College Cross N1 10 G4
College Cross N1 10 G4
College Hill EC4 7 E3
College La NW5 10 B1
College Pk Cl SE13 41 A2
College Pl NW1 10 C5
College Pt E15 13 C3
College Rd NW10 15 E1
College Rd SE21 39 D5
College Row E9 12 B2
College St EC4 7 E3
College Ter E3 19 D2
Collent St E9 12 A3
Collett Rd SE16 25 F4
Collier St N1 17 F1
Collingbourne Rd W12 22 D2
Collingham Gdns SW5 23 C5
Collingham Pl SW5 23 C5
Collingham Rd SW5 23 C5

Collingwood St E1 18 G3
Collins Rd N5 11 B1
Collins St SE3 34 B5
Colls Rd SE15 33 A4
Colman Rd E16 20 F4
Colmore Ms SE15 32 G4
Colnbrook St SE1 25 A4
Colne Ho, Bark. 14 D3
Colne Rd E5 12 C1
Cologne Rd SW11 37 E2
Colombo St SE1 7 B6
Colomb St SE10 34 B1
Columbia WC1 17 E3
Colonnades, The W2 16 C5
Colonnade Wk SW1 24 B5
Colston Rd E7 13 G3
Columbia Rd E2 18 E2
Columbia Rd E13 20 C3
Columbine Av E6 21 A4
Columbine Way SE13 33 G5
Colvestone Cres E8 11 E2
Colville Est N1 11 D5
Colville Gdns W11 16 A5
Colville Hos W11 16 A5
Colville Ms W11 16 A5
Colville Rd W11 16 A5
Colville Sq W11 16 A5
Colville Ter W11 16 A5
Colvin Rd E6 14 A4
Colwell Rd SE22 39 E3
Colwith Rd W6 29 E2
Colyer Cl N1 17 F1
Colyton Rd SE22 39 G3
Combe Av SE3 34 C3
Combedale Rd SE10 34 D1
Combemartin Rd SW18 36 G5
Comber Gro SE5 32 C3
Combermere Rd SW9 38 F1
Comeragh Ms W14 29 G1
Comeragh Rd W14 29 G1
Comerford Rd SE4 40 C2
Comet Cl E12 13 G1
Comet Pl SE8 33 E3
Comet St SE8 33 E3
Comfort St SE15 32 E2
Commercial Rd E1 18 F5
Commercial Rd E14 19 A5
Commercial St E1 18 E3
Commercial Way SE15 32 E3
Commerell St SE10 34 B1
Commodore St E1 19 C3
Common, The E15 13 B3
Commondale SW15 36 E1
Common Mile Cl SW4 38 D3
Common Rd SW13 36 C1
Commonwealth Av W12 22 D1
Community La N7 10 D2
Community Rd E15 13 A2
Compayne Gdns NW6 9 C4
Compton Av E6 20 G1
Compton Av N1 11 A3
Compton Cl E3 19 E4
Compton Cl NW1 11 A3
Compton Rd N1 11 A3
Compton Rd NW10 15 F3
Compton St EC1 18 A3
Compton Ter N1 11 A3
Comus Pl SE17 25 D5
Comyn Rd SW11 37 F2
Comyns Cl E16 20 C4
Concanon Rd SW2 38 F3
Concert Hall App SE1 6 H6
Concorde Dr E6 21 B5
Condell Rd SW8 31 C4
Condover Cres SE18 35 D3
Condray Pl SW11 30 F3
Conduit Ct WC2 6 E3
Conduit Ms SE18 35 E1

Conduit Ms W2 16 E5
Conduit Pl W2 16 E5
Conduit Rd SE18 35 D1
Conduit St W1 24 B1
Coney Way SW8 31 F2
Congleton Gro SE18 35 E1
Congo Rd SE18 35 F1
Congreve Rd SE9 42 A3
Congreve St SE17 25 D5
Congreve Wk E16 20 G4
Coniger Rd SW6 30 B5
Coningham Rd W12 22 D3
Conington Rd SE13 33 F5
Coniston Av, Bark. 14 G4
Coniston Av, Well. 42 D2
Coniston Ho SE5 32 B3
Coniston Way N7 10 E4
Coniston Ho SE5 32 B3
Conlan St W10 15 G3
Conley Rd NW10 8 A3
Conley St SE10 34 B1
Connaught Br E16 27 G2
Connaught Ms NW10 8 A5
Connaught Pl W2 16 F5
Connaught Rd E16 27 G2
Connaught Rd NW10 8 A5
Connaught Rd SE18 35 C1
Connaught Sq W2 16 G5
Connaught St W2 16 F5
Conrad Ho N16 11 D2
Consort Rd SE15 32 G4
Constantine Rd NW3 9 F1
Constitution Hill SW1 24 B3
Constitution Ri SE18 35 C4
Content St SE17 25 C5
Conway Rd SE18 28 F5
Conway Rd E13 20 D3
Conway St W1 17 C4
Conyer St E3 19 C1
Cook's Rd E15 19 F1
Cooks Rd SE17 32 A2
Coolfin Rd E16 20 D5
Coombe Rd W4 29 A1
Coombs St N1 18 A1
Coomer Pl SW6 30 A2
Cooper Pl SW6 30 A2
Cooper Rd NW10 8 C2
Coopersale Rd E9 12 B2
Coopers Cl E1 19 A3
Coopers La NW1 17 D1
Coopers Rd SE1 32 E1
Copeland Dr E14 26 E5
Copeland Rd SE15 32 F1
Copenhagen Pl E14 19 D5
Copenhagen St N1 10 E5
Cope Pl W8 23 D4
Cope St SE16 26 B5
Copleston Pas SE15 39 E1
Copleston Rd SE15 39 E1
Copley St E1 19 B4
Coppelia Rd SE3 41 C2
Copperas St E8 33 F2
Copperfield Rd E3 19 C3
Copperfield St SE1 25 A3
Copper Row SE1 25 E2
Coppice Dr SW15 36 D4
Coppock Cl SW11 38 F1
Copse Cl SE7 34 E2
Copsewood Cl, Sid. 42 G3
Copthall Av EC2 7 G1
Copthall Bldgs EC2 7 F1
Copthall Cl EC2 7 F1
Copthorne Av SW12 38 D5
Coptic St WC1 17 E4
Coral St SE1 24 G3
Coram St WC1 17 E3
Corbden Cl SE15 32 E4
Corbet Ct EC3 7 G2
Corbiere Ho N1 11 D5
Corbridge Cres E2 18 G1
Corbylands Rd, Sid. 42 G5
Cordelia Cl SE24 39 A2
Cordelia St E14 19 F5
Cordwell Rd SE13 41 B3
Corelli Rd SE3 35 A5
Corfield St E2 18 G2
Coriander Av E14 20 A5
Corinne Rd N19 10 C1
Cork St W1 6 A4
Cork St Ms W1 6 A4
Corlett St NW1 16 F4
Cormont Rd SE5 31 F5
Cormorant Rd E7 13 C1
Cornelia St N7 10 F3
Corner Grn SE3 34 D5
Corner Reach Way W4 29 A3
Corney Rd W4 29 A2
Cornflower Ter SE22 39 G4
Cornhill EC3 7 G2
Cornmill La SE13 40 F1
Cornmow Dr NW10 8 B2
Cornwall Av E2 19 A2
Cornwall Av, Well. 42 G1
Cornwall Cres W11 22 G1
Cornwall Gdns NW10 8 D3
Cornwall Gdns SW7 23 D4
Cornwall Gro W4 29 A1
Cornwalls Wk SE9 42 B1
Cornwall Ms S SW7 23 D4
Cornwall Rd SE1 6 J5
Cornwall Sq SE11 32 A1
Cornwood Dr E1 19 A5
Corona Rd SE12 41 D5
Coronation Rd E13 20 E2
Coronet St N1 18 D2
Corporation Row EC1 17 G3
Corporation St E15 20 C3
Corporation St N7 10 E2
Corrance Rd SW2 38 E2
Corry Dr SW9 39 A2
Corsham St N1 18 C2
Corsica St N5 11 A3
Cortayne Rd SW6 30 A5
Cortis Rd SW15 36 D4
Cortis Ter SW15 36 D4
Corunna Rd SW8 31 C4
Corunna Ter SW8 31 C4
Cosbycote Av SE24 39 B3
Cosmur Cl W12 22 B4
Cossall Wk SE15 32 G4
Cosser St SE1 24 G4
Costa St SE15 32 F5
Cosway St NW1 16 F4
Cotall St E14 19 E5
Cotleigh Rd NW6 9 B4
Cotswold Gdns E6 20 G2
Cottage Grn SE5 32 C3
Cottage Gro SW9 38 E1
Cottage Pl SW3 23 F4
Cottage St E14 26 F1
Cottesmore Gdns W8 23 C4
Cottingham Rd SW8 31 F3
Cotton Row SW11 37 D1
Cottons La SE1 7 G5
Cotton St E14 26 G1
Coulgate St SE4 40 C1
Coulson St SW3 23 G5
Coulter Rd W6 22 D4
Councillor St SE5 32 B1
County Gro SE5 32 B4
County Rd E6 21 D4
County St SE1 25 B4
Coupland Pl SE18 35 E1
Courland Gro SW8 31 D4
Courland St SW8 31 D4
Courtenay St SE11 32 A1
Courtfield Gdns SW5 23 C5
Courtfield Rd SW7 23 C5
Court Gdns N7 10 G3
Courthill Rd SE13 40 G2
Courthope Rd NW3 9 G1
Courtlands Av SE12 41 E3
Court La SE21 39 D4
Court La Gdns SE21 39 D5
Courtmead Cl SE24 39 B4
Courtnell St W2 16 B5
Courtrai Rd SE23 40 C4
Court Yd SE9 42 A4
Courtyard, The, N1 10 F4
Cousin La EC4 7 F4
Cousthurst Rd SE3 34 E2
Covelees Wall E6 21 C5
Covent Gdn WC2 6 F3
Coventry Rd E1 18 G3
Coventry Rd E1 18 G3
Coventry St W1 6 C4
Coverdale Rd NW2 8 F4
Coverdale Rd W12 22 D2
Coverdales, The, Bark. 21 F1
Coverley Cl E1 18 F4
Cowbridge La, Bark. 14 D4
Cowcross St EC1 18 A4
Cowdenbeath Path N1 10 F5
Cow Leaze E6 21 C5
Cowley Rd SW9 31 G4
Cowley Rd SW14 36 A1
Cowley Rd W3 22 B2
Cowper Av E6 14 A4
Cowper Rd N16 11 D2
Cowper St EC2 18 C3
Cowthorpe Rd SW8 31 D4
Coxmount Rd SE7 34 G1
Coxwell Rd SE18 35 F1
Crabtree Cl E2 18 E1
Crabtree La SW6 29 F3
Craigerne Rd SE3 34 E3
Craighton Rd SE18 35 D5
Craignair Rd SW2 38 G5
Craig's Ct SW1 6 E5
Craigton Rd SE9 42 B2
Cramond Cl W6 29 G2
Crampton St SE17 25 B5
Cranberry La E16 20 B3
Cranbourne Rd, Bark. 14 F5
Cranbourn All WC2 6 D3
Cranbourne Rd E15 12 G1
Cranbourn St WC2 6 D3
Cranbrook Rd SE8 33 E4
Cranbrook Rd W4 29 A1
Cranbury Rd SW6 30 C5
Crane Ct EC4 7 A2
Crane Gro N7 10 G3
Crane Mead SE16 26 B5
Crane St SE10 34 A1
Crane St SE15 32 E4
Cranfield Rd SE4 40 D1
Cranford St E1 26 A1
Cranhurst Rd NW2 8 E2
Cranleigh Gdns, Bark. 14 F4
Cranleigh Ms SW11 30 F5
Cranleigh St NW1 17 C1
Cranley Gdns SW7 30 D1
Cranley Ms SW7 23 D5
Cranley Pl SW7 23 E5
Cranmer Rd E13 13 E1
Cranmer Rd SW9 31 G3
Cranmer Ct SW4 38 D1
Cranston Est N1 18 C1
Cranston Rd SE23 40 B1
Cranswick Rd SE16 32 G1
Cranwell Cl E3 19 F3
Cranwood St EC1 18 C2
Cranworth Gdns SW9 31 G4
Craster Rd SW2 38 F5
Crathie Rd SE12 41 E4
Craven Gdns, Bark. 21 G1
Craven Hill W2 23 D1
Craven Hill Gdns W2 23 D1
Craven Hill Ms W2 23 D1
Craven Pk NW10 8 A5
Craven Pk Ms NW10 8 A5
Craven Pas WC2 6 E5
Craven Rd W2 23 D1
Craven St WC2 6 E5
Craven Ter W2 23 D1
Crawford St SE5 32 B5
Crawford Pl W1 16 F5
Crawford Rd SE5 16 F5
Crawford St W1 16 G4
Crawthew Gro SE22 39 E2
Crayford Rd N7 10 D1
Crealock St SW18 37 C4
Creasy Est SE1 25 D4
Crebor St SE22 39 F4
Crediton Hill NW6 9 C2
Crediton Rd NW10 8 F6
Credon Rd E13 20 F1
Credon Rd SE16 32 G1
Creechurch La EC3 7 J2
Creechurch Pl EC3 7 J2
Creed La EC4 7 C2
Creek Rd SE8 33 E2
Creek Rd SE10 33 E2
Creekside SE8 33 F3
Crefeld Cl W6 29 F2
Creighton Av E6 20 G1
Creighton Rd NW6 15 F1
Cremer St E2 18 E1
Cremorne Rd SW10 30 D3
Crescent, The SW13 29 B5
Crescent, The W3 15 A5
Crescent Arc SE10 33 G2
Crescent Gro SW4 38 C2
Crescent La SW4 38 D3
Crescent Pl SW3 23 F5
Crescent Rd E6 13 F5
Crescent Rd E13 13 D5
Crescent Rd SE18 35 D1
Crescent Row EC1 18 B3
Crescent St N1 10 F4
Crescent Way SE4 40 E1
Cresford Rd SW6 30 C4
Cresset Rd E9 12 A3
Cresset St SW4 38 D1
Cressfield Cl NW5 10 A2
Cressingham Rd SE13 40 G1
Cresswell Gdns SW5 30 D1
Cresswell Pk SE3 41 C1
Cresswell Rd SW10 30 D1
Cressy Ct W6 22 D4
Cressy Pl E1 19 A4
Cressy Rd NW3 9 G2
Crestway SW15 36 D4
Creton St SE18 28 C4
Crewdson Rd SW9 31 G3
Crewe Pl NW10 15 B2
Crews St E14 26 E5
Crewys Rd SE15 32 G5
Cricketers Cl SE11 25 A5
Cricketfield Rd E5 11 G1
Cricklewood La NW2 8 F1
Crieff Rd SW18 37 D4
Crimscott St SE1 25 D4
Crimsworth Rd SW8 31 D4
Crinan St N1 17 E1
Cringle St SW8 31 C3
Crispian Cl NW10 8 A1
Crispin St E1 18 E4
Crisp Rd W6 29 E1
Cristowe Rd SW6 30 A5
Croft, The NW10 15 B1
Crofters Way NW1 10 D5
Croftongate Way SE4 40 C3
Crofton Pk Rd SE4 40 D4
Crofton Rd E13 20 E3
Crofton Rd SE5 32 D4
Crofts St E1 25 F1
Croft St SE8 26 D5
Crogsland Rd NW1 10 A4
Crome Rd NW10 8 A3
Cromer St WC1 17 E2
Cromer Vil Rd SW18 37 A4
Cromford Rd SW18 37 B3
Crompton St W2 16 E3
Cromwell Av W6 29 D1
Cromwell Cres SW5 23 B5

Name	Ref.
Cromwell Gdns SW7	23 E4
Cromwell Gro W6	22 E4
Cromwell Ms SW7	23 E5
Cromwell Pl SW7	23 E5
Cromwell Rd E7	13 F4
Cromwell Rd SW5	23 C5
Cromwell Rd SW7	23 D5
Cromwell Rd SW9	32 A4
Cromwell Twr EC2	18 B4
Crondace Rd SW6	30 B4
Crondall St N1	18 C1
Cronin St SE17	24 C5
Crooke Rd SE8	33 C1
Crookham Rd SW6	30 A4
Crookston Rd SE9	42 C1
Croombs Rd E16	20 F4
Crooms Hill SE10	34 A3
Crooms Hill Gro SE10	33 G3
Cropley St N1	18 C1
Crosby Rd E7	13 D3
Crosby Row SE1	25 C3
Crosby Sq EC3	7 H2
Crosby Wk SW2	38 G5
Crosier Cl SE3	35 A4
Cross Av SE10	34 A2
Crossbrook Rd SE3	35 A5
Crossfield Rd NW3	9 E4
Crossfield St SE8	33 E3
Crossford St SW9	31 F5
Cross La EC3	7 H4
Crosslet Vale SE10	33 F4
Crossley St N7	10 G3
Crossmount Ho SE5	32 B3
Cross Rd SE5	32 D5
Cross St N1	11 A5
Cross St SW13	29 A5
Crossthwaite Av SE5	39 C2
Crosswall EC3	25 E1
Crossway N16	11 D2
Croston St E8	11 F5
Crowder St E1	25 G1
Crowhurst Cl SW9	31 G5
Crowland Ter N1	11 C4
Crown Cl E3	12 E5
Crown Cl NW6	9 C3
Crown Ct SE12	41 E4
Crown Ct WC2	6 F2
Crowndale Rd NW1	17 C1
Crownfield Rd E15	13 A2
Crownhill Rd NW10	8 B5
Crown Ms W6	22 C3
Crown Office Row EC4	6 J3
Crown Pas SW1	5 B6
Crown Pl EC2	18 D4
Crownstone Rd SW2	38 G3
Crown St SE5	32 B5
Crown Wds La SE9	35 D5
Crown Wds La SE18	35 D5
Crown Wds Way SE9	42 F3
Crows Rd E15	20 A2
Crows Rd, Bark.	14 D3
Crowthorne Rd W10	15 F5
Croxley Rd W9	16 A2
Croxted Cl SE21	39 B5
Croxted Rd SE21	39 B5
Croxted Rd SE24	39 B5
Croyde Cl, Sid.	42 G5
Croydon Rd E13	20 C3
Crozier Ter E9	12 B2
Crucifix La SE1	25 D3
Cruden St N1	11 A5
Cruikshank Rd E15	13 B1
Cruikshank St WC1	17 G2
Crutched Friars EC3	7 J3
Crystal Palace Rd SE22	39 F2
Cuba St E14	26 E3
Cubitt St WC1	17 F2
Cubitts Yd WC2	6 F3
Cubitt Ter SW4	38 C1
Cudham St SE6	40 G5
Cudworth St E1	18 G4
Cuff Cres SE9	41 G4
Cuff Pt E2	18 E2
Culford Gdns SW3	23 G5
Culford Gro N1	11 D3
Culford Rd N1	11 D3
Cullingworth Rd NW10	8 C2
Culloden Cl SE16	32 F1
Culloden St E14	19 G5
Cullum St EC3	7 H3
Culmore Rd SE15	32 D4
Culmstock Rd SW11	38 A3
Culross St W1	24 A1
Culvert Pl SW11	31 A5
Culvert Rd SW11	30 G5
Cumberland Av, Well.	42 G1
Cumberland Cl E8	11 E3
Cumberland Cres W14	22 G5
Cumberland Gate W1	23 G1
Cumberland Mkt NW1	17 B2
Cumberland Pk NW10	15 C2
Cumberland Rd E12	13 G1
Cumberland Rd E13	20 E4
Cumberland Rd SW13	29 B4
Cumberland St SW1	31 B1
Cumming St N1	17 F1
Cunard Pl EC3	7 J2
Cunard Wk SE16	26 C5
Cundy Rd E16	20 F5
Cundy St SW1	24 A5
Cunningham Pl NW8	16 E3
Cupar Rd SW11	31 A4
Cureton St SW1	24 D5
Curlew St SE1	25 E3
Curricle St W3	22 A2
Cursitor St EC4	6 J1
Curtain Rd EC2	18 D3
Curtis St SE1	25 E5
Curtis Way SE1	25 E5
Curve, The W12	22 C1
Curwen Rd W12	22 C3
Curzon Cres NW10	8 B4
Curzon Gate W1	24 A2
Curzon St W1	24 A2
Custom Ho Reach SE16	26 D3
Custom Ho Wk EC3	7 H4
Cut, The SE1	24 G3
Cutcombe Rd SE5	32 B5
Cuthbert St W1	16 E3
Cuthill Wk SE5	32 C4
Cutlers Gdns EC1	7 J1
Cutler St E1	7 J1
Cyclops Wk E14	26 E5
Cygnus Business Cen NW10	8 B3
Cynthia St N1	17 F1
Cyntra Pl E8	11 G4
Cypress Gdns SE4	40 C3
Cyprus Pl E2	19 A1
Cyprus Pl E6	28 C1
Cyprus St E2	19 A1
Cyrena Rd SE22	39 E4
Cyril Mans SW11	30 G4
Cyrus St EC1	18 A3
Czar St SE8	33 E2

D

Name	Ref.
Dabin Cres SE10	33 G4
Dacca St SE8	33 D2
Dace Rd E3	12 E4
Dacre Gdns SE13	41 B1
Dacre Pk SE13	41 B1
Dacre Pl SE13	41 B1
Dacre Rd E13	13 E5
Dacre St SW1	24 D4
Daffodil Gdns, Ilf.	14 D2
Daffodil St W12	22 B2
Dagenham Gdns NW10	15 F1
Dagmar Gdns SE5	32 D4
Dagmar Ter N1	11 A5
Dagnall St SW11	30 G5
Dagonet Rd SW12	38 B1
Dahlia Gdns, Ilf.	14 D3
Dairsie Rd SE9	42 C1
Dairy Cl NW10	8 C5
Dairy La SE18	28 B5
Dairy Ms SW9	38 E1
Daisy La SW6	37 B3
Dakota Gdns E6	21 A3
Dalberg Rd SW2	38 G3
Dalby Rd SW18	37 D2
Dalby St NW5	10 B3
Dale Cl SE3	34 D5
Daleham Gdns NW3	9 E2
Daleham Ms NW3	9 E3
Dalehead NW1	17 C1
Dale Rd SE17	32 A2
Dale St W4	29 A1
Daley St E9	12 B3
Daley Thompson Way SW8	31 B5
Dalgarno Gdns W10	15 E4
Dalgarno Way W10	15 E3
Dalgleish St E14	19 C5
Daling Way E3	12 C5
Dallinger Rd SE12	41 C4
Dalling Rd W6	22 D4
Dallington St EC1	18 A3
Dalmain Rd SE23	40 B5
Dalmeny Av N7	10 D1
Dalmeyer Rd NW10	8 B3
Dalrymple Rd SE4	40 C2
Dalston La E8	11 E3
Dalwood St SE5	32 D4
Dalyell Rd SW9	38 E1
Dame St N1	18 B1
Damien St E1	18 G5
Danbury St N1	18 A1
Danby St SE15	39 E1
Dancer Rd SW6	30 A4
Dando Cres SE3	41 E1
Dandridge Cl SE10	34 C1
Danebury Av SW15	36 A4
Danecroft Rd SE24	39 B3
Danehurst St SW6	29 G4
Danesdale Rd E9	12 C3
Danesfield SE5	32 D2
Daneville Rd SE5	32 C4
Daniel Gdns SE15	32 E3
Daniels Rd SE15	40 A1
Dansey Pl W1	6 C3
Dante Rd SE11	25 A5
Danvers St SW3	30 E2
Daphne St SW18	37 D4
D'Arblay St W1	6 B2
Darfield Rd SE4	40 D3
Darfield Way W10	15 F5
Darfur St SW15	36 F1
Darien Rd SW11	37 E1
Darlan Rd SW6	30 A3
Darley Rd SW11	37 G4
Darling Rd SE4	40 E1
Darling Row E1	18 G3
Darnley Ho E14	19 C5
Darnley Rd E9	11 G3
Darrell Rd SE22	39 F3
Darsley Dr SW8	31 E4
Dartford St SE17	32 B2
Dartmouth Cl W11	16 A5
Dartmouth Gro SE10	33 G4
Dartmouth Hill SE10	33 G4
Dartmouth Pk Rd NW5	10 B1
Dartmouth Pl W4	29 A2
Dartmouth Rd NW2	8 F3
Dartmouth Row SE10	33 G5
Dartmouth St SW1	24 D3
Dartmouth Ter SE10	34 A4
Dart St W10	15 G2
Darwell Cl E6	21 C1
Darwin St SE17	25 C5
Datchelor Pl SE5	32 C4
Date St SE17	32 B1
Daubeney Rd E5	12 C1
Daubeney Twr SE8	26 D5
Dault Rd SW18	37 D4
Davenant St E1	18 F4
Davenport Rd SE6	40 F4
Daventry St NW1	16 F4
Davern Cl SE10	27 C5
Davey Cl N7	10 F3
Davey St SE15	32 E2
Davidge St SE1	25 A3
David Lee Pt E15	13 B5
Davidson Gdns SW8	31 E3
Davies La E11	13 A3
Davies St W1	24 B1
Davis Rd W3	22 B2
Davis St E13	20 E1
Davisville Rd W12	22 C3
Dawes Rd SW6	29 G3
Dawes St SE17	32 C1
Dawlish Dr, Ilf.	14 G1
Dawlish Rd NW2	8 F3
Dawson Av, Bark.	14 G4
Dawson Cl SE18	28 E5
Dawson Hts Est SE22	39 F5
Dawson Pl W2	23 B1
Dawson Rd NW2	8 E2
Dawson St E2	18 E1
Daylesford Av SW15	36 C2
Days La, Sid.	42 G5
Dayton Gro SE15	33 A1
Deacon Ms N1	11 C4
Deacon Rd NW2	8 C2
Deacon Way SE17	25 B5
Deal Porters Way SE16	26 A4
Deal St E1	18 F4
Dealtry Rd SW15	36 E2
Dean Bradley St SW1	24 E4
Deancross St E1	19 A5
Deanery Rd E15	13 B3
Deanery St W1	24 A2
Dean Farrar St SW1	24 D4
Dean Rd NW2	8 E3
Dean Ryle St SW1	24 E5
Deans Bldgs SE17	25 C5
Deans Ct EC4	7 C2
Dean Stanley St SW1	24 E4
Dean St E7	13 D2
Dean St W1	6 C1
Dean Trench St SW1	24 E4
De Beauvoir Cres N1	11 D5
De Beauvoir Est N1	11 D5
De Beauvoir Rd N1	11 D5
De Beauvoir Sq N1	11 D5
Decima St SE1	25 D4
De Crespigny Pk SE5	32 C5
Deeley Rd SW8	31 D4
Deepdene Gdns SW2	38 F5
Deepdene Rd SE5	39 B2
Deerdale Rd SE24	39 B2
Deerhurst Rd NW2	8 F3
Dee St E14	19 G5
Defiance Wk SE18	28 B4
Dekker Rd SE21	39 D4
Delafield Rd SE7	34 E1
Delaford Rd SE16	32 G1
Delaford St SW6	29 G3
Delamere Ter W2	16 C4
Delancey St NW1	10 B5
De Laune St SE17	32 A1

Delaware Rd W9 16 C3
Delawyk Cres SE24 19 E5
Delhi St N1 10 B5
Delia St SW18 37 C5
Delisle Rd SE28 28 G2
Delius Gro E15 20 A1
Dell Cl E15 21 A5
Dellow St E1 25 G1
Delme Cres SE3 34 E5
Deloraine St SE8 33 E4
Delorme St W6 32 B2
Delverton Rd SE17 32 A1
Delvino Rd SW6 30 B4
De Morgan Rd SW6 37 C1
Dempster Rd SW18 37 D3
Denbigh Cl NW10 8 A4
Denbigh Cl W11 23 A1
Denbigh Pl SW1 31 C1
Denbigh Rd E6 20 G2
Denbigh Rd W11 23 A1
Denbigh St SW1 24 C5
Denbigh Ter W11 23 A1
Dene Cl SE4 40 C1
Denham St SE10 34 D1
Denham Way, Bark. 14 G5
Denholme Rd W9 16 A2
Denman Rd SE15 30 B4
Denman St W1 6 C4
Denmark Gro N1 17 G1
Denmark Hill SE5 32 B4
Denmark Hill Est SE5 39 C2
Denmark Pl WC2 6 D1
Denmark Rd NW6 16 A1
Denmark Rd SE5 32 B4
Denmark Rd E13 20 E4
Denmark St WC2 6 D2
Denne Ter E8 11 E5
Dennetts Rd SE14 33 A4
Denning Cl NW8 16 D2
Denning Rd NW3 9 B3
Dennington Pk Rd NW6 9 B3
Dennison Pt E15 12 G4
Denny St SE11 31 G1
Densham Rd E15 13 B5
Denton St SW18 37 C4
Dents Rd SW11 37 G4
Denyer St SW3 23 F5
Denzil Rd NW10 8 B2
Deodar Rd SW15 36 G2
Depot App NW2 8 F1
Deptford Br SE8 33 E4
Deptford Bdy SE8 33 E4
Deptford Ch St SE8 33 E2
Deptford Ferry Rd E14 26 E5
Deptford Grn SE8 33 E2
Deptford High St SE8 33 E2
Deptford Strand SE8 26 D5
Deptford Wf SE8 26 D5
Derby Rd E7 13 F4
Derby Rd E9 12 B5
Derbyshire St E2 18 F2
Dericote St E8 11 F5
Derifall Cl E6 21 B4
Dering St W1 5 B1
Dermody Gdns SE13 41 A3
Dermody Rd SE13 41 A3
Derry St W8 23 C3
Dersingham Av E12 14 C2
Derwent Gro SE22 39 E2
Derwent St SE10 34 B1
Desborough Cl W2 16 C4
Desenfans Rd SE21 39 D4
Desford Rd E16 20 B3
Desmond St SE14 33 C2
Devalls Cl E6 28 C1
Devas St E3 19 F3
Devenay Rd E15 13 C4
Deventer Cres SE22 39 D3
De Vere Gdns W8 23 D3
Deverell St SE1 25 C4

Devereux Ct WC2 6 J2
Devereux La SW13 29 D3
Devereux Rd SW11 37 G4
Devonia Rd N1 18 A1
Devonport Rd W12 22 D3
Devonport St E1 19 A5
Devon Rd, Bark. 14 G5
Devons Est E3 19 F2
Devonshire Cl E15 13 B1
Devonshire Cl W1 5 A5
Devonshire Dr SE10 33 E3
Devonshire Gro SE15 32 G2
Devonshire Ms S W1 17 B4
Devonshire Ms W W1 17 B4
Devonshire Pas W4 29 A1
Devonshire Pl W1 17 A3
Devonshire Rd E16 20 E5
Devonshire Rd W4 29 A1
Devonshire Sq EC2 7 H1
Devonshire St W1 17 A4
Devonshire St W4 29 A1
Devonshire Ter W2 16 D5
Devons Rd E3 19 E4
Devon St SE15 32 G2
Dewar St SE15 39 F1
Dewberry Gdns E6 21 A4
Dewberry St E14 19 G4
Dewey Rd N1 17 G1
Dewhurst Rd W14 22 F4
Dewsbury Rd NW10 8 C2
D'Eynsford Rd SE5 32 C3
Diadem Ct W1 6 C2
Dial Wk, The W8 23 C3
Diamond St SE15 32 D3
Diamond Ter SE10 33 G4
Diana Ho SW13 29 B4
Dibden St N1 11 A5
Dicey Av NW2 8 D2
Dickens Est SE1 25 F3
Dickens Est SE16 25 E3
Dickens Ho NW6 16 B2
Dickens Rd E6 20 G1
Dickens Sq SE1 25 B4
Dickens St SW8 31 B5
Dickson Rd SE9 42 A1
Digby Rd E9 12 B3
Digby St E2 19 A2
Dighton Ct SE5 32 B2
Dighton Rd SW18 37 D3
Dilke St SW3 30 G2
Dimond Cl E7 13 D1
Dimson Cres E3 19 E3
Dingle Gdns E14 26 E1
Dingley Pl EC1 18 B2
Dingley Rd EC1 18 B2
Dingwall Rd SW18 37 D5
Dinsdale Rd SE3 34 C2
Dinsmore Rd SW12 38 B5
Dirleton Rd E15 13 C1
Disbrowe Rd W6 29 G2
Discovery Wk E1 25 G2
Disraeli Cl E13 13 D3
Disraeli Rd SW15 36 G2
Diss St E2 18 E2
Distaff La EC4 7 D3
Distillery Rd W6 29 E1
Distin St SE11 24 G5
Ditch All SE10 33 F4
Ditchburn St E14 26 G1
Divis Way SW15 36 D4
Dixon Ho W10 15 F5
Dixon Rd SE14 33 C4
Dixon's All SE16 25 G3
Dobell Rd SE9 42 B3
Dobree Av NW10 8 D4
Dobson Cl NW6 9 E4
Doby Ct EC4 7 E3
Dockers Tanner Rd E14 26 E4
Dockhead SE1 25 E3
Dock Hill Av SE16 26 B3
Dockland St E16 28 C2
Dockley Rd SE16 25 F4

Dock Rd E16 27 C1
Dockside Rd E16 27 G1
Dock St E1 25 F1
Docwra's Bldgs N1 11 D3
Doddington Gro SE17 32 A2
Doddington Pl SE17 32 A2
Dodson St SE1 24 G3
Dod St E14 19 D5
Doggett Rd SE6 40 E5
Dog Kennel Hill SE22 39 D2
Dog Kennel Hill Est SE22 39 D1
Dog La NW10 8 A3
Doherty Rd E13 20 D3
Dolben St SE1 7 B6
Dolby Rd SW6 30 A5
Dolland St SE11 31 F1
Dolman St SW4 38 F2
Dolphin La E14 26 F1
Dolphin Sq SW1 31 C1
Dolphin Sq W4 29 A3
Dombey St WC1 17 F4
Domett Cl SE5 39 C2
Dominica Cl E13 20 F1
Donald Rd E13 13 E5
Donaldson Rd NW6 9 A5
Donaldson Rd SE18 35 C4
Donegal St N1 17 F1
Doneraile St SW6 29 F5
Dongola Rd E1 19 C4
Dongola Rd E13 20 E2
Dongola Rd N1 19 C4
Donkey All SE22 39 F5
Donne Ct SE24 39 B4
Donne Pl SW3 23 F5
Donnington Rd NW10 8 D1
Don Phelan Cl SE5 32 C4
Doon St SE1 6 J6
Dorando Cl W12 22 D2
Doran Gro SE18 35 G3
Doran Wk E15 12 G4
Dora St E14 19 D5
Dorchester Cl SE24 39 B3
Dorchester Dr SE24 39 B3
Dorchester Gro W4 29 A1
Dordrecht Rd W3 22 A2
Dore Av E12 14 C2
Doria Rd SW6 30 A5
Doric Way NW1 17 D2
Doris Rd E7 13 D4
Dorking Cl SE8 33 D2
Dorlcote Rd SW18 37 F5
Dorman Way NW8 16 E1
Dormay St SW18 37 C3
Dormer Cl E15 13 C3
Dornberg Cl SE3 34 D3
Dorncliffe Rd SW6 29 G5
Dorney NW3 9 F4
Dornfell St NW6 9 A2
Dorothy Rd SW11 37 G1
Dorrington St EC1 17 G4
Dorset Bldgs EC4 7 B2
Dorset Est E2 18 E2
Dorset Pl E15 13 A3
Dorset Ri EC4 7 B2
Dorset Rd E7 13 F4
Dorset Rd SW8 31 F3
Dorset Sq NW1 16 G3
Dorset St W1 17 A4
Dorville Cres W6 22 D4
Dorville Rd SE12 41 C3
Dothill Rd SE18 35 F3
Doughty Ms WC1 17 F3
Doughty St WC1 17 F3
Douglas Rd E16 20 D4
Douglas Rd N1 11 B4
Douglas Rd NW6 9 A5
Douglas Rd SW1 24 D5
Douglas Way SE8 33 D3
Douro Pl W8 23 C4
Douro St E3 19 E1
Dove App E6 21 A4
Dove Ct EC2 7 F2
Dovedale Rd SE22 39 G3

Dovehouse Mead, Bark. 21 F1
Dovehouse St SW3 30 E1
Dove Ms SW5 23 D5
Dovercourt Est N1 11 C3
Dovercourt Rd SE22 39 D4
Doverfield Rd SW2 38 E4
Dover Ho Rd SW15 36 C2
Dover Rd N1 11 C3
Dover Row E2 11 F5
Dover Pk Dr SW15 36 D4
Dover St W1 24 B1
Dover Yd W1 6 A5
Doves Yd N1 10 G5
Dowdeswell Cl SW15 36 A2
Dowdney Cl NW5 10 C2
Dowgate Hill EC4 7 F3
Dowland St W10 15 G1
Dowlas St SE5 32 D3
Downfield Cl W9 16 C3
Downham Rd N1 11 C4
Downings E6 21 C5
Downing St SW1 24 E3
Downman Rd SE9 42 A1
Down Pl W6 22 D5
Downsell Rd E15 12 G1
Downshire Hill NW3 9 E1
Downside Cres NW3 9 F2
Downs Pk Rd E5 11 E2
Downs Pk Rd E8 11 E2
Downs Rd E5 11 F1
Down St W1 24 B2
Downtown Rd SE16 26 C3
Dowson Cl SE5 39 C2
Doyle Gdns NW10 8 C5
D'Oyley St SW1 24 A5
Draco St SE17 32 B2
Dragon Rd SE15 32 D2
Dragoon Rd SE8 33 D1
Drake Cl W12 22 A3
Drakefell Rd SE4 33 B5
Drakefell Rd SE14 33 B5
Drake Rd SE4 40 E1
Drakes Ctyd NW6 9 A4
Drakes Wk E6 14 B5
Drapers Rd E15 13 A1
Drawdock Rd SE10 27 F2
Drawell Cl SE18 35 G1
Draycott Av SW3 23 F5
Draycott Pl SW3 23 G5
Draycott Ter SW3 23 G5
Drayford Cl W9 16 A3
Dray Gdns SW2 38 F3
Drayson Ms W8 23 B3
Drayton Gdns SW10 30 D1
Drayton Pk N5 10 G2
Drayton Rd NW10 8 B5
Dresden Cl NW6 9 C3
Dressington Av SE4 40 E4
Drew Rd E16 27 E2
Driffield Rd E3 19 C1
Dromore Rd SW15 36 G4
Droop St W10 15 G3
Drovers Pl SE15 32 G3
Druce Rd SE21 39 D4
Druid St SE1 25 D3
Drummond Cres NW1 17 D2
Drummond Gate SW1 31 D1
Drummond Rd SE16 25 G4
Drummond St NW1 17 C3
Drury La WC2 6 F2
Dryad St SW15 36 F1
Dryburgh Rd SW15 36 D1
Dryden Ct SE11 24 G5
Dryden Rd, Well. 35 G4
Dryden St WC2 6 F2
Drysdale St N1 18 D2
Dublin Av E8 11 F5
Du Cane Cl W12 15 E5
Du Cane Rd W12 15 B5

Duchess of Bedford's Wk W8 23 B3
Duchess St W1 17 B4
Duchy St SE1 7 A5
Ducie St SW4 38 B4
Duckett St E1 19 B3
Duck La W1 6 C2
Dudden Hill La NW10 8 B1
Dudley Rd NW6 15 G1
Dudley Rd, Ilf. 14 D1
Dudley St W2 16 E4
Dufferin St EC1 19 B5
Duff St E14 19 F5
Dufour's Pl W1 6 B2
Dugard Way SE11 25 A5
Duke Humphrey Rd SE3 34 B4
Duke of Wellington Av SE18 28 D4
Duke of Wellington Pl SW1 24 A2
Duke of York Sq SW3 23 G5
Duke of York St SW1 6 B5
Dukes Ct E6 14 C5
Dukes La W8 23 B3
Dukes Pl EC3 7 J2
Dukes Rd E6 14 C5
Duke's Rd WC1 17 D2
Duke St W1 6 B5
Duke St W1 17 A5
Duke St Hill SE1 7 G5
Dulford St W11 22 D3
Dulka Rd SW11 37 G3
Dulwich Rd SE24 38 G3
Dulwich Village SE21 39 D4
Dumbarton Rd SW2 38 E4
Dumbreck Rd SE9 42 B2
Dunbar Rd E7 13 D3
Dunblane Rd SE9 42 A1
Dunboyne Rd NW3 9 G2
Dunbridge St E2 18 F3
Duncan Gro W3 15 A5
Duncannon St WC2 6 E4
Duncan Rd E8 11 G5
Duncan St N1 18 A1
Duncan Ter N1 18 A1
Duncombe Hill SE23 40 C5
Duncrievie Rd SE13 41 A4
Duncroft SE18 35 G3
Dundalk Rd SE4 40 C1
Dundas Rd SE15 33 A5
Dundee Rd E13 20 E1
Dundee St E1 25 G2
Dundonald Rd NW10 8 F5
Dunelm St E1 19 B1
Dunford Rd N7 10 F1
Dungarvan Av SW15 36 C2
Dunlace Rd E5 12 A1
Dunloe St E2 18 E1
Dunmore Rd NW6 8 G5
Dunmow Rd E15 13 A1
Dunnock Rd E6 21 A5
Dunns Pas WC1 6 F1
Dunn St E8 11 E2
Dunollie Rd NW5 10 C2
Dunoon Rd SE23 40 A5
Dunraven Rd W12 22 C2
Dunsany Rd W14 22 F4
Dunstable Rd SE9 39 G4
Dunstans Gro SE22 39 G4
Dunstans Rd SE22 39 F5
Dunster Ct EC3 7 H3
Dunster Gdns NW6 9 A4
Dunston Rd E8 11 E5
Dunston Rd SW11 31 A5
Dunston St E8 11 E5
Dunton Rd SE1 32 E1
Dunvegan Rd SE9 42 B2
Dupree Rd SE7 34 E1
Durand Gdns SW9 31 F4
Durands Wk SE16 26 D3

Durant St E2 18 F1
Durban Rd E15 20 B2
Durham Ho St WC2 6 F4
Durham Ri SE18 35 F1
Durham Rd E12 13 G1
Durham Rd E16 20 B3
Durham Row E1 19 C4
Durham St SE11 31 F1
Durham Ter W2 16 C5
Durrell Rd SW6 30 A4
Durrington Rd E5 12 C1
Dursley Cl SE3 34 F5
Dursley Gdns SE3 34 G4
Dursley Rd SE3 34 F5
Durward St E1 18 G4
Durweston St W1 16 G6
Dutton St SE10 33 G4
Dye Ho La E3 12 E5
Dyers La SW15 36 D2
Dylan Rd SE24 39 A2
Dylways SE5 39 C2
Dymock St SW6 37 C1
Dyne Rd NW6 9 B4
Dynham Rd NW6 9 B4
Dyott St WC1 6 E1
Dyson Rd E15 13 C3

E

Eagle Ct EC1 18 A4
Eagle Pl SW1 6 B4
Eaglesfield Rd SE18 35 D3
Eagle St WC1 17 F4
Eagle Wf Rd N1 18 B1
Ealdham Sq SE9 41 F2
Eamont St NW8 9 E5
Eardley Cres SW5 30 B1
Earldom Rd SW15 36 E2
Earlham Gro E7 13 C2
Earlham St WC2 6 D2
Earl Ri SE18 28 F5
Earls Ct Gdns SW5 23 C5
Earls Ct Rd SW5 23 B5
Earls Ct Rd W8 23 B4
Earls Ct Sq SW5 30 C1
Earlsferry Way N1 10 F4
Earlsfield Rd SW18 37 B5
Earlsmead Rd NW10 15 E1
Earls Ter W8 23 A4
Earlsthorpe Ms SW12 38 A4
Earlston Gro E9 11 G5
Earl St EC2 18 C4
Earls Wk W8 23 A4
Earlswood St SE10 34 B1
Earnshaw St WC2 6 D1
Earsby St W14 22 G5
East Acton La W3 22 A1
East Arbour St E1 19 B5
East Av E12 14 A4
Eastbourne Ms W2 16 D5
Eastbourne Rd E15 13 B5
Eastbourne Ter W2 16 D5
Eastbrook Rd SE3 34 E3
Eastbury Av, Bark. 14 G5
Eastbury Ct, Bark. 14 G5
Eastbury Gro W4 29 A1
Eastbury Ter E1 19 B3
Eastcastle St W1 6 A1
Eastcheap EC3 7 G3
Eastcombe Av SE7 34 E2
Eastcote St SW9 31 F5
East Cross Cen E15 12 E3
East Cross Route E3 12 D4
East Cross Route E9 12 D3
Eastdown Pk SE13 41 A2
East Dulwich Gro SE22 39 D4
East Dulwich Rd SE15 39 E2
East Dulwich Rd SE22 39 E2

Eastern Gateway E16 27 F1
Eastern Rd E13 20 E1
Eastern Rd SE4 40 E2
East Ferry Rd E14 26 F4
Eastfield St E14 19 C4
East Ham Ind Est E6 21 A3
East Ham Manor Way E6 21 C5
East Harding St EC4 7 A1
East Hill SW18 37 C3
East India Dock Rd E14 19 E5
Eastlake Rd SE5 32 A5
Eastlands Cres SE21 39 E4
East La SE16 25 G3
Eastmoor Pl SE7 27 G4
Eastmoor St SE7 27 G4
East Mt St E1 18 G4
Eastney St SE10 34 A1
East Parkside SE10 27 B3
East Rd N1 18 C1
East Rochester Way SE9 42 G2
East Rochester Way, Sid. 42 G2
East Row W10 15 G3
East Smithfield E1 25 E1
East St SE17 32 B1
East St, Bark. 14 E4
East Surrey Gro SE15 32 E3
East Tenter St E1 18 E5
Eastview Av SE18 35 G3
Eastway E9 12 D3
Eastway Commercial Cen E9 12 E2
Eaton Cl SW1 24 A5
Eaton Dr SW9 39 A2
Eaton Gate SW1 24 A5
Eaton La SW1 24 B4
Eaton Ms N SW1 24 A4
Eaton Ms S SW1 24 B4
Eaton Ms W SW1 24 B4
Eaton Pl SW1 24 A4
Eaton Row SW1 24 B4
Eaton Sq SW1 24 A4
Eaton Ter SW1 24 A5
Ebbisham Dr SW8 31 F2
Ebbsfleet Rd NW2 8 G1
Ebdon Way E1 41 E1
Ebenezer St N1 18 C2
Ebley Cl SE15 32 E2
Ebner St SW18 37 C3
Ebor St E1 18 E3
Ebsworth St SE23 40 B5
Ebury Br SW1 31 B1
Ebury Br Est SW1 31 B1
Ebury Br Rd SW1 31 A1
Ebury Ms SW1 24 B5
Ebury Ms E SW1 24 B5
Ebury Sq SW1 24 A5
Ebury St SW1 24 A5
Ecclesbourne Rd N1 11 B4
Eccles Rd SW11 37 G2
Eccleston Br SW1 24 B5
Eccleston Ms SW1 24 A4
Eccleston Pl SW1 24 B5
Eccleston Sq SW1 24 B5
Eccleston St SW1 24 A4
Eckford St N1 17 G1
Eckstein Rd SW11 37 F2
Eclipse Rd E13 20 E4
Edbrooke Rd W9 16 B3
Eddiscombe Rd SW6 30 A5
Eddystone Rd SE4 40 C3
Eddystone Twr SE8 26 C5
Edenbridge Rd E9 12 B4
Eden Gro N7 10 F2
Edenhurst Av SW6 37 A1
Edensor Gdns W4 29 A3
Edensor Rd W4 29 A3
Edenvale St SW6 30 C5
Edgar Kail Way SE22 39 D2

Edgarley Ter SW6 29 G4
Edgar Rd E3 19 F2
Edge Hill SE18 35 D2
Edgeley Rd SW4 38 D2
Edgeworth Rd SE9 41 F2
Edgware Rd W2 16 F5
Edinburgh Gate SW1 23 G3
Edinburgh Ho W9 16 D2
Edinburgh Rd E13 20 E1
Edis St NW1 10 A5
Edith Gro SW10 30 D2
Edithna St SW9 38 E1
Edith Rd E6 13 G4
Edith Rd W14 22 G5
Edith Row SW6 30 C4
Edith St E2 18 F1
Edith Ter SW10 30 D3
Edith Vil W14 23 A5
Edmeston Cl E9 12 C3
Edmond Halley Way SE10 27 B2
Edmund Hurst Dr E6 21 D4
Edmund St SE5 32 C3
Edna St SW11 30 F4
Edrich Ho SW4 31 E4
Edric Rd SE14 33 B3
Edward Cl NW2 8 F1
Edwardes Sq W8 23 B4
Edward Pl SE8 33 D2
Edward Sq N1 10 G4
Edward Ms W1 17 A5
Edward St E16 20 D3
Edward St SE8 33 D2
Edward St SE14 33 C3
Edward Temme Av E15 13 C4
Edwin Av E6 21 C1
Edwin St E1 19 A3
Edwin St E16 20 D4
Effie Pl SW6 30 B3
Effie Rd SW6 30 B3
Effingham Rd SE12 41 B3
Effra Par SW2 38 G3
Effra Rd SW2 38 G2
Egbert St NW1 10 A5
Egerton Cres SW3 23 F5
Egerton Dr SE10 33 F4
Egerton Gdns NW10 8 E5
Egerton Gdns SW3 23 F4
Egerton Gdns Ms SW3 23 F4
Egerton Pl SW3 23 F4
Egerton Ter SW3 23 F4
Eglantine Rd SW18 37 D3
Eglinton Hill SE18 35 D2
Eglinton Rd SE18 35 C2
Egliston Ms SW15 36 E1
Egliston Rd SW15 36 E1
Egmont St SE14 33 B3
Eider Cl E7 13 C2
Eighth Av E12 14 B1
Eisenhower Dr E6 21 A4
Elaine Gro NW5 10 A2
Elam Cl SE5 32 A5
Elam St SE5 32 A5
Eland Rd SW11 37 G1
Elba Pl SE17 32 B5
Elbe St E16 20 D5
Elbury Dr E16 20 D5
Elcho St SW11 30 F3
Elcot Av SE15 32 G3
Elderfield Rd E5 12 A1
Elderflower Way E15 13 C4
Eldersie Rd SE9 42 C3
Elder St E1 18 E4
Eldon Gro NW3 9 E2
Eldon Rd W8 23 C4
Eldon St EC2 18 C4
Eldred Rd, Bark. 14 G5
Eleanor Cl SE16 26 B3
Eleanor Rd E8 11 G4
Eleanor Rd E15 13 C3
Eleanor St E3 19 E2

Electric Av SW9 38 G2
Electric La SW9 38 G2
Elephant & Castle SE1 25 A5
Elephant La SE16 26 A3
Elephant Rd SE17 25 B5
Elfindale Rd SE24 39 B3
Elford Cl SE3 41 E2
Elfort Rd N5 10 G1
Elf Row E1 26 A1
Elgar St SE16 26 C4
Elgin Av W9 16 C2
Elgin Av W9 22 D3
Elgin Cl W12 22 D3
Elgin Cres W11 22 G3
Elia Ms N1 18 A1
Elias Pl SW8 31 G2
Elia St N1 18 A1
Elibank Rd SE9 42 C2
Elim Est SE1 25 D4
Elim Way E13 20 D3
Eliot Gdns SW15 36 C2
Eliot Hill SE13 33 G5
Eliot Ms NW8 16 D1
Eliot Pl SE3 40 G1
Eliot Pl SE3 34 B5
Eliot Vale SE3 34 A5
Elizabeth Av N1 11 B4
Elizabeth Br SW1 24 B5
Elizabeth Est SE17 32 C2
Elizabeth Fry Pl SE18 35 A5
Elizabeth Gdns W3 22 B2
Elizabeth Ms NW3 9 F3
Elizabeth Rd E6 13 G5
Elizabeth St SW1 24 A5
Elizabeth Ter SE9 42 B4
Elkington Rd E13 20 E3
Elkstone Rd W10 16 A4
Ellaline Rd W6 29 F2
Elland Rd SE15 40 A2
Ellenborough Pl SW15 36 C2
Ellen St E1 18 F5
Ellerby St SW6 29 F4
Ellerdale Rd NW3 9 D2
Ellerdale St SE13 40 F2
Ellerslie Gdns NW10 8 C2
Ellerslie Rd W12 22 D2
Ellerslie Sq Ind Est SW2 38 E3
Ellerton Rd SW13 29 C4
Ellery St SE15 32 G5
Ellesmere Rd E3 19 C1
Ellesmere Rd NW3 9 F3
Ellesmere St E14 19 F5
Ellingfort Rd E8 11 G4
Ellingham Rd E15 13 A1
Ellingham Rd W12 22 C3
Ellington St N7 10 G3
Elliot Cl E15 13 B4
Elliot Rd SW9 32 A3
Elliott Rd W4 22 A5
Elliott Sq NW3 9 F4
Elliotts Row SE11 25 A5
Elliscombe Rd SE7 34 F1
Ellisfield Dr SW15 36 B5
Ellison Rd SW13 29 B5
Ellis St SW1 23 G5
Elliston Ho SE18 28 C5
Ellsworth St E2 18 G2
Elm Bk Gdns SW13 29 A5
Elmbrook Gdns SE9 42 A2
Elm Cl EC4 6 J3
Elmcroft St E5 12 A1
Elmdene Rd SE18 35 D1
Elmer Rd SE6 40 G5
Elmfield Way W9 16 B4
Elm Friars Wk NW1 10 D4
Elm Grn W3 15 A5
Elm Grn W3 15 A5
Elm Gro SE15 32 E5
Elm Gro Rd SW13 29 C5
Elmhurst Rd E7 13 E4
Elmhurst St SW4 38 D1
Elmington Est SE5 32 C3

Elmington Rd SE5 32 C4
Elmira St SE13 40 F1
Elmley St SE18 28 F5
Elmore St N1 11 B4
Elm Pk SW2 38 F4
Elm Pk Gdns SW10 30 E1
Elm Pk La SW3 30 E1
Elm Pl SW7 30 E1
Elm Quay Ct SW8 31 D2
Elm Rd E7 13 C3
Elms, The SW13 36 B1
Elms Cres SW4 38 D3
Elmshaw Rd SW15 36 C3
Elmslie Pt E3 19 D4
Elms Ms W2 23 E1
Elms Rd SW4 38 C3
Elmstone Rd SW6 30 B4
Elm St WC1 17 F3
Elm Ter SE9 42 C4
Elm Tree Cl NW8 16 E2
Elm Tree Rd NW8 16 E2
Elm Way NW10 8 A1
Elmwood Cl SW14 31 B4
Elmwood Rd SE24 39 C3
Elrington Rd E8 11 F3
Elsa St E1 19 C4
Elsdale St E9 12 A3
Elsenham Rd E12 14 C2
Elsham Rd W14 22 G3
Elsham Ter W14 22 G3
Elsiemaud Rd SE4 40 D3
Elsie Rd SE22 39 E2
Elsley Rd SW11 37 G1
Elspeth Rd SW11 37 G2
Elsted St SE17 25 C5
Elstow Cl SE9 42 C3
Elstree Gdns, Ilf. 14 E2
Elswick Rd SE13 33 F5
Elswick St SW6 30 D5
Elsworthy Ri NW3 9 F4
Elsworthy Rd NW3 9 F5
Elsworthy Ter NW3 9 F4
Elsynge Rd SW18 37 E3
Eltham Grn SE9 41 F3
Eltham Grn Rd SE9 41 E3
Eltham High St SE9 42 B4
Eltham Hill SE9 41 G3
Eltham Palace Rd SE9 41 F4

Eltham Pk Gdns SE9 42 C2
Eltham Rd SE9 41 F3
Eltham Rd SE12 41 F3
Elthiron Rd SW6 30 B4
Elthruda Rd SE13 41 A4
Elsley Rd, Ilf. 14 D1
Elton Ho E3 12 D5
Elton Pl N16 11 D2
Eltringham St SW18 37 D2
Elvaston Ms SW7 23 D4
Elvaston Pl SW7 23 D4
Elverson Ms SE8 33 F5
Elverson Rd SE8 33 F5
Elverton St SW1 24 D5
Elvis Rd NW2 8 E3
Elwin St E2 18 F2
Elwyn Gdns SE12 41 D5
Elystan Pl SW3 30 F1
Elystan St SW3 23 F5
Embankment SW15 29 F5
Embankment Gdns SW3 30 G2
Embankment Pl WC2 6 F5
Emba St SE16 25 F3
Emberton SE5 32 D2
Embleton Rd SE13 40 F1
Emden St SW6 30 C4
Emerald Cl E16 21 A5
Emerald Ct WC1 17 F2
Emerson St SE1 7 D5
Emery Hill St SW1 24 C4
Emily Pl N7 10 G1
Emlyn Gdns W12 22 A3
Emlyn Rd W12 22 A3

Emma Rd E13 20 C1
Emma St E2 18 G1
Emmott Cl E1 19 C4
Emperor's Gate SW7 23 C4
Empire Wf Rd E14 27 A5
Empress Ms SE5 32 B5
Empress Pl SW6 30 B1
Empress St SE17 32 B2
Empson St E3 19 F3
Emu Rd SW8 31 B5
Enbrook St W10 15 G2
Enclave, The SW13 36 B1
Enderby St SE10 34 B1
Endlesham Rd SW12 38 A5
Endsleigh Gdns WC1 17 D3
Endsleigh Pl WC1 17 D3
Endsleigh St WC1 17 D3
Endwell Rd SE4 40 D3
Endymion Rd SW2 38 F4
Enfield Rd N1 11 D4
Enford St W1 16 G4
Engate St SE13 40 G2
Engineer Cl SE18 35 C2
Englands La NW3 9 G3
Englefield Rd N1 11 C4
Englewood Rd SW12 38 B4
Engleheart Rd SE6 40 F5
Englewood Rd SW12 38 A5
English Grds SE1 7 H6
English St E3 19 D3
Enid St SE16 25 E3
Enmore Rd SW15 36 E2
Ennerdale Ho E3 19 D3
Ennersdale Rd SE13 41 A3
Ennismore Av W4 22 B5
Ennismore Gdns SW7 23 F3
Ennismore Gdns Ms SW7 23 F4
Ennismore Ms SW7 23 F3
Ennismore St SW7 23 F4
Ennis Rd SE18 35 E2
Ensign St E1 25 F1
Enslin Rd SE9 42 C4
Enterprise Way NW10 15 C2
Enterprise Way SW18 37 B2

Enterprise Way SE8 26 D5
Epirus Ms SW6 30 B3
Epirus Rd SW6 30 A3
Epping Cl E14 26 E5
Epple Rd SW6 30 A4
Epworth St EC2 18 C3
Erasmus St SW1 24 D5
Erconwald St W12 15 B5
Erebus Dr SE28 28 E4
Eresby Pl NW6 9 B4
Erica St W12 22 C1
Eric Clarke La, Bark. 21 D3
Eric Cl E7 13 D1
Eric Ct E7 13 D1
Eric Rd E7 13 D1
Eric St E3 19 D2
Erindale SE18 35 F2
Erindale Ter SE18 35 F2
Erlanger Rd SE14 33 B4
Ermine Rd SE13 40 F1
Ernald Av E6 21 A1
Ernest St E1 19 B3
Erpingham Rd SW15 36 E1
Errington Rd W9 16 A3
Errol St EC1 18 B3
Erskine Rd NW3 9 G4
Erwood Rd SE7 35 A1
Escreet Gro SE18 28 C5
Esk Rd E13 20 D3
Esme Ho SW15 36 B2
Esmeralda Rd SE1 25 F5
Esmond Rd NW6 9 A5
Esmond St SW15 36 G2

Esparto St SW18 37 C5
Essendine Rd W9 16 B3
Essex Ct EC4 6 J2
Essex Ct SW13 29 B5
Essex Pk Ms W3 22 A2
Essex Rd E12 14 A2
Essex Rd N1 11 A5
Essex Rd NW10 8 A4
Essex Rd, Bark. 14 G5
Essex St E7 13 D2
Essex Vil W8 23 B3
Essian St E1 19 C4
Estcourt Rd SW6 30 A3
Esterbrooke St SW1 24 D5
Este Rd SW11 37 F1
Estoria Cl SW2 38 G5
Etchingham Rd E15 12 G1
Eternit Wk SW6 29 E4
Ethelburga St SW11 30 F5
Ethelden Rd W12 22 D2
Ethel Rd E16 20 E5
Etherow St SE22 39 F4
Ethnard Rd SE15 32 G2
Eton Av NW3 9 E4
Eton Cl SW18 37 C5
Eton Coll Rd NW3 9 G3
Eton Gro SE13 41 B1
Eton Rd NW3 9 G4
Eton Rd, Ilf. 14 E2
Eton Vil NW3 9 G3
Etta St SE8 33 C2
Ettrick St E14 19 G5
Eugenia Rd SE16 26 A4
Europa Rd SE18 28 B4
Eustace Rd E6 21 A2
Eustace Rd SW6 30 B3
Eustace Gro NW1 17 D2
Euston Rd N1 17 D3
Euston Rd NW1 17 C2
Euston Sq NW1 17 D2
Euston Sq NW1 17 D2
Euston St NW1 17 C2
Euston Twr NW1 17 C3
Evandale Rd SW9 31 G5
Evangelist Rd NW5 10 B1
Evelina Rd SE15 40 A1
Eveline Lowe Est SE16 25 F4
Evelyn Denington Rd E6 21 A3
Evelyn Gdns SW7 30 E1
Evelyn Rd E16 27 E2
Evelyn Rd E17 33 C1
Evelyn Wk N1 18 C1
Evelyn Yd W1 6 C1
Evenwood Cl SW15 36 G3
Everdon Rd SW13 29 C2
Everest Pl E14 19 G4
Everest Rd SE9 42 B3
Evergreen Sq E8 11 E4
Everilda St N1 10 F5
Everington St W6 29 F2
Eve Rd E11 13 B1
Eve Rd E15 20 B1
Evershott St NW1 17 C1
Eversleigh Rd E6 13 G5
Eversleigh Rd SW11 37 G1
Eversley Rd SE7 34 E2
Everthorpe Rd SE15 39 F1
Evesham Rd E15 13 C5
Evesham St W11 22 F1
Evesham Way SW11 38 A1
Ewald Rd SW6 30 A5
Ewart Rd SE23 40 B5
Ewe Cl N7 10 E3
Ewen Cres SW2 38 G5
Ewer St SE1 7 D6
Ewhurst Cl E1 19 A4
Ewhurst Rd SE4 40 D4
Excel Ct WC2 6 D3
Excelsior Gdns SE13 33 G5
Exchange Ct WC2 6 F4

Exchange Sq EC2 18 D4
Exeter Rd E16 20 D4
Exeter Rd NW2 6 F3
Exeter St WC2 6 E3
Exeter Way SE14 33 D3
Exhibition Cl W12 22 E1
Exhibition Rd SW7 23 E4
Exmoor St W10 15 F3
Exmouth Mkt EC1 17 G3
Exmouth Pl E8 11 G4
Exning Rd E16 20 C3
Exon St SE17 32 D1
Exton St SE1 6 J6
Eynella Rd SE22 39 E5
Eynham Rd W12 15 E5
Eyot Gdns W6 29 B1
Eythorne Rd SW9 31 G4
Ezra St E2 18 E2

F

Fabian Rd SW6 30 A3
Fabian Rd E6 21 B3
Factory Rd E16 28 A2
Fairacres SW15 36 C2
Fairbairn Grn SW9 31 G4
Fairby Rd SE12 41 E3
Faircharm Trd Est SE8 33 F3
Fairclough St E1 18 F5
Faircross Av, Bark. 14 E3
Fairdale Gdns SW15 36 D2
Fairfax Gdns SE3 34 G4
Fairfax Ms SW15 36 E2
Fairfax Pl NW6 9 D4
Fairfax Pl W14 22 G4
Fairfax Rd NW6 9 D4
Fairfax Rd W4 22 A4
Fairfield Cl N8 8 C5
Fairfield Dr SW18 37 C3
Fairfield Gro SE7 34 G1
Fairfield Rd E3 19 E1
Fairfield Rd, Ilf. 14 B4
Fairfield St SW18 37 C3
Fairfoot Rd E3 19 E3
Fairhazel Gdns NW6 9 C3
Fairholme Rd W14 29 G1
Fairland Rd E15 13 C3
Fairlawn SE7 34 F2
Fairlawn Gdns SE23 40 A5
Fairlight Av NW10 15 A1
Fairmount Rd SW2 38 F4
Fairoak Dr SE9 42 F3
Fairthorn Rd SE7 34 D1
Fairview Pl SW2 38 F5
Fairway, The W3 15 A5
Fairway Gdns, Ilf. 14 E3
Fakruddin St E1 18 F3
Falconberg Ct W1 6 D1
Falconberg Ms W1 6 C1
Falcon Cl SE1 7 C5
Falcon Ct EC4 6 J2
Falcon Gro SW11 37 F1
Falcon La SW11 37 F1
Falcon Pk Ind Est NW10 8 B2
Falcon Rd SW11 30 F5
Falcon St E13 20 D2
Falcon Ter SW11 37 F1
Falcon Way E14 26 F5
Falconwood Av, Well. 35 F5
Falconwood Par, Well. 42 G2
Falkirk Ho W9 16 C2
Falkirk St N1 18 D1
Falkland Rd NW5 10 C2
Falmouth Cl SE12 41 C3
Falmouth Rd SE1 25 B4
Falmouth St E15 13 A2
Fann St EC1 18 B3
Fann St EC2 18 B3
Fanshawe Av, Bark. 14 E3
Fanshaw St N1 18 D2
Fanthorpe St SW15 36 E1

Faraday Rd E15 13 C3
Faraday Rd W10 15 G4
Faraday Way SE18 27 G4
Fareham St W1 6 C1
Faringford Rd E15 13 B4
Farjeon Rd SE3 34 G3
Farleigh Rd N16 11 E1
Farley Ms SE6 40 G5
Farley Rd SE6 40 F5
Farlow Rd SW15 36 F1
Farlton Rd SW18 37 C5
Farmdale Rd SE10 34 D1
Farmers Rd SE5 32 A3
Farm La SW6 30 B2
Farm St W1 24 B1
Farnaby Rd SE9 41 F2
Farncombe St SE16 25 F3
Farnham Royal SE11 31 F1
Faroe Rd W14 22 F4
Farrance St E14 19 D5
Farrell Ho E1 19 A5
Farrier St NW1 10 B4
Farrier Wk SW10 30 D2
Farringdon La EC1 17 G3
Farringdon Rd EC1 17 G3
Farringdon St EC4 7 B1
Farrins Rents SE16 26 C2
Farrow La SE14 33 A3
Farthingale Wk E15 13 A2
Fashion St E1 18 E4
Fassett Rd E8 11 F3
Fassett Sq E8 11 F3
Faulkner St SE14 33 A4
Favart Rd SW6 30 B4
Faversham Rd SE6 40 D5
Fawcett Cl SW11 30 E5
Fawcett Rd NW10 8 B5
Fawcett St SW10 30 D2
Fawe Pk Rd SW15 37 A2
Fawe St E14 19 F4
Fawley Rd NW6 9 C2
Fawnbrake Av SE24 39 A3
Fawn Rd E13 20 F1
Fearon St SE10 34 D1
Feathers Pl SE10 34 A2
Featherstone St EC1 18 C3
Featley Rd SW9 39 A1
Felday Rd SE13 40 A4
Felden St SW6 30 A4
Felgate Ms W6 22 D5
Felixstowe Rd NW10 15 D2
Fellbrigg Rd SE22 39 E3
Fellbrigg St E1 18 E1
Fellows Rd NW3 9 E3
Felsberg Rd SW2 38 E4
Felsham Rd SW15 36 F1
Felstead Rd E9 12 D3
Felsted Rd E16 20 G5
Felton St N1 11 C5
Fenchurch Av EC3 7 H2
Fenchurch Bldgs EC3 7 J2
Fenchurch Pl EC3 7 J3
Fenchurch St EC3 7 H3
Fen Ct EC3 7 H3
Fendall St SE1 25 D4
Fenelon Pl W14 23 A5
Fenham Rd SE15 35 C2
Fenn St E9 12 A2
Fentiman Rd SW8 31 E2
Fenton Cl SW9 31 F5
Fentons Av E13 20 E1
Fenwick Gro SE15 39 F1
Fenwick Pl SW9 38 E1
Fenwick Rd SE15 39 F1
Ferdinand St NW1 10 A3
Ferguson Cl E14 26 E5
Fermoy Rd W9 16 A3
Fernbank Ms SW12 38 C4
Fernbrook Cres SE13 41 B4

Fernbrook Rd SE13 41 B4
Ferncliff Rd E8 11 F2
Ferndale Cl SE3 34 C3
Ferndale Rd E7 13 E4
Ferndale Rd SW4 38 E2
Ferndale Rd SW9 38 E2
Ferndale St E16 28 D1
Ferndene Rd SE24 39 B2
Ferndown Rd SE9 41 G5
Fernhead Rd W9 16 A2
Fernhill St E16 28 B2
Fernholme Rd SE15 40 B3
Fernhurst Rd SW6 29 G4
Fernleigh Cl W9 16 A2
Fernshaw Rd SW10 30 D2
Ferns Rd E15 13 C3
Fern St E3 19 E3
Ferntower Rd N5 11 C2
Ferranti Cl SE18 27 G4
Ferrey Ms SW9 31 G5
Ferrier St SW18 37 C2
Ferris Rd SE22 39 F2
Ferry La SW13 29 B2
Ferryman's Quay SW6 30 D5
Ferry Rd SW13 29 C3
Ferry St E14 33 G1
Festing Rd SW15 36 F1
Festoon Way E16 27 G1
Fetter La EC4 7 A2
Ffinch St SE8 33 E3
Fieldgate St E1 18 F4
Fielding Ho NW6 16 B2
Fielding Rd W14 22 F4
Fielding St SE17 32 B2
Field Rd E7 13 C1
Field Rd W6 29 G1
Fields Est E8 11 F4
Field St WC1 17 F2
Fieldway Cres N5 10 G2
Fife Rd E16 20 D4
Fife Rd SW14 36 A1
Fife Ter N1 17 F1
Fifth Av E12 14 B1
Fifth Av W10 15 G2
Filmer Rd SW6 29 G4
Finborough Rd SW10 30 C1
Finch La EC3 7 G2
Finchley Pl NW8 16 E1
Finchley Rd NW3 9 D3
Finchley Rd NW8 9 D3
Finch Ms SE15 32 E3
Finden Rd E7 13 E2
Findhorn St E14 19 G5
Findon Rd W12 22 C3
Fingal St SE10 34 C1
Finland Rd SE4 40 C1
Finland St SE16 26 C4
Finlay St SW6 29 F4
Finnis St E2 18 G2
Finsbury Circ EC2 18 C4
Finsbury Est EC1 17 G2
Finsbury Mkt EC2 18 D3
Finsbury Pavement EC2 18 C4
Finsbury Sq EC2 18 C4
Finsbury St EC2 18 C4
Finsen Rd SE5 39 B1
Finstock Rd W10 15 F5
Firbank Cl E16 20 G4
Firbank Rd SE15 32 G5
Firs Cl SE23 40 B5
First Av E12 14 A1
First Av E13 20 D2
First Av SW14 36 A1
First Av W3 22 B2
First Av W10 16 A3
First St SW3 23 F5
Firth Gdns SW6 29 G4
Fir Trees Cl SE16 26 C2
Fishermans Dr SE16 26 B3
Fisherman's Wk E14 26 E2
Fisher St E16 20 D4
Fisher St WC1 17 F4
Fisherton St NW8 16 E3

Fishguard Way E16 28 D3
Fish St Hill EC3 7 G3
Fitzalan St SE11 24 G5
Fitzgeorge Av W14 22 G5
Fitzgerald Av SW14 36 A1
Fitzgerald Ho E14 19 F5
Fitzhardinge St W1 17 A5
Fitzhugh Gro SW18 37 E4
Fitzjames Av W14 22 G5
Fitzjohn's Av NW3 9 E2
Fitzmaurice Pl W1 24 B1
Fitznal St W18 15 B5
Fitzroy Rd NW1 10 A5
Fitzroy Sq W1 17 C3
Fitzroy St W1 17 C3
Fitzwilliam Rd SW4 38 C1
Fiveways Rd SW9 31 G5
Flamborough St E14 19 C5
Flamsteed Rd SE7 35 A1
Flanchford Rd W12 22 B4
Flanders Rd E6 21 B1
Flanders Rd W4 22 A5
Flanders Way E9 12 B3
Flask Wk NW3 9 E1
Flavell Ms SE10 34 B1
Flaxman Ct W1 6 C2
Flaxman Rd SE5 32 A5
Flaxman Ter WC1 17 D2
Flaxton Rd SE18 35 F4
Fleet Rd NW3 9 F2
Fleet St EC4 6 J2
Fleetwood Cl E16 20 G4
Fleetwood Rd NW10 8 C2
Fleming Rd SE17 32 A2
Fletching Rd SE7 34 F2
Fleur de Lis St E1 18 D3
Flinton St SE17 25 D5
Flintmill Cres SE23 40 E5
Flinton St SE17 25 D5
Flint St SE17 25 C5
Flitcroft St WC2 6 D1
Flodden Rd SE5 32 B4
Flood St SW3 30 F1
Flood Wk SW3 30 F2
Flora Cl E14 19 F5
Flora Gdns W6 22 D5
Floral St WC2 6 E3
Florence Rd E13 13 F5
Florence Rd E6 20 C1
Florence Rd SE14 33 D4
Florence Rd SE16 26 C3
Florence St N1 11 A4
Florence Ter SE14 33 D4
Florian Rd SW15 36 G2
Florida St E2 18 F2
Floss St SW15 29 E5
Flower Wk, The SW7 23 D3
Foal St SE7 34 F1
Fludyer St SE13 41 B2
Foley St W1 17 C4
Folgate St E1 18 D4
Foliot St W12 15 B5
Folkestone Rd E6 21 C1
Follett St E14 19 G5
Folly Wall E14 26 G3
Fontarabia Rd SW11 38 A2
Fontley Way SW15 36 C5
Footpath, The SW15 36 C3
Footscray Rd SE9 42 C4
Fordham St E1 18 F5
Fordingley Rd W9 16 A2
Ford Rd E3 12 C5
Fords Pk Rd E16 20 D5
Ford Sq E1 18 G4
Ford St E3 12 C5
Ford St E16 20 C5
Fordwych Rd NW2 8 G2
Fordyce Rd SE13 40 G4
Foreign St SE5 32 A5
Foreshore SE8 26 D5
Forester Rd SE15 39 G2
Forest Gro E8 11 E4
Forest Hill Rd SE22 39 G3

Street	Ref
Forest Hill Rd SE23	39 G3
Forest La E7	13 B2
Forest Rd E15	13 B2
Fore St EC2	18 B4
Forest Rd E7	13 D1
Forest Rd E8	13 D2
Forest St E7	13 D2
Forest Vw Rd E12	14 A1
Forest Way, Sid.	42 F5
Forfar St W1	31 A4
Formosa St W9	16 C3
Forset St W1	16 F5
Forster Rd SW2	38 C4
Forsyth Gdns SE17	32 A2
Forsythia Cl, Ilf.	14 D2
Fortess Rd NW5	10 B2
Forthbridge Rd SW11	38 A2
Fortis Cl E16	20 F5
Fort Rd SE1	25 E5
Fort St E16	27 E2
Fortune Gate Rd NW10	8 A5
Fortune Grn Rd NW6	9 B1
Fortune St EC1	18 B3
Fortune Way NW10	15 A2
Forty Acre La E16	20 E4
Foskett Rd SW6	30 A5
Fossdene Rd SE7	34 E1
Fossil Rd SE13	40 E1
Foster La EC2	**7 D1**
Foster Rd E13	20 D3
Foster Rd W3	22 A1
Fothergill Cl E13	20 D3
Foubert's Pl W1	**6 A2**
Foulden Rd N16	11 E1
Foulis Ter SW7	30 E1
Founders Ct EC2	**7 F1**
Foundry Cl SE16	26 C2
Fountain Ct EC4	**6 J3**
Fountain Ms NW3	9 G3
Fountain Pl SW9	31 G4
Fountain Sq SW1	24 B5
Fount St SW8	31 D3
Fournier St E1	19 E1
Four Seasons Cl E3	19 E1
Fourth Av E12	14 B1
Fourth Av W10	15 G3
Fowler Cl SW11	37 E1
Fowler Rd E7	13 D1
Fownes St SW11	37 F1
Foxberry Rd SE4	40 C1
Foxborough Gdns SE4	40 E4
Fox Cl E1	19 A3
Fox Cl E16	20 D4
Foxcote SE5	32 D1
Foxcroft Rd SE18	35 D4
Foxes Dale SE3	41 D1
Foxglove St W12	22 B1
Foxhole Rd SE18	35 A3
Fox Hollow Cl SE18	35 G3
Foxley Rd SW9	31 G3
Foxmore St SW11	30 G4
Fox Rd E16	20 C4
Foxwell St SE4	40 C1
Foxwood Rd SE3	41 C3
Foyle Rd SE3	34 C2
Framfield Rd N5	11 A2
Frampton Pk Rd E9	12 A3
Frampton St NW8	16 E3
Francemary Rd SE4	40 E3
Frances St SE18	28 B5
Frances Chichester Way SW11	31 A4
Francis St E15	13 B2
Francis St SW1	24 C5
Franconia Rd SW4	38 C3
Frankfurt Rd SE24	39 B3
Frankham St SE8	33 F4
Frankland Cl SE16	25 G4
Franklin Cl SE13	33 F4
Franklin Pas SE9	42 A1
Franklin Pl SE13	33 F4
Franklin's Row SW3	30 G1
Franklyn Rd NW10	8 B4
Frank St E13	20 D3
Fraser St W4	29 A1
Frazier St SE1	24 G3
Frean St SE16	25 F4
Frederick Cl W2	23 F1
Frederick Cres SW9	32 A3
Frederick Pl SE18	35 D1
Frederick's Pl EC2	**7 F2**
Frederick St WC1	17 F2
Freedom St SW11	30 G5
Freegrove Rd N7	10 E2
Freemantle St SE17	32 D1
Freemasons Rd E16	20 E4
Freke Rd SW11	38 A1
Fremont St E9	12 A5
French Ordinary Ct EC3	**7 J3**
Frendsbury Rd SE4	40 C2
Frensham St SE15	32 E5
Frere St SW11	30 F5
Freshfield Av E8	11 E1
Fresh Wharf Rd, Bark.	14 D5
Freston Rd W10	22 F1
Freston Rd W11	22 F1
Friars Cl SE1	**7 C6**
Friars Mead E14	26 G4
Friars Ms SE9	42 C3
Friars Rd E6	21 C2
Friar St EC4	**7 C2**
Friary St SW1	**6 B6**
Friary Est SE15	32 F2
Friary Rd SE15	32 F3
Friday St EC4	**7 D2**
Friendly St SE8	33 E4
Friend St EC1	18 A2
Friern Rd SE22	39 F4
Frimley Way E1	19 B3
Frinstead Ho W10	22 F1
Frinton Rd E6	20 G2
Friston St SW6	30 C5
Frith Rd E11	12 G1
Frith St W1	**6 C2**
Frithville Gdns W12	22 E1
Frobisher Rd E6	21 B5
Frobisher St SE10	34 B2
Frogley Rd SE22	39 E2
Frogmore SW18	37 B3
Frognal NW3	9 D2
Frognal Cl NW3	9 D3
Frognal Gdns NW3	9 D2
Frognal Ri NW3	9 D1
Frognal Way NW3	9 D1
Froissart Rd SE9	41 G3
Frome St N1	18 B1
Frostic Wk E1	18 E4
Froude St SW8	31 B5
Fry Rd E6	20 E1
Fry Rd NW10	8 B5
Fulford St SE16	25 G3
Fulham Bdy SW6	30 B3
Fulham High St SW6	29 G5
Fulham Palace Rd SW6	29 F3
Fulham Palace Rd W6	29 E1
Fulham Pk Gdns SW6	30 A5
Fulham Pk Rd SW6	30 A5
Fulham Rd SW3	30 D2
Fulham Rd SW6	30 A5
Fulham Rd SW10	30 C3
Fullerton Rd SW18	37 D3
Fulmead St SW6	30 D4
Fulmer Rd E16	20 G4
Fulthorp Rd SE3	34 C5
Fulwood Pl WC1	17 F4
Furber St W6	22 D4
Furley Rd SE15	32 F3
Furlong Rd N7	10 G3
Furmage St SW18	37 D5
Furness Ho SW18	15 C1
Furness Rd SW6	30 C5
Furnival St EC4	**6 J1**
Furrow La E9	12 A2
Further Grn Rd SE6	41 B5
Furzefield Rd SE3	34 E2
Furze St E3	19 E4
Fyfield Ct E7	13 D3
Fyfield Rd SW9	38 G1
Fynes St SW1	24 D5

G

Street	Ref
Gables Cl SE5	32 D4
Gabrielle Cl NW3	9 F3
Gabriel St SE23	40 B5
Gabriel's Wf SE1	**6 J5**
Gad Cl E13	20 E2
Gadwall Way SE28	28 F3
Gainsborough Av E12	14 C2
Gainsborough Rd E15	20 B2
Gainsborough Rd W4	22 B5
Gainsford St SE1	25 E3
Gairloch Rd SE5	32 D5
Gaisford St NW5	10 C3
Gaitskell Ct SW11	30 F5
Galata Rd SW13	29 C3
Galbraith St E14	26 G4
Galena Rd W6	22 D5
Galesbury Rd SW18	37 D4
Gales Gdns E2	18 G2
Gale St E3	19 E4
Galleywall Rd SE16	25 G5
Gallia Rd N5	11 A2
Gallions Rd SE7	27 E5
Gallions Roundabout E16	28 D1
Gallon Cl SE7	27 F5
Gallosson Rd SE18	28 G5
Galloway Rd W12	22 C2
Galsworthy Av E14	19 C4
Galsworthy Rd NW2	8 G1
Galton St W10	15 G3
Galveston Rd SW15	37 A3
Galway St EC1	18 B2
Gambetta St SW8	31 B5
Gambia St SE1	**7 C6**
Gamlen Rd SW15	36 F2
Ganton St W1	**6 A3**
Garden Cl SW15	36 D5
Garden Ct EC4	**6 J3**
Garden Rd NW8	16 D2
Garden Row SE1	25 A4
Gardens, The SE22	39 F2
Garden St E1	19 B4
Gardiner Av NW2	8 E2
Gardner Rd E13	20 E3
Gardners La EC4	**7 D3**
Garfield Rd E13	20 C3
Garfield Rd SW11	38 A1
Garford St E14	26 E1
Garibaldi St SE18	28 G5
Garland Rd SE18	35 F3
Garlick Hill EC4	**7 E3**
Garlinge Rd NW2	9 A3
Garnet Rd NW10	8 A3
Garnet St E1	26 A1
Garnett Cl SE9	42 B1
Garnett Rd NW3	9 G2
Garnies Cl SE15	32 E3
Garratt La SW18	37 C3
Garratt La SW18	37 D2
Garrick St WC2	**6 E3**
Garsington Ms SE4	40 D1
Garthorne Rd SE23	40 B5
Garton Pl SW18	37 D4
Gartons Way SW11	37 D1
Garvary Rd E16	20 E5
Garway Rd W2	16 C5
Gascoigne Pl E2	18 E2
Gascoigne Rd, Bark.	14 E5
Gascony Av NW6	9 B4
Gascoyne Rd E9	12 B4
Gaselee St E14	26 G1
Gaskarth Rd SW12	38 B4
Gaskell St SW4	31 E5
Gaskin St N1	11 A5
Gastein Rd W6	29 F2
Gataker St SE16	25 G4
Gatcombe Rd E16	27 D2
Gatcombe Rd N19	16 F3
Gateley Rd SW9	38 F1
Gate Ms SW7	23 F3
Gate St WC2	**6 G1**
Gateway SE17	32 B2
Gateway Ind Est NW10	15 B2
Gateway Retail Pk E6	21 D3
Gateways, The SW3	23 G5
Gatliff Rd SW1	31 B1
Gatonby St SE15	32 E4
Gatwick Rd SW18	37 A5
Gauden Cl SW4	38 D1
Gauden Rd SW4	31 D5
Gautrey Rd SE15	33 A5
Gautrey Sq E6	21 B5
Gavestone Cres SE12	41 E5
Gavestone Rd SE12	41 E5
Gavin St SE18	28 G5
Gawber St E2	19 A2
Gay Cl NW2	8 D2
Gaydon Ho W2	16 C4
Gayfere St SW1	24 E4
Gayford Rd W12	22 B3
Gayhurst Rd E8	11 F4
Gay Rd E15	20 A1
Gay St SW15	36 F1
Gayton Cres NW3	9 E1
Gayton Rd NW3	9 E1
Gayville Rd SW11	37 G4
Gaywood Est SE1	25 A4
Gaywood St SE1	25 A4
Geary Rd NW10	8 C2
Geary St N7	10 F2
Gedling Pl SE1	25 E5
Geere Rd E15	13 C5
Gee St EC1	18 B3
Geffrye St E2	18 E1
Geldart Rd SE15	32 G3
Gellatly Rd SE14	33 A5
General Gordon Pl SE18	28 D5
General Wolfe Rd SE10	34 A4
Genesta Rd SE18	35 D2
Geneva Dr SW9	38 G2
Genoa Av SW15	36 E3
Geoffrey Cl SE5	32 B5
Geoffrey Gdns E6	21 A1
Geoffrey Rd SE4	40 D1
George Beard Rd SE8	26 D5
George Ct WC2	**6 F4**
George Inn Yd SE1	**7 F6**
George La SE13	40 G4
George Mathers Rd SE11	25 A5
George Row SE16	25 F3
George's Rd N7	10 F2
George St E16	20 C5
George St W1	17 A5
George St, Bark.	14 E4
George Yd EC3	**7 G2**
George Yd W1	24 A1
Georgiana St NW1	10 C5
Geraldine Rd SW18	37 D3
Geraldine St SE11	25 A4
Gerald Rd E16	20 C5
Gerald Rd SW1	24 A5
Gerard Rd SW13	29 B4
Gerards Cl SE16	33 A1
Germander Way E15	20 B2
Gernon Rd E3	19 C1
Gerrard Pl W1	**6 D3**
Gerrard Rd N1	18 A1
Gerrard St W1	**6 C3**
Gerridge St SE1	24 G4
Gertrude St SW10	30 D2

Gervase St SE15 32 G3
Giant Arches Rd
SE24 32 B1
Gibbins Rd E15 12 G6
Gibbon Rd E15 33 A5
Gibbon Rd W3 39 C2
Gibbs Grn W14 30 A1
Gibraltar Wk E2 18 E2
Gibson Rd SE11 24 F5
Gibson Sq N1 10 G5
Gibson St SE10 34 B1
Gideon Rd SW11 38 B1
Giffin St SE8 33 E3
Gifford St N1 10 E4
Gift La E15 19 B5
Gilbert Cl SE18 35 B4
Gilbert Rd SE11 24 F5
Gilbert St E15 13 B1
Gilbert St W1 17 A5
Gilbeys Yd NW1 10 A4
Gilden Cres NW5 10 A2
Gilkes Cres SE21 39 D4
Gilkes Pl SE21 39 D4
Gill Av E16 20 D5
Gillender St E3 19 G3
Gillender St E14 19 G3
Gillett Av E6 21 A1
Gillett St N16 11 D2
Gillfoot NW1 17 C1
Gillian St SE13 40 F3
Gillies St NW5 10 A2
Gilling Ct NW3 9 F3
Gillingham St SW1 24 B5
Gillman Dr E15 13 C5
Gill St E14 19 D5
Gilmore Rd SE13 41 A2
Gilpin Rd E5 12 C1
Giltspur St EC1 7 C1
Gipsy La SW15 36 C1
Giraud St E14 19 F5
Girdlers Rd W14 22 F5
Girdwood Rd SW18 36 G5
Gironde Rd SW6 30 A3
Girton Vil W10 15 F5
Given Wilson Wk
E13 20 C1
Gladding Rd E12 13 G1
Glade, The SE7 34 F3
Gladiator St SE23 40 C4
Gladstone Av E12 14 A4
Gladstone St SE1 25 A4
Gladwyn Rd SW15 36 F1
Gladys Rd NW6 9 A2
Glaisher St SE8 33 F2
Glamis Pl E1 26 A1
Glamis Rd E1 26 A1
Glanville Rd SW2 38 E3
Glasbrook Rd SE9 41 G5
Glasgow Ho W9 16 C1
Glasgow Rd E13 20 E1
Glasgow Ter SW1 31 C1
Glasshill St SE1 25 A3
Glasshouse St W1 6 B4
Glasshouse Wk
SE11 31 E1
Glastonbury St
NW6 9 A2
Glaucus St E3 19 F3
Glazbury Rd W14 22 G5
Glebe, The SE3 41 B1
Glebe Pl SW3 30 F2
Glebe Rd NW10 8 B3
Glebe Rd SW13 29 C5
Glebe St W4 29 A1
Gleckhow Gdns
SW5 23 C5
Gledstanes Rd W14 29 G1
Glegg Pl SW15 36 F1
Glenaffric Av E14 27 A5
Glenalvon Way
SE18 28 A5
Glenarm Rd E5 12 A2
Glenavon Rd E15 13 B4

Glenbrook Rd NW6 9 B2
Glencairne Cl E16 20 G4
Glendall St SW9 38 F2
Glendarvon St
SW15 36 F1
Glendower Pl SW7 23 E5
Glendun Rd W3 22 A1
Glenelg Rd SW2 38 E3
Glenesk Rd SE9 42 C1
Glenfinlas Way SE5 32 A3
Glenforth St SE10 34 C1
Glengall Gro E14 26 E4
Glengall Gro E14 26 F4
Glengall Rd NW6 9 A5
Glengall Rd SE15 32 E2
Glengall Ter SE15 32 E2
Glengarnock Av E14 26 G5
Glengarry Rd SE22 39 D3
Glenhouse Rd SE9 42 C3
Glenhurst Av NW5 10 A1
Glenilla Rd NW3 9 F3
Glenister Rd SE10 34 C1
Glenister St E16 28 C2
Glenlea Rd SE9 42 B3
Glenloch Rd NW3 9 F3
Glenluce Rd SE3 34 D3
Glenlyon Rd SE9 42 C3
Glenmore Rd NW3 9 F3
Glenparke Rd E7 13 E3
Glen Rd E13 20 F3
Glenrosa St SW6 30 D5
Glenroy St W12 15 E5
Glensdale Rd SE4 40 D1
Glenshiel Rd SE9 42 C3
Glentham Rd
SW13 29 C2
Glenthorne Rd W6 22 E5
Glenton Rd SE13 41 B2
Glentworth St NW1 16 G3
Glenure Rd SE9 42 C3
Glenville Gro SE8 33 D3
Glenville Ms SW18 37 C5
Glenworth Av E14 27 A5
Gliddon Dr E5 11 G1
Gliddon Rd W14 22 G5
Globe Pond Rd
SE16 26 C2
Globe Rd E1 19 A2
Globe Rd E2 19 A2
Globe Rd E15 13 C2
Globe Rope Wk E14 26 G5
Globe St SE1 25 B4
Gloucester Circ
SE10 33 G3
Gloucester Ct EC3 7 J4
Gloucester Cres
NW1 10 B5
Gloucester Gate
NW1 17 B1
Gloucester Gro Est
SE15 32 D2
Gloucester Ho NW6 16 D5
Gloucester Ms NW1 16 D5
Gloucester Ms W2 16 D3
Gloucester Pl NW1 16 G4
Gloucester Pl W1 16 G4
Gloucester Sq W2 23 D4
Gloucester Sq E2 16 E5
Gloucester St SW1 31 C1
Gloucester Ter W2 23 E1
Gloucester Wk W8 23 B3
Gloucester Way EC1 17 G2
Glycena Rd SW11 37 G1
Glynde St SE4 40 D4
Glyndon Rd SE18 28 E5
Glynfield Rd NW10 8 A4
Goaters All SW6 30 A3
Godalming Rd E14 19 F4
Godbold Rd E15 20 B2
Godfrey Hill SE18 28 A5
Godfrey Rd SE18 28 B5
Godfrey St E15 19 G1
Godfrey St SW3 30 F1
Goding St SE11 31 E1

Godliman St EC4 7 D2
Godman Rd SE15 32 G5
Godolphin Rd W12 22 D3
Godson St N1 17 G1
Godwin Rd E7 13 E1
Goffers Rd SE3 34 A4
Golborne Rd W10 15 G4
Golden Jubilee Br
SE1 6 F5
Golden Jubilee Br
WC2 6 F5
Golden La EC1 18 B3
Golden Sq W1 6 B3
Goldfinch Rd SE28 28 F4
Goldhawk Rd W6 22 B5
Goldhawk Rd W12 22 C4
Goldhurst Ter NW6 9 C4
Golding St E1 18 F5
Goldington Cres
NW1 17 D1
Goldington St NW1 17 D1
Goldman Cl E2 18 F3
Goldney Rd W9 16 B3
Goldsboro Rd SW8 31 D4
Goldsmith Av E12 14 A3
Goldsmith Rd SE15 32 F4
Goldsmith's Row E2 18 F1
Goldsmith's Sq E2 18 F1
Goldsmith St EC2 7 E1
Goldsworthy Gdns
SE16 26 A5
Goldwin Cl SE14 33 A4
Goldwing Cl E16 20 D5
Gollogly Ter SE7 34 F1
Gomm Rd SE16 26 A4
Gondar Gdns NW6 9 A2
Gonson St SE8 33 F3
Goodall Rd E11 13 C1
Goodhall St NW10 15 A2
Goodhart Pl E14 26 C1
Goodinge Cl N7 10 E3
Goodman's Stile E1 18 F5
Goodmans Yd E1 25 E1
Goodrich Rd SE22 39 E4
Goodwood Rd NW10 8 A4
Goods Way NW1 17 E1
Goodway Gdns E14 20 A5
Goodwin Cl SE16 25 F4
Goodwin Rd W12 22 C3
Goodwins Ct WC2 6 E3
Goodwood Rd
SE14 33 C3
Goosander Way
SE28 28 F4
Gooseley La E6 21 C2
Gophir La EC4 7 F3
Gopsall St N1 11 C5
Gordon Av SW14 36 A2
Gordonbrook Rd
SE4 40 E3
Gordon Cl W12 15 E5
Gordon Gro SE5 32 A5
Gordon Ho Rd
NW5 10 A1
Gordon Pl W8 23 B3
Gordon Rd E15 12 G1
Gordon Rd SE15 32 G5
Gordon Rd, Bark. 14 G5
Gordon Rd, Sid. 42 G3
Gordon St WC1 17 D3
Gordon St WC1 17 D3
Gorefield Pl NW6 16 B1
Gore Rd E9 12 A5
Gore St SW7 23 D4
Goring Rd EC3 7 J1
Gorleston St W14 22 G5
Gorman Rd SE18 28 B5
Gorse Rd SW11 37 G4
Gorsuch St E2 18 E2
Gosfield St W1 17 C4
Goslett Yd WC2 6 D2
Gosling Way SW9 31 G4
Gospel Oak Est
NW5 9 G2
Gosset St E2 18 E2

Gosterwood St
SE8 33 C2
Goswell Rd EC1 18 A2
Gough Rd E15 13 C1
Gough Sq EC4 7 A1
Gough St WC1 17 F3
Goulden Ho App
SW11 30 F5
Goulston St E1 18 E5
Goulton Rd E5 11 G1
Gourock Rd SE9 42 C3
Govier Cl E15 13 B4
Gowan Av SW6 29 G4
Gowan Rd NW10 8 D3
Gower Cl SW4 38 C4
Gower Ms WC1 17 D4
Gower Pl WC1 17 C3
Gower Rd E7 13 D3
Gower St WC1 17 C3
Gower's Wk E1 18 F5
Gowlett Rd SE15 39 F1
Gowrie Rd SW11 38 A1
Gracechurch St EC3 7 G3
Grace's All E1 25 F1
Graces Ms SE5 32 D5
Graces Rd SE5 32 D5
Grace St E3 19 F2
Grafton Cres NW1 10 B3
Grafton Ho E3 19 E2
Grafton Pl NW1 17 D2
Grafton Rd NW5 10 A2
Grafton Sq SW4 38 C1
Grafton St W1 24 B1
Grafton Ter NW5 9 G2
Grafton Way W1 17 C3
Grafton Way WC1 17 C3
Graham Rd E8 11 F3
Graham Rd E13 20 D3
Graham St N1 18 A1
Graham St N1 18 A1
Graham Ter SW1 24 A5
Granard Av SW15 36 D3
Granard Rd SW12 37 G5
Granary Rd E1 18 G3
Granary St NW1 10 D1
Granby Rd SE9 35 B5
Granby St E2 18 E3
Granby Ter NW1 17 C1
Grand Dep Rd
SE18 35 C1
Grandison Rd
SW11 37 G3
Grand Junct Wf N1 18 B1
Grand Union Cres
E8 11 F4
Grand Union Wk
NW1 10 B4
Granfield St SW11 30 E4
Grange, The SE1 25 E4
Grange Ct WC2 6 H2
Grange Gro N1 11 A3
Grangehill Rd SE9 42 B1
Grange Pl NW6 9 B4
Grange Rd E13 20 C2
Grange Rd NW10 8 D3
Grange Rd SE1 25 D5
Grange Rd SW13 29 C4
Grange Rd, Ilf. 14 D1
Grange Rd N1 11 C5
Grange Wk SE1 25 D4
Grangewood St E6 13 F5
Grange Yd SE1 25 E4
Gransden Av E8 11 G4
Grantbridge St N1 18 A1
Grantham Rd E12 14 C1
Grantham Rd SW9 31 E5
Grantham Rd W4 29 A3
Grantley St E1 19 B2
Grant Rd SW11 37 E2
Grant's Quay Wf
EC3 7 G4
Grant St E13 20 D2
Grantully Rd W9 16 C2
Granville Ct N1 11 C5
Granville Gro SE13 40 G1
Granville Pk SE13 40 G1
Granville Pl W1 17 A5

Granville Rd NW6	16	B1
Granville Rd SW18	37	B5
Granville Sq SE15	32	D3
Granville Sq WC1	17	F2
Grape St WC2	**6**	**E1**
Grasmere Rd E13	20	D1
Gratton Rd W14	22	G4
Gravel Pit La SE9	42	E3
Gravesend Rd W12	22	C1
Grayling Sq E2	18	D2
Grayshott Rd SW11	31	A5
Gray's Inn WC1	17	G4
Gray's Inn Rd WC1	17	F2
Great Bell All EC2	**7**	**F1**
Great Castle St W1	17	C5
Great Cen St NW1	16	G4
Great Cen Way NW10	8	A2
Great Chapel St W1	**6**	**C1**
Great Ch La W6	29	F1
Great Coll St SW1	24	E4
Great Cross Av SE10	34	B3
Great Cumberland Pl W1	16	G5
Great Dover St SE1	25	B3
Great Eastern Rd E15	13	A4
Great Eastern St EC2	18	D2
Greatfield Av E6	21	B3
Greatfield Cl SE4	40	E2
Greatfields Rd, Bark.	14	F5
Great George St SW1	24	D3
Great Guildford St SE1	**7**	**D5**
Great James St WC1	17	F4
Great Marlborough St W1	**6**	**A2**
Great Maze Pond SE1	25	C3
Great New St EC4	**7**	**A3**
Greatorex St E1	18	E5
Great Ormond St WC1	17	E4
Great Percy St WC1	17	F2
Great Peter St SW1	24	D4
Great Portland St W1	17	B3
Great Pulteney St W1	**6**	**B3**
Great Queen St WC2	**6**	**F2**
Great Russell St WC1	**6**	**D1**
Great St. Helens EC3	**7**	**H1**
Great St. Thomas Apostle EC4	**7**	**E3**
Great Scotland Yd SW1	**6**	**E6**
Great Smith St SW1	24	D4
Great Spilmans SE22	39	D3
Great Suffolk St SE1	**7**	**C6**
Great Sutton St EC1	18	A3
Great Swan All EC2	**7**	**F1**
Great Titchfield St W1	**6**	**A1**
Great Twr St EC3	**7**	**H3**
Great Trinity La EC4	**7**	**E3**
Great Western Rd W2	16	A4
Great Western Rd W9	16	A4
Great Western Rd W11	16	A4
Great W Rd W6	29	B1
Great Winchester St EC2	**7**	**G1**
Great Windmill St W1	**6**	**C3**
Greek Ct W1	**6**	**D2**
Greek St W1	**6**	**D2**
Greek Yd WC2	**6**	**E3**
Green, The E15	13	B3
Green, The W3	15	A5
Green, The, Well.	42	G2
Greenacres SE9	42	C4
Green Arbour Ct EC1	**7**	**B1**
Greenaway Gdns NW3	9	C1
Green Bk E1	25	G2
Greenbay Rd SE7	34	G3
Greenberry St NW8	16	F1
Greencoat Pl SW1	24	C5
Greencroft Gdns NW6	9	C4
Green Dale SE5	39	C2
Green Dale SE22	39	D3
Green Dragon Ct SE1	**7**	**F5**
Greenfield Rd W4	22	A3
Greenfield Rd E1	18	F4
Greengate St E13	20	D1
Greenham Cl SE1	24	G3
Greenhill SE18	35	B1
Greenhill Gro E12	14	A1
Greenhill Pk NW10	8	A5
Greenhill Rd NW10	8	A5
Greenhill Ter SE18	35	B1
Greenhithe Cl, Sid.	42	G5
Greenholm Rd SE9	42	D3
Green Hundred Rd SE15	32	F2
Greenland Quay SE16	26	B5
Greenland Rd NW1	10	C5
Greenlaw St SE18	28	C5
Greenman St N1	11	B4
Green Pt E15	13	B3
Greenroof Way SE10	27	C4
Green's Ct W1	**6**	**C3**
Green's End SE18	28	D5
Greenshields Ind Est E16	27	E2
Greenside Rd W12	22	C4
Greenslade Rd, Bark.	14	F4
Greenstead Gdns SW15	36	C3
Green St E7	13	E3
Green St E13	13	F5
Green St W1	24	A1
Greenvale Rd SE9	42	B2
Greenview Cl W3	22	A2
Green Way SE9	41	G3
Greenwell St W1	17	B3
Greenwich Ch St SE10	33	G2
Greenwich Foot Tunnel E14	33	G1
Greenwich Foot Tunnel SE10	33	G1
Greenwich High Rd SE10	33	F4
Greenwich Ind Est SE7	27	E5
Greenwich Pk SE10	34	B3
Greenwich Pk St SE10	34	A1
Greenwich Quay SE8	33	F2
Greenwich S St SE10	33	F4
Greenwich Vw Pl E14	26	F4
Greenwood Cl SW1	31	C1
Greenwood Rd E8	11	F3
Greet St SE1	**7**	**A6**
Gregor Ms SE3	34	E5
Gregory Cres SE9	41	G5
Gregory Pl W8	23	C3
Grenada Rd SE7	34	F3
Grenade St E14	26	D1
Grenadier St E16	28	C2
Grendon St NW8	16	F3
Grenfell Rd W11	22	F1
Grenfell Twr W11	22	F1
Grenfell Wk W11	22	F1
Grenville Ms SW7	23	D5
Grenville Pl SW7	23	D4
Grenville St WC1	17	E3
Gresham Rd E6	21	B1
Gresham Rd E16	20	E5
Gresham Rd SW9	38	G1
Gresham St EC2	**7**	**D1**
Gressenhall Rd SW18	37	A4
Gresse St W1	17	D4
Greswell St SW6	29	F4
Greville Hall NW6	16	C1
Greville Pl NW6	16	C1
Greville Rd NW6	9	C5
Greville St EC1	17	G4
Greycoat Pl SW1	24	D4
Greycoat St SW1	24	D4
Grey Eagle St E1	18	E4
Greyfriars Pas EC1	**7**	**C1**
Greyhound Rd NW10	15	D2
Greyhound Rd W6	29	F2
Greyhound Rd W14	29	G2
Greystoke Pl EC4	**6**	**J1**
Grierson Rd SE23	40	B5
Griffin Cl NW10	8	D2
Griffin Manor Way SE28	28	F4
Griffin Rd SE18	35	F1
Grimsby Gro E16	28	D2
Grimston Rd SW6	30	A5
Grinwade Cl SE15	40	A1
Grinling Pl SE8	33	E2
Grinstead Rd SE8	33	C1
Grittleton Rd W9	16	B3
Grocer's Hall Ct EC2	**7**	**F2**
Groombridge Rd E9	12	B4
Groom Cres SW18	37	E5
Grosse Way SW15	36	D4
Grosvenor Av N5	11	B2
Grosvenor Av SW14	36	A1
Grosvenor Ct E14	8	F5
Grosvenor Cres SW1	24	A3
Grosvenor Cres Ms SW1	24	A3
Grosvenor Est SW1	24	D5
Grosvenor Gdns E6	20	G2
Grosvenor Gdns NW2	8	E2
Grosvenor Gdns SW1	24	B4
Grosvenor Gdns SW14	36	A1
Grosvenor Gate W1	23	G1
Grosvenor Hill W1	24	B1
Grosvenor Pk SE5	32	B5
Grosvenor Pl SW1	24	A3
Grosvenor Rd E6	13	G5
Grosvenor Rd E7	13	E3
Grosvenor Rd E11	31	B2
Grosvenor Sq W1	24	A1
Grosvenor St W1	24	B1
Grosvenor Ter SE5	32	A3
Grosvenor Wf Rd E14	27	A5
Grote's Bldgs SE3	34	B5
Grote's Pl SE3	34	B5
Grove, The E15	13	B3
Grove Cotts SW3	30	F2
Grove Cl SE23	40	B5
Grove Cres E15	13	A3
Grove End Rd NW8	16	E2
Grove Hill Rd SE5	39	D1
Groveland Ct EC4	**7**	**E2**
Grovelands Cl SE5	32	D5
Grove La SE5	32	C4
Grove Mkt Pl SE9	42	B4
Grove Ms W6	22	E4
Grove Pk SE5	32	D5
Grove Pas E2	18	G1
Grove Rd E3	12	B5
Grove Rd NW2	8	E3
Grove Rd SW13	29	B5
Grove St SE8	26	D5
Grove Vale SE22	39	D2
Grove Vil E14	26	F1
Groveway SW9	31	F4
Grummant Rd SE15	32	E4
Grundy St E14	19	F5
Guibyon Av SE24	39	A3
Guerin Sq E3	19	D2
Guernsey Gro SE24	39	B5
Guibal Rd SE12	41	D5
Guildford Gro SE10	33	F4
Guildford Rd E6	21	A5
Guildford Rd SW9	31	E4
Guildhall Yd EC2	**7**	**F1**
Guildhouse St SW1	24	C5
Guild Rd SE7	34	G1
Guilford Pl WC1	17	F3
Guilford St WC1	17	E3
Guilsborough Cl NW10	8	A4
Guinness Cl E9	12	C4
Guinness Trust Bldgs SE11	32	A1
Guinness Trust Bldgs SW9	39	A2
Guion Rd SW6	30	A5
Gulliver St SE16	26	D4
Gunmakers La E3	12	C5
Gunner La SE18	35	C1
Gunnery Ter SE18	28	E5
Gunning St SE18	28	G5
Gunpowder Sq EC4	**7**	**A1**
Gunstor Rd N16	11	D1
Gun St E1	18	E4
Gunter Gro SW10	30	D2
Gunterstone Rd W14	22	G5
Gunthorpe St E1	18	E4
Gunwhale Cl SE16	26	B2
Gurdon Rd SE7	34	D1
Gurney Cl, Bark.	14	D3
Gurney Rd E15	13	B2
Gurney Rd SW6	37	D1
Gutter La EC2	**7**	**E1**
Guyscliff Rd SE13	40	G3
Guy St SE1	25	C3
Gwendolen Av SW15	36	F3
Gwendolen Cl SW15	36	F3
Gwendoline Av E13	13	E5
Gwendwr Rd W14	29	G1
Gwyn Cl SW6	30	D3
Gwynne Rd SW11	30	E5
Gylcote Cl SE5	39	C2

H

Haarlem Rd W14	22	F4
Haberdasher St N1	18	C2
Hackford Rd SW9	31	F4
Hackford Wk SW9	31	F4
Hackney Rd E2	18	E2
Hadden Rd SE28	28	G4
Haddonfield SE8	26	B5
Haddo St SE10	33	F2
Hadleigh St E2	19	A3
Hadleigh Wk E6	21	A5
Hadley St NW1	10	B3
Hadrian Est E2	18	F1
Hadrian St SE10	34	B1
Hadyn Pk Rd W12	22	C3
Hafer Rd SW11	37	G2
Haggerston Rd E8	11	E4
Ha-Ha Rd SE18	35	B2
Haig Rd E13	20	F2
Haig Rd W E13	20	F2
Haimo Rd SE9	41	G3
Hainford Cl SE4	40	B2

Hainton Cl SE1 18 G5
Halcomb St N1 11 D5
Haldane Rd E6 20 G2
Haldane Rd SW6 30 A3
Haldon Rd SW18 37 A3
Hale Rd E6 21 A3
Hale St E14 26 F1
Halesworth Rd
SE13 40 F1
Half Moon Cres N1 17 F1
Half Moon La SE24 39 B4
Half Moon St W1 24 B2
Halford Rd SW6 30 B2
Halfway St, Sid. 42 F5
Halkin Arc SW1 23 G4
Halkin Pl SW1 24 A4
Halkin St SW1 24 A3
Hall, The SE3 41 D1
Hallam Rd SW13 36 D1
Hallam St W1 16 C2
Halley Gdns SE13 41 A2
Halley Rd E7 13 F3
Halley Rd E12 13 G3
Halley St E14 19 C4
Hallfield Est W2 16 D5
Hallford St N1 11 B4
Halliwell Rd SW2 38 F4
Hall Pl W2 16 E3
Hall Rd E6 14 B5
Hall Rd NW8 16 D3
Hall St EC1 3 A2
Hallsville Rd E16 20 C5
Hall Twr W2 16 E3
Hallywell Cres E6 21 B4
Halons Rd SE9 42 C5
Halsbrook Rd SE3 41 G1
Halsbury Rd W12 22 D2
Halsey St SW3 23 G5
Halsmere Rd SE5 32 A4
Halston Cl SW11 37 G4
Halstow Rd NW10 15 F2
Halstow Rd SE10 34 D1
Halton Cross St N1 11 A5
Halton Rd N1 11 A4
Hambalt Rd SW4 38 C3
Hambledon Rd
SW18 37 A5
Hambledown Rd,
Sid. 42 F5
Hamble St SW6 37 C1
Hambridge Way
SW2 38 G5
Hameway E6 21 C3
Hamfrith Rd E15 13 C3
Hamilton Cl NW8 16 E2
Hamilton Gdns
NW8 16 D2
Hamilton Pk N5 11 A1
Hamilton Pk W N5 11 A1
Hamilton Pl W1 24 A2
Hamilton Rd E15 20 B2
Hamilton Rd NW10 8 C2
Hamilton Rd W4 22 A3
Hamilton Rd, Ilf. 14 D1
Hamilton Ter NW8 16 C1
Hamlea Cl SE12 41 C3
Hamlet, The SE5 39 C1
Hamlet Gdns W6 22 C5
Hamlets Way E3 19 D3
Hammersmith Br
SW13 29 D1
Hammersmith Br
W6 29 D1
Hammersmith Br Rd
W6 29 E1
Hammersmith Bdy
W6 22 E5
Hammersmith Flyover
W6 29 E1
Hammersmith Gro
W6 22 E4
Hammersmith Rd
W6 22 F5
Hammersmith Rd
W14 22 F5

Hammersmith Ter
W6 29 C1
Hammond St NW5 10 C3
Ham Pk Rd E7 13 C4
Ham Pk Rd E15 13 C4
Hampson Way SW8 31 F4
Hampstead Grn
NW3 9 F2
Hampstead High St
NW3 9 D1
Hampstead Hill Gdns
NW3 9 E1
Hampstead Rd
NW1 17 C1
Hampton Cl NW6 16 B2
Hampton Rd E7 13 E2
Hampton Rd, Ilf. 14 C1
Hampton St SE1 25 A5
Hampton St SE17 25 A5
Ham Yd W1 6 C3
Hanameel St E16 27 D2
Hanbury St E1 18 E2
Hancock Rd E3 19 G2
Hand Ct WC1 17 F3
Handel St WC1 17 E3
Handen Rd SE12 41 B3
Handforth Rd SW9 31 G3
Handley Rd E9 12 A4
Hands Wk E16 20 D5
Hanging Sword All
EC4 7 A2
Hankey Pl SE1 25 C3
Hannell Rd SW6 29 C3
Hannibal Rd E1 19 A4
Hannington Rd
SW4 38 B1
Hanover Av E16 27 D2
Hanover Gdns SE11 31 G2
Hanover Gate NW1 16 F2
Hanover Pk SE15 32 F4
Hanover Pl WC2 6 F2
Hanover Rd NW10 8 C2
Hanover Sq W1 17 B5
Hanover St W1 17 B5
Hanover Ter NW1 16 F2
Hans Cres SW1 23 G4
Hansler Rd SE22 39 E3
Hanson Cl SW12 38 B5
Hanson St W1 17 C4
Hans Pl SW1 23 G4
Hans Rd SW3 23 G4
Hanway Pl W1 6 C1
Hanway St W1 6 C1
Harben Rd NW6 9 D4
Harberson Rd E15 13 C5
Harbet Rd W2 16 E4
Harbinger Rd E14 26 F5
Harbledown Rd
SW6 30 B4
Harbord St SW6 29 F4
Harborough Av,
Sid. 42 G5
Harbour Av SW10 30 D4
Harbour Ex Sq E14 26 F3
Harbour Rd SE5 39 B1
Harbridge Av
SW15 36 B5
Harbut Rd SW11 37 E2
Harcourt Av E12 14 B1
Harcourt Rd E15 20 C1
Harcourt Rd SE4 40 C2
Harcourt St W1 16 F4
Harcourt Ter SW10 30 C1
Hardens Manorway
SE7 27 G4
Harders Rd SE15 32 G5
Hardinge Rd NW10 8 D5
Hardinge St E1 19 A5
Hardman Rd SE7 34 E1
Hardwicke St, Bark. 14 E5
Hardwick St EC1 17 G2
Hardy Rd SE3 34 C3
Hare & Billet Rd
SE3 34 A4
Harebell Dr E6 21 C4
Hare Ct EC4 6 J2

Harecourt Rd N1 11 B3
Haredale Rd SE24 39 B2
Haredon Cl SE23 40 A5
Harefield Ms SE4 40 D1
Harefield Rd SE4 40 D1
Hare Row E2 18 G1
Hare St SE18 28 C4
Hare Wk N1 18 D1
Harewood Av NW1 16 F3
Harewood Rd NW10 8 C5
Harfield Gdns SE5 39 D1
Harford St E1 19 C3
Hargood Rd SE3 34 F3
Hargwyne St SW9 38 F1
Harlescott Rd SE15 40 B2
Harlesden Gdns
NW10 8 B5
Harlesden La NW10 8 C5
Harlesden Rd NW10 8 C5
Harleyford Rd SE11 31 F2
Harleyford St SE11 31 G2
Harley Gdns SW10 30 D1
Harley Gro E3 19 D2
Harley Pl W1 17 B4
Harley Rd NW3 9 E4
Harley Rd NW10 15 A5
Harley St W1 17 B3
Harlinger St SE18 28 A4
Harmood St NW1 10 B4
Harmsworth St
SE17 32 A1
Harold Est SE1 25 D4
Harold Gibbons Ct
SE7 34 F2
Harold Pl SE11 31 G1
Harold Rd E13 13 E5
Harp All EC4 7 B1
Harper Rd E6 21 B5
Harper Rd SE1 25 B4
Harp La EC3 7 H4
Harpley Sq E1 19 A2
Harpour Rd, Bark. 14 E3
Harpsden St SW11 31 A4
Harpur St WC1 17 F4
Harraden Rd SE3 34 F3
Harrap St E14 26 G1
Harriet Ms SE28 28 F4
Harriet Way E6 21 B4
Harriet St E8 11 F5
Harriet Tubman Cl
SW2 38 G5
Harriet Wk SW1 23 G3
Harrington Gdns
SW7 23 C5
Harrington Rd SW7 23 E5
Harrington Sq NW1 17 C1
Harrington St NW1 17 C2
Harrington Way
SE18 27 G4
Harriott Cl SE10 27 C5
Harrison St WC1 17 E2
Harris St SE5 32 C2
Harroway Rd SW11 30 E5
Harrowby St W1 16 F4
Harrowgate Rd E9 12 C3
Harrow La E14 26 G1
Harrow Pl E1 7 J1
Harrow Rd E6 14 A5
Harrow Rd E11 15 D2
Harrow Rd W2 16 A3
Harrow Rd W9 16 A3
Harrow Rd W10 15 F3
Harrow Rd, Bark. 14 G5
Harrow Rd, Ilf. 14 G5
Hartfield Ter E3 19 E1
Hartham Cl N7 10 E2
Hartham Rd N7 10 E2

Hartmann Rd E16 27 G2
Harton St SE8 33 E4
Hartshorn All EC3 7 J2
Hartshorn Gdns E6 21 C3
Harts La SE14 33 C3
Harts La, Bark. 14 D3
Hart St EC3 7 J3
Hartswood Gdns
W12 22 B4
Hartswood Rd W12 22 B3
Hartsworth Cl E13 20 C1
Hartville Rd SE18 28 G5
Harvard Rd SE13 40 G3
Harvey Gdns SE7 34 F1
Harvey Rd SE5 32 C4
Harvey Rd, Ilf. 14 D2
Harvey St N1 11 C5
Harvist Est N7 10 G1
Harvist Rd NW6 15 F1
Harwood Rd SW6 30 B3
Harwood Ter SW6 30 C4
Haselrigge Rd SW4 38 D2
Hasker St SW3 23 F5
Haslam Cl N1 10 G4
Haslam St SE15 32 E3
Hassendean Rd
SE3 34 E2
Hassett Rd E9 12 B3
Hassop Rd NW2 8 F1
Hasted Rd SE7 34 G1
Hastings Cl SE15 32 F3
Hastings Ho SE18 28 B5
Hastings St SE18 28 E4
Hastings St WC1 17 E2
Hatcham Pk Rd
SE14 33 B4
Hatcham Rd SE15 33 A2
Hatcliffe Cl SE3 41 C1
Hatfield Rd E15 13 B2
Hatfields SE1 7 A5
Hathaway Cres E12 14 B3
Hatherley Gdns E6 20 G1
Hatherley Gro W2 16 C5
Hathorne Cl SE15 32 G5
Hatton Cl SE18 35 F3
Hatton Gdn EC1 17 G4
Hatton Pl EC1 17 G3
Hatton Wall EC1 17 G4
Haul Rd NW1 17 E1
Havannah St E14 26 E3
Havelock Rd N1 10 E5
Havelock Ter SW8 31 B3
Haverfield Rd E3 19 C2
Haverstock Hill
NW3 9 F2
Haverstock Rd
NW3 10 A2
Haverstock St N1 18 A1
Havil St SE5 32 D3
Hawarden Gro
SE24 39 B5
Hawes St N1 11 A4
Hawgood St E3 19 E4
Hawkesbury Rd
SW15 36 D3
Hawkshead Rd
NW10 8 B4
Hawkshead Rd W4 22 A3
Hawkslade Rd
SE15 40 B3
Hawksmoor Cl
SE18 35 G1
Hawksmoor St W6 29 F2
Hawkstone Rd
SE16 26 A5
Hawley Cres NW1 10 B4
Hawley Rd NW1 10 B4
Hawley St NW1 10 B4
Hawstead Rd SE6 40 F4
Hawthorn Av E3 12 D5
Hawthorn Cl N1 11 D3
Hawthorn Rd NW10 8 C4
Hawtrey Rd NW3 9 F4
Hay Cl E15 13 B4
Haycroft Gdns
NW10 8 C5

Street	Ref		Street	Ref		Street	Ref		Street	Ref
Haycroft Rd SW2	38 E3		Helix Rd SW2	38 F4		Herringham Rd SE7	27 F4		High St N E12	14 A2
Hay Currie St E14	19 F5		Helmet Row EC1	18 B3		Hersant Cl NW10	8 C5		High St S E6	21 B1
Hayday Rd E16	20 D4		Helmsley Pl E8	11 G4		Herschell Rd SE23	40 C5		High Timber St EC4	7 D1
Haydon Wk SW11	38 F2		Helsinki Sq SE16	26 C4		Hersham Cl SW15	36 C5		Highway, The E1	25 G1
Hayes Gro SE15	39 E2		Hemans St SW8	31 D3		Hertford Av SW14	36 A3		Highway, The, E14	25 G1
Hay Hill W1	24 B1		Hemberton Rd SW9	38 E1		Hertford Rd N1	11 D5		Hilary Cl SW6	30 C3
Hayles St SE11	25 A5		Hemingford Rd N1	10 F5		Hertford Rd, Bark.	14 D4		Hilary Rd W12	15 B5
Haymarket SW1	6 C4		Hemlock Rd W12	22 B2		Hertford St W1	24 B2		Hilda Rd E6	13 G4
Haymarket Arc SW1	6 C4		Hemming St E1	18 F3		Hertsmere Rd E14	26 E1		Hilda Rd E16	20 B3
Haymerle Rd SE15	32 F2		Hemp Wk SE17	25 B5		Hervey Rd SE3	34 E4		Hilda Ter SW9	31 G5
Haynes Cl SE3	41 B1		Hemstal Rd NW6	9 B4		Hesketh Pl W11	22 G1		Hildyard Rd SW6	30 B2
Hay's Galleria SE1	7 H5		Henchman St W12	15 B5		Hesper Ms SW5	30 C1		Hiley Rd NW10	15 E2
Hay's La SE1	7 H6		Henderson Rd E7	13 F3		Hesperus Cres E14	26 F5		Hilgrove Rd NW6	9 D4
Hay's Ms W1	24 B1		Henderson Rd SW18	37 F5		Hessel St E1	18 G5		Hillbeck Cl SE15	33 A3
Hay St E2	11 F5		Hendrick Av SW12	37 G4		Hestercombe Av SW6	29 G5		Hillcourt Rd SE22	39 G4
Hayter Rd SW2	38 E3		Heneage La EC3	7 J2		Hester Rd SW11	30 F3		Hillcroft Rd E6	21 D4
Hayward Gdns SW15	36 E4		Heneage St E1	18 E2		Heston St SE14	33 D4		Hilldrop Cres N7	10 D2
Hazelbourne Rd SW12	38 B4		Hengist Rd SE12	41 E5		Hetherington Rd SW4	38 E2		Hilldrop Est N7	10 D2
Hazel Cl SE15	32 F5		Hengrave Rd SE23	40 B5		Hetley Rd W12	22 D2		Hilldrop La N7	10 D2
Hazeldon Rd SE4	40 C3		Henley Cross SE3	41 E1		Hevelius Cl SE10	34 C1		Hilldrop Rd N7	10 D2
Hazelmere Rd NW6	9 B5		Henley Dr SE1	25 E5		Heverham Rd SE18	28 G5		Hillend SE18	35 C4
Hazel Rd NW10	15 E2		Henley Rd E16	28 B3		Hewer St W10	15 F4		Hillersdon Av SW13	29 C5
Hazlebury Rd SW6	36 D5		Henley Rd NW10	8 E5		Hewison St E3	19 D1		Hillfield Ct NW3	9 F2
Hazlewell Rd SW15	36 D3		Henley, Rd. Ilf.			Hewlett Rd E3	19 C1		Hillfield Rd NW6	9 A2
Hazlewood Cres W10	15 G3		Henley St SW11	31 A5		Heyford Av SW8	31 E3		Hillgate Pl SW12	38 B5
Hazlitt Rd W14	22 G4		Henniker Gdns E6	20 G2		Heygate St SE17	25 B5		Hillgate Pl W8	23 B2
Headfort Pl SW1	24 A3		Henniker Pt E15	13 B3		Heyworth Rd E5	11 G1		Hillgate St W8	23 B2
Headlam Rd SW4	38 D4		Henniker Rd E15	13 A2		Heyworth Rd E15	13 C2		Hillier Rd SW11	37 G4
Headlam St E1	18 G3		Henning St SW11	30 F4		Hibbert St SW11	37 D1		Hillingdon St SE5	32 A2
Head St E1	19 B5		Henrietta Cl SE8	33 E2		Hichisson Rd SE15	40 A3		Hillingdon St SE17	32 A2
Heald St SE14	33 D4		Henrietta Pl W1	17 B5		Hickin Cl SE7	27 G3		Hillman Dr W10	15 E3
Healey St NW1	10 B3		Henrietta St E15	12 G2		Hickling Rd, Ilf.	14 D2		Hillman St E8	11 G3
Hearn St EC2	18 D3		Henrietta St WC2	6 F3		Hickman Cl E16	20 G4		Hillmarton Rd N7	10 E2
Heathcote St WC1	17 F3		Henriques St E1	18 F5		Hickmore Wk SW4	38 C1		Hillmead Dr SW9	39 A2
Heath Dr NW3	9 C1		Henry Addlington Cl E6			Hicks Cl SW11	37 F1		Hillreach SE18	35 B1
Heatherbank SE9	35 B5		Henry Dent Cl SE5	39 C2		Hicks St SE8	33 C1		Hill Rd NW8	16 D1
Heather Cl E1	21 D4		Henry Dickens Ct W11	22 F2		Hide Pl SW1	24 D5		Hillsborough Rd SE22	39 D3
Heather Cl SE13	41 A5		Henry Jackson Rd SW15	36 F1		Hide Twr SW1	24 D5		Hillside Cl NW8	16 C1
Heather Cl SW8	38 B1		Henry Rd E6	21 A1		High Br SE10	34 A1		Hillsleigh Rd W8	23 A2
Heathfield Cl E16	20 G4		Henryson Rd SE4	40 E3		Highbridge Rd, Bark.	14 D5		Hills Pl W1	6 A2
Heathfield Gdns SE3	34 B5		Henshall St N1	11 C3		High Br Wf SE10	34 A1		Hill St W1	24 B2
Heathfield Pk NW2	8 E3		Henshaw St SE17	25 C5		Highbrook Rd SE3	41 G1		Hilltop Rd NW6	9 B4
Heathfield Rd SW18	37 D4		Henslowe Rd SE22	39 F3		Highbury Cor N5	10 G3		Hill Vw Dr SE28	28 G2
Heathfield Sq SW18	37 E5		Henson Av NW2	8 E2		Highbury Cres N5	10 G3		Hill Vw Dr, Well.	35 G5
Heath Hurst Rd NW3	9 F1		Henstridge Pl NW8	16 F1		Highbury Est N5	11 B2		Hillworth Rd SW2	38 G5
Heathla SE3	34 A5		Henty Cl SW11	30 F3		Highbury Gra N5	11 A1		Hillyard St SW9	31 G4
Heathlee Rd SE3	41 C2		Henty Wk SW15	36 D3		Highbury Gro N5	11 A3		Hilly Flds Cres SE4	40 E1
Heathmans Rd SW6	30 A4		Henwick Rd SE9	41 G1		Highbury New Pk N5	11 B2		Hilsea St E5	12 A1
Heath Ri SW15	36 F4		Hepscott Rd E9	12 E4		Highbury Pl N5	11 A3		Hinckley Rd SE15	39 F2
Heath Rd SW8	31 B5		Herbal Hill EC1	17 G3		Highbury Sta Rd N1	10 G3		Hind Ct EC4	7 A2
Heath Side NW3	9 E1		Herbert Gdns NW10	15 D1		Highbury Ter N5	11 A2		Hinde St W1	17 A5
Heathstan Rd W12	15 C5		Herbert Rd E12	14 A1		Highbury Ter Ms N5	11 A2		Hind Gro E14	19 E5
Heath St NW3	9 D1		Herbert Rd SE18	35 C3		Highcliffe Dr SW15	36 B4		Hindmans Rd SE22	39 F3
Heathview Gdns SW15	36 E5		Herbert St E13	20 D1		Highcombe SE7	34 F2		Hindrey Rd E5	11 G2
Heathwall St SW11	37 G1		Herbert St NW5	10 A3		Highdown Rd SW15	36 D4		Hinstock Rd SE18	35 E2
Heathway SE3	34 C3		Herbrand St WC1	17 E3		Highfield Cl SE13	41 A5		Hinton Rd SE24	39 A1
Heathwood Gdns SE7	28 A5		Hercules St N7	24 F4		Highgate Rd NW5	10 B1		Hippodrome Pl W11	22 G1
Heaton Rd SE15	39 F1		Hereford Ho NW6	16 B5		High Gro SE18	15 B1		Hitchin Sq E3	19 C1
Heaven Tree Cl N1	11 B2		Hereford Rd W2	16 B5		Highshore Rd SE15	32 E5		Hither Fm Rd SE3	41 F1
Heavitree Cl SE18	35 F1		Hereford Sq SW7	23 D5		High St E13	20 D1		Hither Grn La SE13	40 D3
Heavitree Rd SE18	35 F1		Hereford St E2	18 F3		High St E15	13 B1		Hobart Pl SW1	24 B4
Heber Rd NW2	8 F2		Heritage Cl SW9	39 A1		High St (Harlesden) NW10	15 B1		Hobbes Wk SW15	36 D3
Heber Rd SE22	39 E4		Hermitage, The SW13	29 B4		High St N E6	14 A5		Hobday St E14	19 F4
Hebron Rd W6	22 D4		Hermitage Row E8	11 F2					Hobury St SW10	30 D2
Hector St SE18	28 G5		Hermitage St W2	16 E4					Hockley Av E6	21 A1
Heddington Gro N7	10 F2		Hermitage Wall E1	25 F2					Hockley Ms, Bark.	21 G1
Heddon St W1	6 A3		Hermit Rd E16	20 C4					Hocroft Rd NW2	9 A1
Hedgers Gro E9	12 C3		Hermit St EC1	18 A2					Hodnet Gro SE16	26 B5
Hedgley St SE12	41 C3		Herndon Rd SW18	37 D3					Hofland Rd W14	22 F4
Heigham Rd E6	13 G4		Herne Hill SE24	39 B4					Hogarth Business Pk W4	29 A2
Heights, The SE7	34 F1		Herne Hill Rd SE24	39 B1					Hogarth Cl E16	20 G4
Heiron St SE17	32 A2		Herne Pl SE24	39 A3					Hogarth Ct EC3	7 J3
Helby Rd SW4	38 D4		Heron Cl NW10	8 A3					Hogarth La W4	29 A2
Helder Gro SE12	41 C5		Heron Pl SE16	26 C2					Hogarth Rd SW5	23 C5
Helena Rd E13	20 C1		Heron Quay E14	26 E2					Hogarth Roundabout W4	29 A3
Helena Rd NW10	8 D2		Heron Rd SE24	39 B2					Holbeach Gdns, Sid.	42 G4
			Herrick St SW1	24 D5					Holbeach Rd SE6	40 E5
			Herries St W10	15 G1					Holbeck Row SE15	32 F3
									Holbein Ms SW1	31 A1
									Holbein Pl SW1	24 A5

Holberton Gdns
NW10 15 D2
Holborn EC1 17 G4
Holborn Rd E13 20 E3
Holborn Viaduct
EC1 17 G4
Holbrooke St E9 10 E1
Holbrook Rd E15 20 C1
Holburne Cl SE3 34 F4
Holburne Gdns
SE3 34 G4
Holburne Rd SE3 34 F4
Holcombe St W9 29 D1
Holcroft Rd E9 12 A4
Holdenby Rd SE4 40 C3
Holden St SW11 31 A5
Holford St WC1 17 G2
Holgate Av SW11 37 E1
Holland Gdns W14 22 G4
Holland Gro SW9 31 G3
Holland Pk W8 23 A3
Holland Pk W11 22 G3
Holland Pk Av W11 22 G3
Holland Pk Gdns
W14 22 G2
Holland Pk Ms W11 22 G2
Holland Pk Rd W14 23 A4
Holland Pk
Roundabout W11 22 F3
Holland Rd E6 14 B5
Holland Rd E15 20 B2
Holland Rd W14 8 C5
Holland Rd W14 22 F3
Holland St SE1 7 C5
Holland St W8 23 A3
Holland Vil Rd W14 22 G3
Holland Wk W8 23 A3
Hollen St W1 6 C1
Holles St W1 17 B5
Holley Rd W3 22 A3
Hollingbourne Rd
SE24 39 B3
Hollington Rd E6 21 B2
Holloway Rd E6 21 B2
Holloway Rd N7 10 F1
Hollybush Gdns E2 18 G2
Holly Bush Hill
NW3 9 D1
Hollymount Cl
SE10 33 G4
Holly St E8 11 E3
Holly Wk NW3 9 D1
Hollywood Rd
SW10 30 D2
Holman Rd SW11 30 E5
Holmbush Rd
SW15 36 G4
Holmcote Gdns N5 11 B2
Holmdale Rd NW6 9 F4
Holmdene Av SE24 39 B3
Holmead Rd SW6 30 C3
Holmefield Ct NW3 9 F3
Holme Lacey Rd
SE12 41 C4
Holme Rd E6 14 A5
Holmesley Rd
SE23 40 C4
Holmes Rd NW5 10 B2
Holmes Ter SE1 24 G3
Holmewood Gdns
SW2 38 F5
Holmewood Rd
SW2 38 F5
Holmside Rd SW12 38 A4
Holms St E2 18 C2
Holness Rd E15 13 C3
Holroyd Rd SW15 36 E2
Holton St E1 19 B3

Holt Rd E16 28 A2
Holwood Pl SW4 38 D2
Holybourne Av
SW15 36 C5
Holyhead Cl E3 19 E2
Holyport Rd SW6 29 E3
Holyrood St SE1 7 H6
Holywell Cl SE3 34 D2
Holywell La EC2 18 D3
Holywell Row EC2 18 D3
Homefield Rd W4 22 B5
Homefield St N1 18 D1
Homeleigh Rd
SE15 40 B3
Homer Dr E14 26 E5
Homer Rd E9 12 C2
Homer Rd E9 12 C3
Homer Row W1 16 F4
Homer St W1 16 F4
Homerton Gro E9 12 B2
Homerton High St
E9 12 A2
Homerton Rd E9 12 C2
Homerton Row E9 12 A2
Homestall Rd SE22 40 A3
Homestead Rd
SW6 30 A3
Honeybourne Rd
NW6 9 C2
Honeybrook Rd
SW12 38 C5
Honey La EC2 7 E2
Honeyman Cl NW6 8 F4
Honeywell Rd
SW11 37 G4
Honeywood Rd
NW10 15 B1
Honiton Rd NW6 16 A1
Honley Rd SE6 40 F5
Honor Oak Pk SE23 40 A4
Honor Oak Ri SE23 40 A4
Hood Ct EC4 7 A2
Hooper Rd E16 20 D5
Hooper St E1 18 F5
Hopedale Rd SE7 34 E2
Hopefield Av NW6 15 G1
Hope St SW11 37 E1
Hopewell St SE5 32 C3
Hop Gdns WC2 6 E4
Hopkins St W1 6 B2
Hop St SE10 27 C5
Hopton Gdns SE1 7 C5
Hopton St SE1 7 C5
Hopwood Rd SE17 32 C2
Horace Rd E7 13 H1
Horatio St E2 18 E1
Horbury Cres W11 23 B1
Horder Rd SW6 29 G4
Horizon Way SE7 27 E5
Horle Wk SE5 32 A5
Hormead Rd W9 16 A3
Hornbeam Cl, Ilf. 14 F2
Hornby Cl NW3 9 E4
Horncastle Cl SE12 41 D5
Horncastle Rd SE12 41 D5
Horne Way SW15 29 E5
Hornfair Rd SE7 27 D5
Horn La SE10 27 D5
Horn Link Way SE10 27 D5
Horn Pk Cl SE12 41 E3
Horn Pk La SE12 41 E3
Hornsey St N7 10 F2
Hornshay St SE14 33 A2
Hornton Pl W8 23 B3
Hornton St W8 23 B3
**Horse & Dolphin Yd
W1** 6 D3
Horseferry Pl SE10 33 G2
Horseferry Rd E14 26 C1
Horseferry Rd SW1 24 D5

Horsell Rd N5 10 G2
Horselydown La
SE1 25 E3
Horse Ride SW1 6 C6
Horseshoe Cl E14 33 G1
Horsfeld Gdns SE9 42 A3
Horsfeld Rd SE9 41 G3
Horsford Rd SW2 38 F3
Horsley St SE17 32 C2
Horsmonden Rd
SE4 40 D3
Horton Av NW2 8 G1
Horton Rd E8 11 G3
Horton St SE13 40 F1
Hosier La EC1 18 A4
Hoskins Cl E16 20 F5
Hoskins St SE10 34 A1
Hotham Rd SW15 36 E1
Hotham St E15 13 B5
Hotspur St SE11 31 G1
Houghton St WC2 6 H2
Houndsditch EC3 7 J1
Hoveden Rd NW2 9 B2
Howard Cl NW2 8 G1
Howard Rd E6 21 B1
Howard Rd N16 11 C1
Howard Rd NW2 8 F1
Howard Rd, Bark. 14 F5
Howard Rd, Ilf. 14 D5
Howards La SW15 36 D2
Howards Rd E13 20 D2
Howbury Rd SE15 40 A1
Howden St SE15 39 F1
Howick Pl SW1 24 C4
Howie St SW11 30 F3
Howitt Rd NW3 9 F3
Howland Est SE16 26 A4
Howland St W1 17 C4
Howland Way SE16 26 C3
Howletts Rd SE24 39 B4
Howley Pl W2 16 D4
Howsman Rd SW13 29 C2
Howson Rd SE4 40 C2
Hows St E2 18 E1
Hoxton Sq N1 18 D2
Hoxton St N1 11 D5
Hoylake Rd W3 15 A5
Hoy St E16 20 C5
Hubbard St E15 13 B5
Hubert Gro SW9 38 E1
Hubert Rd E6 20 G2
Huddart St E3 19 D4
Huddleston Cl E2 19 A1
Huddlestone Rd E7 13 G1
Huddlestone Rd
NW2 8 D3
Huddleston Rd N7 10 D1
Hudson Pl SE18 35 E1
Hugging St SW15 36 F2
Huggin Ct EC4 7 E3
Huggin Hill EC4 7 E3
Hugh Astor Ct SE1 13 A2
Hugh Dalton Av
SW6 30 A2
Hugh Gaitskell Cl
SW6 30 A2
Hugh St SW1 24 B5
Hugon Rd SW6 37 C1
Hugo Rd N19 10 C1
Huguenot Pl E1 18 E4
Huguenot St SW18 37 D3
Hull Cl SE16 26 B3
Hulse Av, Bark. 14 F3
Humber Dr W10 15 F3
Humber Rd SE3 34 C2
Humberstone Rd
E13 20 F2
Humbolt Rd W6 29 G2
Humphrey St SE1 32 E1
Hungerford Br SE1 6 F5
Hungerford Br WC2 6 F5
Hungerford La WC2 6 E5
Hunsdon Rd SE14 33 B2
Hunt Cl W11 22 G1
Hunter Rd, Ilf. 14 D2

Hunter St WC1 17 E3
Hunter Wk E13 20 D1
Huntingdon St E16 20 C5
Huntingdon St N1 10 F4
Huntingfield Rd
SW15 36 C2
Huntley St WC1 17 C3
Huntley St WC1 18 F3
Hunt's Cl SE3 34 D5
Hunt's Ct WC2 6 D4
Hunts La E15 19 G1
Huntsman St SE17 25 C5
Hurlingham Business
Pk SW6 37 B1
Hurlingham Ct
SW6 37 A1
Hurlingham Gdns
SW6 37 A1
Hurlingham Rd
SW6 30 A5
Hurlingham Sq
SW6 37 B1
Hurren Cl SE3 41 B1
Hurry Cl E15 13 B4
Hurstbourne Gdns,
Bark. 14 G3
Hurst St SE24 39 A4
Hurstway Wk W11 22 F1
Huson Cl NW3 9 F4
Hutchings St E14 26 E3
Hutton St EC4 7 A2
Huxbear St SE4 40 D3
Huxley St W10 15 G2
Hyacinth Cl, Ilf. 14 D3
Hyde Cl E13 20 D1
Hyde Pk SW7 23 G2
Hyde Pk W1 23 G2
Hyde Pk W2 23 G2
Hyde Pk Cor W1 24 A3
Hyde Pk Cres W2 16 F5
Hyde Pk Gdns W2 23 E1
Hyde Pk Gdns SW7 23 D3
Hyde Pk Pl W2 23 F1
Hyde Pk Sq W2 16 F5
Hyde Pk St W2 16 F5
Hyderabad Way
E15 13 B4
Hyde Rd N1 11 C5
Hyde Vale SE10 33 G3
Hyndman St SE15 32 G2
Hythe Rd NW10 15 C3
Hythe Rd Ind Est
NW10 15 C2

I

Ibbotson Av E16 20 C5
Iceland Rd E3 12 E5
Ida St E14 19 G5
Idmiston Rd E15 13 C2
Idol La EC3 7 H4
Idonia St SE8 33 D3
Iffley Rd W6 22 D4
Ifield Rd SW10 30 C2
Ilbert St W10 15 F2
Ilchester Gdns W2 23 C1
Ilchester Pl W14 23 A4
Ilderton Rd SE15 33 A3
Ilderton Rd SE16 32 G1
Ilex Rd NW10 8 B3
Iliffe St SE17 32 A1
Ilkley Rd E16 20 F4
Ilminster Gdns
SW11 37 F2
Imber St N1 11 C5
Imperial Coll Rd
SW7 23 D4
Imperial Rd SW6 30 C4
Imperial Sq SW6 30 C4
Imperial St E3 19 G2
Imperial Wf SW6 30 D5
Inca Dr SE9 42 D5
Indescon Ct E14 26 F3
India Pl WC2 6 G3
India Way W12 22 C1
Indus Rd SE7 34 F3

Ingal Rd E13	20 D3	Ivy St N1	18 D1	Jodrell Rd E3	12 D5
Ingate Pl SW8	31 B4	Ixworth Pl SW3	30 F1	**John Adam St** WC2	**6 F4**
Ingelow Rd SW8	31 B5			John Aird Cl SW18	16 D4
Ingersoll Rd W12	22 D2	**J**		John Archer Way	
Ingestre Pl W1	**6 B2**			SW18	37 E4
Ingestre Rd E7	13 D1	Jacaranda Gro E8	11 E4	John Ashby Cl	
Ingestre Rd NW5	10 B1	Jack Clow Rd E15	20 B1	SW2	38 E4
Ingham Rd NW6	9 B1	Jack Cornwell St		John Barnes Wk	
Ingleborough St		E12	14 C1	E15	13 C3
SW9	31 G5	Jack Dash Way E6	21 A3	John Burns Dr,	
Ingledew Rd SE18	35 C3	Jackman St E8	11 G5	Bark.	14 G4
Inglesham Wk E9	12 D3	Jackson Cl E9	12 A4	John Campbell Rd	
Ingleside Gro SE3	34 C2	Jackson Rd N7	10 F1	N16	11 D2
Inglethorpe St		Jackson Rd, Bark.	14 G1	**John Carpenter St**	
SW6	29 F4	Jackson St SE18	35 C2	EC4	**7 B3**
Ingleton St SW9	31 G5	Jack Walker Ct N5	11 A1	John Cornwell VC Ho	
Inglewood Cl E14	26 E5	Jacobs Ho E13	20 F2	E12	14 C1
Inglewood Rd NW6	9 B2	Jacob St SE1	25 E3	John Felton Rd	
Inglis St SE5	32 A4	Jade Cl E16	20 G5	SE16	25 F3
Ingrave St SW11	37 E1	Jaggard Way		John Fisher St E1	25 F1
Inigo Jones Rd SE7	35 A3	SW12	37 G5	John Harrison Way	
Inigo Pl WC2	**6 E3**	Jago Cl SE18	35 E2	SE10	27 C4
Inkerman Rd NW5	10 B3	Jago Wk SE5	32 C3	John Islip St SW1	24 E5
Inman Rd NW10	8 A5	Jamaica Rd SE1	25 E3	John Maurice Cl	
Inman Rd SW18	37 D5	Jamaica Rd SE16	25 E3	SE17	25 B5
Inner Circle NW1	17 A2	Jamaica St E1	19 A5	John Penn St SE13	33 F4
Inner Temple La EC4	**6 J2**	James Av NW2	8 E2	John Princes St W1	17 B5
Innes Gdns SW15	36 D4	Jameson Ct E2	19 A1	John Roll Way	
Inniskilling Rd E13	20 F1	Jameson St W8	23 B2	SE16	25 F4
Institute Pl E8	11 G2	James Sinclair Pt		John Ruskin St SE5	32 A3
Inverine Rd SE7	34 E1	E13	13 F5	John Silkin La SE8	33 B1
Invermore Pl SE18	28 E5	James St W1	17 A5	John's Ms WC1	17 F3
Inverness Ms E16	28 E2	James St, Bark.	14 E4	John Smith Av	
Inverness Pl W2	23 C1	Jamestown Rd		SW6	30 A3
Inverness Ter W2	23 C1	NW1	10 B5	Johnson Cl E8	11 F5
Inverton Rd SE15	40 B2	Jamestown Way		Johnson's Pl SW1	31 C1
Invicta Plaza SE1	**7 B5**	E14	27 A1	John Spencer Sq	
Invicta Rd SE3	34 D3	Jamuna Cl E14	19 C4	N1	11 A3
Inville Rd SE17	32 C1	Janet St E14	26 E4	Johnstone Rd E6	21 B2
Inwen Ct SE8	33 C1	Janeway St SE16	25 F3	John St E15	13 C5
Inworth St SW11	30 F5	Janson Rd E15	13 B2	John St WC1	17 F3
Iona Cl SE6	40 E5	Jardine Rd E1	26 B1	John Williams Cl	
Ireland Yd EC4	**7 C2**	Jarrow Rd SE16	26 A5	SE14	33 B2
Irene Rd SW6	30 B4	Jarrow Way E9	12 C1	John Wilson St	
Iris Cl E6	21 A3	Jasmine Cl, Ilf.	14 D2	SE18	28 C4
Iron Br Cl NW10	8 A2	Jasper Rd E16	20 G5	John Woolley Cl	
Iron Mill Rd SW18	37 C5	Jasper Rd SE19	23 D3	SE13	41 B2
Ironmonger La EC2	**7 F2**	Jay Ms SW7	23 D4	**Joiner St** SE1	**7 G3**
Ironmonger Row		Jebb Av SW2	38 E4	Jonathan St SE11	31 F1
EC1	18 B2	Jebb St E3	19 E1	Joseph Hardcastle Cl	
Irving Gro SW9	31 F5	Jedburgh Rd E13	20 F2	SE14	33 B2
Irving Rd W14	22 F4	Jedburgh St SW11	38 A2	Josephine Av SW2	38 F3
Irving St WC2	**6 D3**	Jeddo Rd W12	22 B3	Joseph St E3	19 D3
Irwin Av SE18	35 G3	Jeffreys Rd SW4	31 E5	Joubert St SW11	30 G5
Irwin Gdns NW10	8 D5	Jeffreys St NW1	10 B4	Jowett St SE15	32 E5
Isabella Rd E9	12 A2	Jeffrey's Wk E14	31 E5	Joyce Wk SW2	38 G4
Isabella St SE1	**7 B6**	Jeger Av E2	11 E5	Jubilee Cres E14	26 G4
Isabel St SW9	31 F4	Jeken Rd SE9	41 F2	Jubilee Pl SW3	30 F1
Isambard Ms E14	26 G4	Jelf Rd SW2	38 G3	Jubilee St E1	19 A5
Isis Cl SW15	36 E2	Jenkins La E6	21 C1	Judd St WC1	17 E2
Island Row E14	19 D5	Jenkins La, Bark.	21 D1	Jude St E16	20 C5
Isla Rd SE18	35 E2	Jenkins Rd E13	20 E3	Juer St SW11	30 F4
Islington Grn N1	11 A5	Jenner Ho SE3	34 B2	Julian Pl E14	33 F1
Islington High St		Jenner Pl SW13	29 D2	Juliette Rd E13	20 C1
N1	18 A1	Jennings Rd SE22	39 E4	Junction App SE13	40 G1
Islington Pk St N1	10 G4	Jephson Rd E7	13 F4	Junction App SW11	37 F1
Islip St NW5	10 C2	Jephtha Rd SW18	37 B4	Junction Rd E13	20 E1
Ismailia Rd E7	13 F3	Jerdan Pl SW6	30 B3	Junction Rd N19	10 C1
Ivanhoe Rd SE5	39 E1	Jeremiah St E14	19 F5	Juniper Cres NW1	10 A4
Ivatt Pl W14	30 A1	**Jermyn St** SW1	**6 A5**	Juniper La E6	21 A4
Iveagh Cl E9	12 B5	Jerningham Rd		Juniper Rd, Ilf.	14 C1
Iveley Rd SW4	31 C5	SE14	33 C5	Juniper St E1	26 A1
Iverna Ct W8	23 B4	Jerome Cres NW8	16 F3	Juno Way SE14	33 B2
Iverna Gdns W8	23 B4	Jerrard St SE13	40 F1	Jupiter Way N7	10 F3
Iverson Rd NW6	9 A3	Jersey Rd, Ilf.	14 D1	Jupp Rd E15	13 A4
Ives Rd E16	20 B4	Jessica Rd SW18	37 D4	Jupp Rd W E15	12 G5
Ives St SW3	23 F5	Jessup Cl SE18	28 E5	Jutland Cl N19	10 E1
Ivestor Ter SE23	40 A5	Jewry St EC3	18 E5	Jutland Rd E13	20 D5
Ivimey St E2	18 F2	Jew's Row SW18	37 D2	Jutland Rd SE6	40 G5
Ivor Pl NW1	16 G3	Jeymer Av NW2	8 D2	Juxon St SE11	24 F5
Ivor St NW1	10 C4	Jeypore Rd SW18	37 D5		
Ivybridge La WC2	**6 F4**	Joan Cres SE9	41 G5	**K**	
Ivydale Rd SE15	40 B1	**Joan St** SE1	**7 B6**		
Ivy Rd NW2	8 E1	Jocelyn St SE15	32 F4	Kambala Rd SW11	37 E1
Ivy Rd SE4	40 D2	Jockey's Flds WC1	17 F4	Kara Way NW2	8 F1
		Jodane St SE8	26 D5	Kashmir Rd SE7	34 G3
				Kassala Rd SW11	30 G4

Katella Trd Est,	
Bark.	21 G2
Katherine Gdns	
SE9	41 G2
Katherine Rd E6	13 G4
Katherine Rd E7	13 F2
Kathleen Rd SW11	37 G1
Kay Rd SW9	31 E5
Kay St E2	18 F1
Kean St WC2	**6 G2**
Keats Gro NW3	9 E1
Keats Rd, Well.	35 G4
Keel Cl SE16	26 B2
Keeley St WC2	**6 G2**
Keeling Rd SE9	41 G3
Keep, The SE3	34 D5
Keetons Rd SE16	25 G4
Keevil Dr SW19	36 F5
Keildon Rd SW11	37 G2
Keith Gro W12	22 C3
Keith Rd, Bark.	21 F1
Kelbrook Rd SE3	42 A1
Kelfield Gdns W10	15 E5
Kelland Rd E13	20 D3
Kellaway Rd SE3	34 F5
Keller Cres E12	13 G1
Kellerton Rd SE13	41 B3
Kellett Rd SW2	38 G2
Kelly Av SE15	32 E3
Kelly St NW1	10 B3
Kelman Cl SW4	31 D5
Kelmore Gro SE22	39 F2
Kelmscott Gdns	
W12	22 C4
Kelmscott Rd SW11	37 F3
Kelross Rd N5	11 A1
Kelsall Cl SE3	34 E5
Kelsey St E2	18 G3
Kelson Ho E14	26 G4
Kelso Pl W8	23 C4
Kelvedon Ho SW8	31 E4
Kelvedon Rd SW6	30 A3
Kelvington Rd	
SE15	40 B3
Kelvin Rd N5	11 A1
Kemble St WC2	**6 G2**
Kemerton Rd SE5	39 B1
Kemeys St E9	12 C2
Kempe Rd NW6	15 F1
Kemplay Rd NW3	9 E1
Kemp's Ct W1	**6 B2**
Kempsford Gdns	
SW5	30 B1
Kempsford Rd SE11	24 G5
Kempson Rd SW6	30 B4
Kempthorne Rd	
SE8	26 C5
Kempton Rd E6	14 B5
Kempt St SE18	35 C2
Kemsing Rd SE10	34 D1
Kemsley SE13	40 G3
Kenbury St SE5	32 B1
Kenchester Cl SW8	31 E3
Kendal Av, Bark.	14 G4
Kendal Cl SW9	32 A3
Kendal Rd SE18	35 A4
Kendal Pl SW15	37 A3
Kendal Rd NW10	8 C1
Kendal St W2	16 F5
Kender St SE14	33 A3
Kendoa Rd SW4	38 D2
Kendrick Pl SW7	23 E5
Kenilford Rd SW12	38 B5
Kenilworth Gdns	
SE18	35 D5
Kenilworth Rd E3	19 C1
Kenilworth Rd NW6	9 A5
Kenley Wk W11	22 G1
Kenmont Gdns	
NW10	15 D2
Kenmure Rd E8	11 G2
Kennard Rd E15	13 A4
Kennard St E16	28 B2
Kennard St SW11	31 A5
Kennedy Cl E13	20 D1
Kennedy Rd, Bark.	14 G5

Kenneth Av, Ilf.   14 D1
Kenneth Cres NW2   8 D2
Kennet Rd W9   16 A3
Kennet St E1   25 F2
Kennet Wf La EC4   7 E3
Kennings Way SE11   31 G1
Kenning Ter N1   11 D5
Kennington La SE11   31 F1
Kennington Oval
  SE11   31 F2
Kennington Pk
  SW9   31 G3
Kennington Pk Gdns
  SE11   32 A2
Kennington Pk Rd
  SE11   31 G2
Kennington Pk Rd
  SE11   31 G2
Kennington Rd SE1   24 G4
Kennington Rd
  SE11   24 G5
Kensal Rd W10   15 G3
Kensington Av E12   14 A3
Kensington Ch St
  W8   23 C3
Kensington Ch St
  W8   23 B2
Kensington Ch Wk
  W8   23 C3
Kensington Ct W8   23 C3
Kensington Ct Pl
  W8   23 C3
Kensington Gdns
  W2   23 D2
Kensington Gdns Sq
  W2   16 C5
Kensington Gate
  W8   23 D4
Kensington Gore
  SW7   23 E3
Kensington High St
  W8   23 B4
Kensington High St
  W14   22 G5
Kensington Mall
  W8   23 B2
Kensington Palace
  Gdns W8   23 B3
Kensington Pk Gdns
  W11   23 A1
Kensington Pk Rd
  W11   23 A1
Kensington Pl W8   23 B2
Kensington Rd SW7   23 E3
Kensington Rd W8   23 C3
Kensington Sq W8   23 C3
Kentish Bldgs SE1   7 F6
Kentish Town Rd
  NW1   10 B4
Kentish Town Rd
  NW5   10 B4
Kentlea Rd SE28   28 G3
Kentmere Rd SE18   28 G3
Kenton Rd E9   12 B3
Kenton St WC1   17 E3
Kent Pas NW1   16 G2
Kent St E2   18 E1
Kent St E13   20 F2
Kent Ter NW1   16 F2
Kentwell Cl SE4   40 C2
Kentwode Grn
  SW13   29 C3
Kenward Rd SE9   41 F3
Kenway Rd SW5   23 C5
Kenworthy Rd E9   12 C2
Kenwyn Rd SW4   38 D2
Kenya Rd SE7   34 C3
Kenyon St SW6   29 F4
Keogh Rd E15   13 B3
Kepler Rd SW4   38 E2
Keppel Rd E6   14 B4
Keppel Row SE1   7 D6
Keppel St WC1   17 D4
Kerbey St E14   19 F5
Kerfield Cres SE5   32 C4
Kerfield Pl SE5   32 C4

Kerridge Ct N1   11 D3
Kerrison Rd E15   13 A5
Kerrison Rd W5   37 F1
Kerry Ct E16   20 D5
Kerry Path SE14   33 D2
Kerry Rd SE14   33 D2
Kersfield Rd SW15   36 F4
Kersley Ms SW11   30 G5
Kersley St SW11   30 G5
Keslake Rd NW6   15 F1
Keston Rd SE15   39 F1
Kestrel Av SE24   39 A3
Kestrel Ho EC1   18 A2
Keswick Rd SW15   36 G3
Kett Gdns SW2   38 F3
Kevan Ho SE5   32 B3
Keybridge Ho SW8   31 E2
Key Cl E1   18 G3
Keyes Rd NW2   8 F2
Keynsham Gdns
  SE9   42 A3
Keynsham Rd SE9   42 A3
Keyworth Cl E5   12 C1
Keyworth St SE1   25 A4
Khartoum Rd E13   20 E2
Khartoum Rd, Ilf.   14 D2
Khyber Rd SW11   30 F5
Kibworth St SW8   31 F3
Kidbrooke Gdns
  SE3   34 D5
Kidbrooke Gro
  SE3   34 D4
Kidbrooke La SE9   42 A2
Kidbrooke Pk Cl
  SE3   34 E4
Kidbrooke Pk Rd
  SE3   34 E4
Kidbrooke Way SE3   34 E5
Kidderpore Av NW3   9 B1
Kidderpore Gdns
  NW3   9 B1
Kidd Pl SE7   35 A1
Kilburn High Rd
  NW6   9 A4
Kilburn La W9   15 F2
Kilburn La W10   15 F2
Kilburn Pk Rd NW6   16 B2
Kilburn Pl NW6   9 B5
Kilburn Priory NW6   9 B5
Kilburn Sq NW6   9 B5
Kildare Gdns W2   16 B5
Kildare Rd E16   20 D4
Kildare Ter W2   16 B5
Kildoran Rd SW2   38 E3
Kilgour Rd SE23   40 C3
Kilkie St SW6   30 D5
Killarney Rd SW18   37 D4
Killick St N1   17 F1
Killip Cl E16   20 C5
Killowen Rd E9   12 B3
Killyon Rd SW8   31 C5
Killyon Ter SW8   31 C5
Kilmaine Rd SW6   29 G3
Kilmarsh Rd W6   22 E5
Kilmington Rd
  SW13   29 C2
Kilner St E14   19 E4
Kiln Pl NW5   10 A2
Kilravock St W10   15 G2
Kimbell Gdns SW6   29 G4
Kimberley Av E6   21 A1
Kimberley Av SE15   32 G5
Kimberley Rd E16   20 C3
Kimberley Rd NW6   9 B5
Kimberley Rd SW9   31 E5
Kimber Rd SW18   37 B5
Kimbolton Cl SE12   41 C4
Kimpton Rd SE5   32 C4
Kinburn St SE16   26 B3
Kincaid Rd SE15   32 G3
King & Queen St
  SE17   32 B1
King Arthur Cl
  SE15   33 A3
King Charles St
  SW1   24 D3

King David La E1   26 A1
Kingdon Rd NW6   9 B3
King Edward Ms
  SW13   29 C4
King Edwards Ct
  E9   11 G5
King Edwards Rd,
  Bark.   14 F5
King Edward Wk
  SE1   24 G4
Kingfield St E14   26 G5
Kingfisher Ms SE13   40 F3
Kingfisher Sq SE8   33 D2
Kingfisher Cl SE16   21 A4
King Frederik IX Twr
  SE16   26 D4
King George Av
  E16   20 G5
King George St
  SE10   33 G3
Kingham Cl SW18   37 D5
Kingham Cl W11   22 G3
King Henry's Reach
  W6   29 E2
King Henry's Rd
  NW3   9 F4
King Henry St N16   11 D2
King Henry's Wk N1   11 D3
King James St SE1   25 A3
King John St E1   19 B4
King Johns Wk SE9   42 A5
Kinglake St SE17   32 D1
Kingly Ct W1   6 A3
Kingly St W1   6 A3
Kings Arms Yd EC2   7 F1
King's Av SW4   38 D5
Kings Bench Wk
  EC4   7 A2
Kingsbridge Rd
  W10   15 E5
Kingsbridge Rd,
  Bark.   21 F1
Kingsbury Rd N1   11 D3
Kingsbury Ter N1   11 D3
Kingsclere Cl SW15   36 C5
Kings Coll Rd NW3   9 F4
Kingscote St EC4   7 B3
Kingscote Rd E13   13 E5
Kingscroft Rd NW2   9 A3
King's Cross Rd
  WC1   17 F2
Kingsdale Gdns
  W11   22 F2
Kingsdown Av W3   22 A1
Kingsdown Cl W10   15 F5
Kingsford Way E6   21 B4
Kingsgate Pl NW6   9 B4
Kingsgate Rd NW6   9 B4
Kings Gro SE15   32 G3
Kings Head Yd SE1   7 F6
Kings Highway
  SE18   35 G2
Kingshold Rd E9   12 A4
Kingsholm Gdns
  SE9   41 G2
Kingshurst Rd SE12   41 D5
Kingsland Grn E8   11 D1
Kingsland High St
  E8   11 E2
Kingsland Rd E2   18 D1
Kingsland Rd E8   18 D1
Kingsland Rd E13   20 F2
Kingsland Shop Cen
  E8   11 E3
Kingsley Rd E7   13 D4
Kingsley Rd NW6   9 A5
Kingsley St SW11   37 G1
Kings Mall W6   22 E5
Kingsman St SE18   28 B4
Kingsmead Est E9   12 C1
Kingsmead Way E9   12 C1
King's Ms WC1   17 F4
Kingsmill Ter NW8   16 E1

King's Orchard SE9   42 A4
King's Reach Twr
  SE1   7 A5
Kings Rd E6   13 F5
Kings Rd NW10   8 D4
King's Rd SW1   30 G1
King's Rd SW3   30 G1
King's Rd SW6   30 C4
King's Rd SW10   30 C4
King's Rd W10   30 C4
Kingston Rd, Ilf.   14 D1
Kingstown St NW1   10 A5
Kings St E13   20 D3
King St EC2   7 E2
King St SW1   6 B6
Kingsway WC2   6 E3
Kingsway WC2   6 G1
Kingswood Av NW6   8 G5
Kingswood Cl SW8   31 E3
Kingswood Pl SE13   41 B2
Kingswood Rd SW2   38 E4
King William St EC4   7 F2
King William Wk
  SE10   33 G2
Kingwood Rd SW6   29 F4
Kinlet Rd SE18   35 E4
Kinnear Rd W12   22 B3
Kinnerton St SW1   24 A3
Kinnoul Rd W6   29 G2
Kinsale Rd SE15   39 F1
Kinveachy Gdns
  SE7   35 A1
Kipling Est SE1   25 C3
Kipling St SE1   25 C3
Kirby Est SE16   25 G4
Kirby Gro SE1   25 D3
Kirkham Rd E6   21 A5
Kirkham St SE18   35 G2
Kirkland Cl, Sid.   42 G4
Kirkland Wk E8   11 E3
Kirk La SE18   35 E2
Kirkside Rd SE3   34 D2
Kirkwall Pl E2   19 A2
Kirkwood Rd SE15   32 G5
Kirtling St SW8   31 C3
Kirton Rd E13   20 F1
Kirwyn Way SE5   32 A3
Kitcat Ter E3   19 E2
Kitchener Rd E7   13 E3
Kitson Rd SE5   32 C3
Kitson Rd SW13   29 C4
Kitto Rd SE14   33 B5
Klea Av SW4   38 C4
Knapp Cl NW10   8 A3
Knapp Rd E3   19 E3
Knaresborough Pl
  SW5   23 C5
Knatchbull Rd SE5   32 B4
Kneller Rd SE4   40 C2
Knighten St E1   25 F2
Knighthead Pt E14   26 E4
Knightrider St EC4   7 D3
Knightsbridge SW1   23 G3
Knightsbridge SW7   23 F3
Knightsbridge Grn
  SW1   23 G3
Knights Rd E16   27 D3
Knivet Rd SW6   30 B2
Knobs Hill Rd E15   13 G5
Knockholt Rd SE9   41 G3
Knoll Rd SW18   37 D3
Knottisford St E2   19 A2
Knowle Cl SW9   38 G1
Knowles Hill Cres
  SE13   41 A3
Knowles Wk SW4   38 C1
Knowsley Rd SW11   30 G5
Knox Rd E7   13 C3
Knox St W1   16 G4
Knoyle St SE14   33 C2
Kossuth St SE10   34 B1
Kreedman Wk E8   11 F2
Kylemore Rd NW6   9 B4
Kynance Ms SW7   23 C4
Kynance Pl SW7   23 D4
Kyrle Rd SW11   38 A3

L

Laburnum St E2 11 E5
Lacey Wk E3 19 E1
Lackington St EC2 18 C4
Lacon Rd SE22 39 F2
Lacy Rd SW15 36 F2
Ladbroke Gdns
 W11 23 A3
Ladbroke Gro W10 15 F3
Ladbroke Gro W11 15 G5
Ladbroke Rd W11 23 A1
Ladbroke Sq W11 23 A1
Ladbroke Ter W11 23 A1
Ladbroke Wk W11 23 A2
Ladycroft Rd SE13 40 E3
Lady Margaret Rd
 N19 10 C1
Lady Margaret Rd
 NW5 10 C2
Ladysmith Av E6 21 A1
Ladysmith Rd E16 20 C2
Ladysmith Rd SE9 42 E3
Lady Somerset Rd
 NW5 10 B1
Ladywell Hts SE4 40 D4
Ladywell Rd SE13 40 E3
Lafone St SE1 25 E3
Lagado Ms SE16 26 B2
Lainson St SW18 37 B5
Laird Ho SE5 32 B3
Lakedale Rd SE18 35 G2
Laker Pl SW15 37 A4
Lakeside Rd W14 22 F4
Laleham Rd SE6 40 G4
Lalor St SW6 29 G5
Lambert Rd E16 20 E5
Lambert Rd SW2 38 E3
Lambert St N1 10 G4
Lambeth Br SE1 24 E5
Lambeth Br SW1 24 E5
Lambeth High St
 SE1 24 F5
Lambeth Hill EC4 7 D3
Lambeth Palace Rd
 SE1 24 F4
Lambeth Rd SE1 24 F5
Lambeth Rd SE11 24 F5
Lambeth Wk SE11 24 F5
Lamb La E8 11 G4
Lamble St NW5 10 A2
Lambolle Pl NW3 9 F3
Lambolle Rd NW3 9 F3
Lambourne Rd,
 Bark. 14 G4
Lambourn Rd SW4 38 B1
Lambrook Ter SW6 29 G4
Lamb's Conduit St
 WC1 17 F3
Lamb's Pas EC1 18 C4
Lamb St E1 18 E4
Lamerton St SE8 33 E2
Lamington St W6 22 D5
Lammas Rd E9 12 B4
Lammermoor Rd
 SW12 38 B5
Lamont Rd SW10 30 D2
Lamport Rd
 SE12 41 B3
Lamport Cl SE18 28 B5
Lanark Pl W9 16 D3
Lanark Rd W9 16 C1
Lanark Sq E14 26 F4
Lanbury Rd SE15 40 B2
Lancaster Av, Bark. 14 G2
Lancaster Dr NW3 9 F3
Lancaster Gate W2 23 D1
Lancaster Gro NW3 9 E3
Lancaster Ms W2 23 D1
Lancaster Pl WC2 6 G3
Lancaster Rd E7 13 D4
Lancaster Rd NW10 8 C2
Lancaster Rd W11 15 G5
Lancaster St SE1 25 A3
Lancaster Ter W2 23 D1
Lancaster Wk W2 23 D2

Lancefield St W10 16 A2
Lancelot Pl SW7 23 G3
Lanchester Way
 SE14 33 B2
Lancresse Ct N1 11 D5
Landcroft Rd SE22 39 E4
Landells Rd SE22 39 E4
Landford Rd SW15 36 E1
Landmann Way
 SE14 33 B2
Landmark Hts E5 12 C1
Landon Pl SW1 23 G4
Landons Cl E14 26 G2
Landor Rd SW9 38 E1
Landor Wk W12 22 C3
Landridge Rd SW6 30 A5
Landseer Av E12 14 C2
Landstead Rd SE18 35 F3
Lane, The SE3 41 D1
Laneway SW15 36 D3
Lanfranc Rd E3 19 C1
Langbourne Pl E14 33 F1
Langbrook Rd SE3 41 G1
Langdale Cl SE17 32 B2
Langdale Rd SE10 33 G3
Langdon Cres E6 21 C1
Langdon Rd E6 14 C5
Langford Cl E8 11 F2
Langford Grn SE5 39 D1
Langford Pl NW8 16 D1
Langford Rd SW6 30 C5
Langham Pl W1 17 B4
Langham St W1 17 B4
Langland Gdns
 NW3 9 C2
Langler Rd NW10 15 E1
Langley Ct WC2 6 E3
Langley La SW8 31 F2
Langley St WC2 6 E2
Langside Av SW15 36 C2
Lang St E1 19 A3
Langthorn Ct EC2 7 F1
Langthorne St SW6 29 F3
Langton Av E6 21 C2
Langton Ri SE23 39 F4
Langton Rd SW9 32 A3
Langton St SW10 30 D2
Langton Way SE3 34 C4
Langtry Rd NW8 9 B5
Lanhill Rd W9 16 B3
Lanier Rd SE13 40 G4
Lanrick Rd E14 20 A5
Lansbury Est E14 19 F5
Lansbury Gdns
 E14 20 A5
Lanscombe Wk
 SW8 31 E4
Lansdowne Cres
 W11 22 G1
Lansdowne Dr E8 11 F3
Lansdowne Gdns
 SW8 31 E4
Lansdowne Gro
 NW10 8 A1
Lansdowne La SE7 34 G2
Lansdowne Ms SE7 34 G2
Lansdowne Ri W11 22 G1
Lansdowne Ter WC1 17 E3
Lansdowne Wk W11 23 A2
Lansdowne Way
 SW8 31 E4
Lansdown Rd E7 13 F4
Lantern Cl SW15 36 C2
Lanterns Ct E14 26 E3
Lant St SE1 25 B3
Lanvanor Rd SE15 33 A5
Lapford Cl W9 16 A3
Lara Cl SE13 40 G4
Larch Av W3 22 A2
Larch Cl E13 20 E3
Larch Rd NW2 8 E1
Larcom St SE17 25 B5
Larden Rd W3 22 A2

Larkhall La SW4 31 D5
Larkhall Ri SW4 38 C1
Larkhill Ter SE18 35 C4
Lark Row E2 12 A5
Larkspur Cl E6 21 A4
Larnach Rd W6 29 F2
Larpent Av SW15 36 E3
Lassa Rd SE9 42 A3
Lassell St SE10 34 A1
Latchmere Rd
 SW11 30 G5
Latchmere St
 SW11 30 G5
Latham Ho E1 19 B5
Lathom Rd E6 14 B4
Latimer Av E6 14 B5
Latimer Pl W10 15 E5
Latimer Rd E7 13 E1
Latimer Rd E15 15 E5
Latimer Rd SE15 32 F2
Latimer Pl W4 29 A2
Latymer Ct W6 22 F5
Lauderdale Rd W9 16 C2
Lauderdale Twr EC2 18 B4
Launceston Pl W8 23 D4
Launch St E14 26 G4
Laundry Ms SE23 40 C5
Laundry Rd W6 29 G2
Laura Pl E5 12 A1
Laurel Rd SW13 29 C5
Laurel St E8 11 E3
Laurence Pountney
 Hill EC4 7 F3
Laurence Pountney
 La EC4 7 F3
Laurie Gro SE14 33 C4
Lauriston Rd E9 12 B5
Lausanne Rd SE15 33 A4
Lavell St N16 11 C1
Lavender Gdns
 SW11 37 G2
Lavender Gro E8 11 E4
Lavender Hill
 SW11 37 F2
Lavender Pl, Ilf. 14 D2
Lavender Rd SE16 26 C2
Lavender Rd SW11 37 E1
Lavender Sweep
 SW11 37 G2
Lavender Wk SW11 37 G2
Laverstoke Gdns
 SW15 36 C5
Laverton Pl SW5 23 C5
Lavington St SE1 7 C6
Lawford Rd N1 11 D4
Lawford Rd NW5 10 C3
Lawless St E14 26 F1
Lawley St E5 12 A1
Lawn Ho Cl E14 26 G3
Lawn La SW8 31 E2
Lawn Rd NW3 9 G2
Lawnside SE3 41 C4
Lawn Ter SE3 41 B1
Lawrence Av E12 14 C1
Lawrence Cl E3 19 E1
Lawrence La EC2 7 E2
Lawrence Rd E6 13 G5
Lawrence Rd E13 13 E3
Lawrence Rd SE16 20 C4
Lawrence St SW3 30 F2
Lawson Cl E16 20 F4
Lawson Est SE1 25 C4
Lawson St SE1 25 C4
Lawton Rd E3 19 C2
Layard Rd SE16 32 A3
Layard Sq SE16 26 G5
Laycock St N1 10 G3
Laystall St EC1 17 G3
Leabank Sq E9 12 E3
Leacroft Av SW12 38 D5
Leadenhall Mkt EC3 7 H2
Leadenhall Pl EC3 7 H2
Leadenhall St EC3 7 H2
Leader Av E12 14 C2
Leahurst Rd SE13 41 A3

Leamington Cl E12 14 A2
Leamington Rd Vil
 W11 16 A4
Leamore St W6 22 D5
Leamouth Rd E14 20 A5
Leander Ct SE8 33 E4
Leander Rd SW2 38 F4
Learoyd Gdns E6 28 C1
Leather La EC1 17 G4
Leathermarket Ct
 SE1 25 D3
Leathermarket St
 SE1 25 D3
Leathwaite Rd
 SW11 37 G2
Leathwell Rd SE8 33 F5
Lea Valley Wk E3 19 G3
Lea Valley Wk E14 19 F4
Lea Valley Wk E15 19 G2
Lebanon Gdns
 SW18 37 B4
Lebanon Rd SW18 37 B3
Lebrun Sq SE3 41 E1
Lechmere Rd NW2 8 D3
Lecky St SW7 30 E1
Leconfield Av
 SW13 36 B1
Leconfield Rd N5 11 C1
Leda Rd SE18 28 B4
Ledbury Est SE15 32 G3
Ledbury Rd W11 16 A5
Ledbury St SE15 32 F3
Lee Br SE13 40 G1
Lee Ch St SE13 41 B2
Lee Conservancy Rd
 E9 12 D2
Leefern Rd W12 22 C3
Leegate SE12 41 C3
Lee High Rd SE12 41 A1
Lee High Rd SE13 41 A1
Leeke St WC1 17 F2
Leeland Way NW10 8 B1
Lee Pk SE3 41 C2
Leerdam Dr E14 26 G4
Lee Rd SE3 41 C1
Leeson Rd SE24 38 G2
Lees Pl W1 24 A1
Lee St E8 11 E5
Lee Ter SE3 41 B1
Lee Ter SE13 41 B1
Leeway SE8 33 D1
Lefevre Wk E3 12 E5
Lefroy Rd W12 22 B3
Legatt Rd SE9 41 G3
Leggatt Rd E15 19 G1
Legge St SE13 40 G3
Leghorn Rd NW10 15 B1
Leghorn Rd SE18 35 F1
Legion Cl N1 10 G3
Leicester Ct WC2 6 D3
Leicester Pl WC2 6 D3
Leicester Sq WC2 6 D4
Leicester St WC2 6 D3
Leigh Gdns NW10 15 E1
Leigh Rd E6 14 C3
Leigh Rd N5 11 A1
Leigh St WC1 17 E3
Leighton Av E12 14 C2
Leighton Gdns
 NW10 15 D1
Leighton Gro NW5 10 C2
Leighton Pl NW5 10 C2
Leighton Rd NW5 10 D2
Leila Parnell Pl SE7 34 F2
Leinster Gdns W2 23 D1
Leinster Ms W2 23 D1
Leinster Pl W2 16 D5
Leinster Sq W2 16 B5
Leinster Ter W2 23 D1
Leman St E1 18 E5
Lemmon Rd SE10 34 B2
Lemonwell Dr SE9 42 E3
Lemuel St SW18 37 C4
Lena Gdns W6 22 E4
Lendal Ter SW4 38 D1
Lenham Rd SE12 41 C3

Lennon Rd NW2 8 E2
Lennox Gdns NW10 8 B1
Lennox Gdns SW1 23 G4
Lennox Gdns Ms SW1 23 G4
Lens Rd E7 13 F4
Lenthall Rd E8 11 F4
Lenthorp Rd SE10 27 C5
Lenton Path SE17 35 F2
Lenton St SE18 28 F5
Leonard Rd E7 13 D1
Leonard St E16 28 A2
Leonard St EC2 18 C3
Leontine Cl SE15 32 F3
Leopold Rd NW10 8 A4
Leopold St E3 19 D4
Leo St SE15 32 G3
Leppoc Rd SW4 38 D3
Leroy St SE1 25 D5
Leslie Rd E11 12 G1
Leslie Rd E16 20 E5
Lessar Av SW4 38 C3
Lessing St SE23 40 C5
Lester Av E15 20 B2
Letchford Gdns NW10 15 C2
Lethbridge Cl SE13 33 G4
Lettice St SW6 30 A4
Lett Rd E15 13 G3
Lettsom St SE5 32 D5
Lettsom Wk E13 20 D1
Levehurst Way SW4 31 E5
Leven Rd E14 19 G4
Lever St EC1 18 A2
Leverton St NW5 10 C2
Levett Rd, Bark. 14 G3
Lewey Ho E3 19 D3
Lewis Gro SE13 40 G1
Lewis Pl E8 11 F2
Lewis St NW1 10 B3
Lewisham Cen SE13 40 G1
Lewisham High St SE13 40 G1
Lewisham Hill SE13 33 G5
Lewisham Pk SE13 40 F4
Lewisham Rd SE13 33 F4
Lewisham Way SE4 33 D4
Lewisham Way SE14 33 D4
Lexham Gdns W8 23 C4
Lexham Gdns Ms W8 23 C4
Lexham Ms W8 23 B5
Lexington St W1 6 B2
Leybourne Rd NW1 10 B4
Leybridge Ct SE12 41 D3
Leyland Rd SE12 41 D3
Leylang Rd SE14 33 B3
Leysfield Rd W12 22 C3
Leyton Rd E15 13 A2
Leytonstone Rd E15 13 B2
Leywick St E15 20 B1
Liardet St SE14 33 C2
Liberia Rd N5 11 A3
Liberty Ms SW12 38 B4
Liberty St SW9 31 F4
Libra Rd E3 12 D5
Libra Rd E13 20 D1
Library St SE1 25 A3
Lichfield Rd E3 19 C2
Lichfield Rd E6 20 G2
Lichfield Rd NW2 9 C2
Lidcote Gdns SW9 31 G5
Liddell Gdns NW10 15 E1
Liddell Rd NW6 9 B3
Liddington Rd E15 13 C5
Liddon Rd E13 20 E2
Lidfield Rd N16 11 C6
Lidlington Pl NW1 17 C1
Liffler Rd SE18 35 G1
Liffords Pl SW13 29 B5

Lifford St SW15 36 F2
Lighter Cl SE16 26 C5
Lighterman Ms E1 19 B5
Lightermans Rd E14 26 E3
Lilac Pl SE11 24 F5
Lilac St W12 22 C1
Lilburne Gdns SE9 42 A3
Lilburne Rd SE9 42 A3
Lilestone St NW8 16 F3
Lilford Rd SE5 32 A5
Lilian Barker Cl SE12 41 D3
Lillian Rd SW13 29 C2
Lillie Rd SW6 29 G3
Lillieshall Rd SW4 38 B1
Lillie Yd SW6 30 B2
Lily Cl W14 22 G5
Lily Pl EC1 17 G4
Lilyville Rd SW6 30 A4
Limburg Rd SW11 37 G2
Limeburner La EC4 7 B2
Lime Cl E1 25 F2
Lime Gro W12 22 E3
Limeharbour E14 26 F4
Limehouse Causeway E14 26 D1
Limehouse Flds Est E14 19 C4
Limehouse Link E14 26 C1
Limekiln Dr SE7 34 E2
Limerick Cl SW12 38 C5
Limerston St SW10 30 D2
Limes Av SW13 29 B5
Limesford Rd SE15 40 B2
Limes Gdns SW18 37 B4
Limes Gro SE13 40 G2
Lime St EC3 7 H3
Lime St Pas EC3 7 H2
Limes Wk SE15 39 G2
Linacre Cl SE15 39 G1
Linacre Ct W6 29 F1
Linacre Rd NW2 8 D3
Linberry Wk SE8 26 D5
Linchmere Rd SE12 41 C5
Lincoln Ms NW6 9 C2
Lincoln Rd E13 20 E3
Lincoln's Inn Flds WC2 6 G1
Lincoln St SW3 23 G5
Lindal Rd SE4 40 D3
Linden Av NW10 16 C1
Linden Ct W12 22 E2
Linden Gdns W2 23 B1
Linden Gro SE15 39 G1
Linden Ms N1 11 C2
Lindfield Gdns NW3 9 C2
Lindfield St E14 19 E5
Lindisfarne Way E9 12 C1
Lindley St E1 19 A4
Lindore Rd SW11 37 G2
Lindrop St SW6 30 D5
Lindsay Sq SW1 31 D1
Lindsell St SE10 33 G4
Lindsey Ms N1 11 B4
Lindsey St EC1 18 A4
Lind St SE8 33 F5
Linford St SW8 31 C4
Lingards Rd SE13 40 G2
Lingfield Cres SE9 42 F2
Lingham St SW9 31 E5
Ling Rd E16 20 D4
Linhope St NW1 16 G3
Link St E9 12 A3
Linnell Rd SE5 32 D5
Linnet Ms SW12 38 A5
Linom Rd SW4 38 E2
Linscott Rd E5 12 A1
Linsdell Rd, Bark. 14 E5
Linsey St SE16 25 F5
Linstead St NW6 9 B4

Linstead Way SW18 36 G5
Linsted Ct SE9 42 G4
Linton Gdns E6 21 A5
Linton Rd, Bark. 14 E4
Lintons, The, Bark. 14 E4
Linton St N1 11 B5
Linver Rd SW6 30 B5
Linwood Cl SE5 32 E5
Lion Cl SE4 40 E4
Lionel Gdns SE9 41 G3
Lionel Rd SE9 41 G3
Lion Rd E6 21 A5
Liphook Cres SE23 40 A5
Lisburne Rd NW3 9 G1
Lisford St SE15 32 E4
Lisgar Ter W14 22 G2
Liskeard Gdns SE3 34 D4
Lisle St WC2 6 D3
Lismore Circ NW5 10 A2
Lissenden Gdns NW5 10 A2
Lisson Grn Est NW8 16 F3
Lisson Gro NW1 16 E2
Lisson Gro NW8 16 E2
Lisson St NW1 16 F4
Lister Ho SE3 34 B2
Liston Rd SW4 38 C1
Litchfield Av E15 13 B3
Litchfield Gdns NW10 8 C3
Litchfield St WC2 6 D3
Lithos Rd NW3 9 C3
Little Argyll St W1 6 A2
Little Boltons, The, SW5 30 C1
Little Boltons, The, SW10 30 C1
Little Britain EC1 7 D1
Littlebury Rd SW4 38 D1
Little Chester St SW1 24 B4
Littlecombe SE7 34 E2
Littlecombe Cl SW15 36 F4
Littlecote Cl SW19 36 F5
Littlecroft SE9 42 C1
Little Dorrit Ct SE1 25 B3
Little Essex St WC2 6 J3
Little Heath SE7 35 B1
Little Ilford La E12 14 B1
Little Marlborough St W1 6 A2
Little Newport St WC2 6 D3
Little New St EC4 7 A1
Little Portland St W1 6 A1
Little Russell St WC1 17 E4
Little St. James's St SW1 6 A6
Little Trinity La EC4 7 E3
Little Turnstile WC1 6 G1
Littlewood SE13 40 G3
Livermere Rd E8 11 E5
Liverpool Gro SE17 32 C1
Liverpool Rd E16 20 B4
Liverpool Rd N1 17 G1
Liverpool Rd N7 10 G2
Liverpool St EC2 18 D4
Livingstone Rd E15 12 G5
Livingstone Wk SW11 37 E1
Livonia St W1 6 B2
Livsey Cl SE28 28 E3
Lizard St EC1 18 B2
Lizban St SE3 34 E3
Llanover Rd SE18 35 C2
Lloyd Baker St WC1 17 F2
Lloyd Rd E6 14 B5
Lloyd's Av EC3 7 J2
Lloyds Pl SE3 34 B5

Lloyd Sq WC1 17 G2
Lloyd St WC1 17 G2
Loampit Hill SE13 33 E5
Loampit Vale SE13 33 F5
Lochaber Rd SE13 41 B2
Lochaline St W6 29 E2
Lochinvar St SW12 38 B5
Lochnagar St E14 19 G4
Lock Chase SE3 41 B1
Lockesfield Pl E14 33 F1
Lockhart Cl N7 10 F3
Lockhart St E3 19 D3
Lockhurst St E5 12 B1
Lockington Rd SW8 31 B4
Lockmead Rd SE13 40 G1
Locksley St E14 19 D4
Lockwood Sq SE16 25 G4
Loddiges Rd E9 12 A4
Loder St SE15 33 A4
Lodge Av NW10 16 A2
Lodge Rd NW8 16 E2
Lodore St E14 19 G5
Loftie St SE16 25 F3
Lofting Rd N1 10 F4
Loftus Rd W12 22 D2
Logan Ms W8 23 B5
Logan Pl W8 23 B5
Lollard St SE11 24 F5
Loman St SE1 25 A3
Lomas Dr E8 11 E4
Lomas St E1 18 F4
Lombard Ct EC3 7 G3
Lombard La EC4 7 A2
Lombard Rd SW11 30 E5
Lombard St EC3 7 G2
Lombard Wall SE7 27 E4
Lomond Gro SE5 32 C3
Loncroft Rd SE5 32 D2
Londesborough Rd N16 11 D1
London Br EC4 7 G5
London Br SE1 7 G5
London Br St SE1 7 F6
London Br Wk SE1 7 G5
London City Airport E16 28 B2
London Flds E8 11 F3
London Flds E Side E8 11 G4
London Flds W Side E8 11 F4
London La E8 11 F4
London Rd E13 20 D4
London Rd SE1 25 A4
London Rd, Bark. 14 C4
London Shop Pav W1 6 C4
London Silver Vaults WC2 17 G4
London St EC3 7 J3
London St W2 16 E5
London Wall EC2 18 B4
Long Acre WC2 6 E3
Longbeach Rd SW11 37 G1
Longbridge Rd, Bark. 14 G1
Longbridge Way SE13 40 G3
Long Dr W3 15 A5
Longfield Est SE1 25 E5
Longfield St SW18 37 B5
Longford St NW1 17 A3
Longhedge St SW11 31 A5
Longhope Cl SE15 32 D2
Longhurst Rd SE13 41 A3
Long La EC1 18 A4
Long La SE1 25 C4
Longley St SE1 25 F5
Longmoore St SW1 24 C5
Lognor Rd E1 19 B3
Long Pond Rd SE3 34 B4
Long Reach Ct, Bark. 21 F1

Longridge Rd SW5 23 B5
Long Rd SW4 38 B2
Long's Ct WC2 6 C3
Longshore SE8 26 D5
Longstaff Cres SW18 37 B4
Longstaff Rd SW18 37 B4
Longstone Av NW10 8 B4
Long St E2 18 E2
Long Wk SE18 35 D2
Long Wk SW13 29 A5
Longwood Dr SW15 36 C4
Lonsdale Av E6 20 G2
Lonsdale Rd NW6 16 A1
Lonsdale Rd SW13 29 C2
Lonsdale Rd W4 22 B5
Lonsdale Rd W11 16 A5
Lonsdale Sq N1 10 G4
Loraine Rd N7 10 F1
Lord Amory Way E14 26 G3
Lorden Wk E2 18 F2
Lord Hills Rd W2 16 C4
Lord N St SW1 24 E4
Lord Roberts Ter SE18 35 C1
Lordship La SE22 39 E4
Lord St E16 28 A2
Lord Warwick St SE18 28 B4
Lorenzo St WC1 17 F2
Loris Rd W6 22 E4
Lorn Ct SW9 31 G5
Lorne Gdns W11 22 F3
Lorne Rd E7 13 E1
Lorn Rd SW9 31 G5
Lorrimore Rd SE17 32 A2
Lorrimore Sq SE17 32 A2
Lothbury EC2 7 F1
Lothian Rd SW9 32 A4
Lothrop St W10 15 G2
Lots Rd SW10 30 D3
Loudoun Rd NW8 9 D5
Loughborough Pk SW9 39 A2
Loughborough Rd SW9 31 G5
Loughborough St SE11 31 F1
Lough Rd N7 10 F3
Louisa Ho SW15 36 A2
Louisa St E1 19 B3
Louise Rd E15 13 B3
Louvaine Rd SW11 37 E2
Lovage App E5 21 A4
Lovat La EC3 7 H4
Lovegrove St SE1 32 F1
Lovegrove Wk E14 26 G2
Lovelace Grn SE9 42 B1
Love La EC2 7 E1
Love La SE18 28 D5
Lovelinch Cl SE15 33 A2
Lovell Ho E1 11 F5
Loveridge Rd NW6 9 A3
Lovers Wk SE10 34 B2
Lover's Wk W1 24 A2
Love Wk SE5 32 C2
Lowbrook Rd, Ilf. 14 D2
Lowden Rd SE24 39 A2
Lowe Av E16 20 D4
Lowell St E14 19 C5
Lower Addison Gdns W14 22 G3
Lower Belgrave St SW1 24 B4
Lower Clapton Rd E5 11 G2
Lower Common S SW15 36 D1
Lower Grosvenor Pl SW1 24 B4
Lower James St W1 6 B3

Lower John St W1 6 B3
Lower Lea Crossing E14 27 B1
Lower Lea Crossing E16 27 B1
Lower Mall W6 29 D1
Lower Marsh SE1 24 G3
Lower Merton Ri NW3 9 F4
Lower Richmond Rd SW15 36 E1
Lower Rd SE8 26 A4
Lower Rd SE16 26 A4
Lower Sloane St SW1 24 A5
Lower Thames St EC3 7 G4
Lowestoft Ms E16 28 D3
Lowfield Rd NW6 9 B4
Lowman Rd N7 10 F2
Lowndes Cl SW1 24 A4
Lowndes Ct W1 6 A2
Lowndes Pl SW1 24 A4
Lowndes Sq SW1 23 G3
Lowndes St SW1 23 G4
Lowther Gdns SW7 23 E3
Lowther Hill SE23 40 C5
Lowther Rd SW13 29 B4
Lowth Rd SE5 32 B5
Loxford Av E6 20 G1
Loxford La, Ilf. 14 E2
Loxford Rd, Bark. 14 D3
Lubbock St SE14 33 A3
Lucan Pl SW3 23 F5
Lucas Av E13 13 E5
Lucas St SE8 33 E4
Lucerne Rd N5 11 A1
Lucey Rd SE16 25 F4
Lucey Way SE16 25 F4
Lucknow St SE18 35 G3
Lucorn Cl SE13 41 C4
Ludgate Bdy EC4 7 B2
Ludgate Circ EC4 7 B2
Ludgate Hill EC4 7 B2
Ludgate Sq EC4 7 C2
Ludovick Wk SW15 36 A2
Ludwick Ms SE14 33 C3
Lugard Rd SE15 32 G5
Luke Ho E1 18 G5
Luke St EC2 18 D3
Lukin St E1 19 A5
Lullingstone La SE13 41 A5
Lulworth Rd SE15 32 G5
Lumley Ct WC2 6 F4
Lupton St NW5 10 C1
Lupus St SW1 31 B2
Lurgan Av W6 29 F2
Lurline Gdns SW11 31 A4
Luscombe Way SW8 31 E3
Lushington Rd NW10 15 D1
Luton Pl SE10 33 G3
Luton St NW8 16 E3
Luttrell Av SW15 36 D3
Luxborough St W1 17 A3
Luxemburg Gdns W6 22 F5
Luxford St SE16 26 B5
Luxmore St SE4 33 D4
Luxor St SE5 39 B1
Lyall Av SE21 24 A4
Lyall St SW1 24 A4
Lyal Rd E3 19 C1
Lydden Ct SE9 42 F4
Lydden Gro SW18 37 C5
Lydden Rd SW18 37 C5
Lydeard Rd E6 14 B4
Lydford Rd NW2 8 F3
Lydford Rd W9 16 A3
Lydney Cl SE15 32 D3
Lydon Rd SW4 38 C1
Lyford Rd SW18 37 E5
Lyham Cl SW2 38 E4

Lyham Rd SW2 38 E3
Lyme Fm Rd SE12 41 D2
Lyme St NW1 10 C4
Lymington Rd NW6 9 C3
Lympstone Gdns SE15 32 F3
Lyncott Cres SW4 38 B2
Lyncroft Gdns NW6 9 B2
Lyndale NW2 9 A1
Lyndale Cl SE3 34 C2
Lyndhurst Gdns NW3 9 E2
Lyndhurst Gdns, Bark. 14 G3
Lyndhurst Gro SE15 32 D5
Lyndhurst Rd NW3 9 E2
Lyndhurst Sq SE15 32 E4
Lyndhurst Ter NW3 9 E2
Lyndhurst Way SE15 12 C2
Lyneham Wk E5 12 C2
Lynette Av SW4 38 B4
Lyn Ms N16 11 D1
Lynne Way NW10 8 A3
Lynn Rd SW12 38 B5
Lynsted Gdns SE9 41 G1
Lynton Cl NW10 8 A2
Lynton Rd NW6 9 A5
Lynton Rd SE1 25 E5
Lyon Business Pk, Bark. 21 G1
Lyons Pl NW8 16 E3
Lyon St N1 10 F4
Lyric Rd SW13 29 B4
Lysias Rd SW12 38 A4
Lysia St SW6 29 E3
Lytcott Gro SE22 39 E3
Lytham St SE17 32 C1
Lyttelton Cl NW3 9 F4
Lytton Gro SW15 36 E3
Lyveden Rd SE3 34 E3

M
Mableton Pl WC1 17 D2
Mablethorpe Rd SW6 29 G3
Mabley St E9 12 C3
MacArthur Cl E7 13 D3
MacArthur Ter SE7 35 A2
Macaulay Ct SW4 38 B1
Macaulay Rd E6 20 G1
Macaulay Rd SW4 38 B2
Macaulay Sq SW4 38 B2
McAuley Cl SE1 24 G4
McAuley Cl SE9 42 C5
Macaulay Ms SE13 33 G5
Macbean St SE18 28 C4
Macbeth St W6 29 D1
McCall Cres SE7 35 A1
Macclesfield Br NW1 16 F1
Macclesfield Rd EC1 7 E...
Macclesfield St W1 6 D3
McCullum Rd E3 12 D5
McDermott Cl SW11 37 F1
McDermott Rd SE15 39 F1
Macdonald Rd E7 13 D1
McDowall Cl E16 20 D4
McDowall Rd SE5 32 B4
Macduff Rd SW11 31 A4
Mace St E2 19 B1
McEwen Way E15 13 A3
Macfarlane Rd W12 22 E2
McGrath Rd E15 13 C2
Macgregor Rd E16 20 F4
McGregor Rd W11 16 A5
Machell Rd SE15 40 A1
Mackay Rd SW4 38 B1
Mackennal St NW8 16 F1
Mackenzie Rd N7 10 F3
Mackenzie Wk E14 26 E2

McKerrell Rd SE15 32 F4
Mackeson Rd NW3 9 G1
Mackie Rd SW2 38 G5
Macklin St WC2 6 F1
Macks Rd SE16 25 F5
Mackworth St NW1 17 C2
Maclean Rd SE23 40 C4
Macleod St SE17 32 B1
Maclise Rd W14 22 G3
McMillan St SE8 33 E2
McNeil Rd SE5 32 D5
Macoma Rd SE18 35 F2
Macoma Ter SE18 35 F2
Maconochies Rd E14 33 F1
Macquarie Way E14 26 F5
Macroom Rd W9 16 A2
Mac's Pl EC4 6 J1
Maddams St E3 19 F3
Maddock Way SE17 32 A2
Maddox St W1 24 B1
Madeline Gro, Ilf. 14 F2
Madinah Rd E8 11 F3
Madras Pl N7 10 G3
Madras Rd, Ilf. 14 D1
Madrid Rd SW13 29 C4
Madrigal La SE5 32 A3
Madron St SE17 32 D1
Mafeking Av E6 20 G1
Mafeking Rd E16 20 C3
Magdalene Gdns E6 21 C3
Magdalen St SE1 7 H6
Magee St SE11 31 G2
Magnolia Pl SW4 38 E3
Magpie All EC4 7 A2
Magpie Cl E7 13 C2
Maguire St SE1 25 E3
Mahogany Cl SE16 26 C2
Maida Av W2 16 D4
Maida Vale W9 16 C1
Maiden La NW1 10 D4
Maiden La SE1 7 E5
Maiden La WC2 6 F4
Maiden Rd E15 13 B4
Maidenstone Hill SE10 33 G4
Maidstone Bldgs Ms SE1 7 E6
Maitland Pk Est NW3 9 G3
Maitland Pk Rd NW3 9 G3
Maitland Pk Vil NW3 9 G3
Maitland Rd E15 13 C3
Majendie Rd SE18 35 F1
Major Rd E15 12 G2
Makins St SW3 23 F5
Malabar St E14 26 E4
Malbrook Rd SW15 36 D2
Malcolm Pl E2 19 A3
Malcolm Rd E1 19 A3
Malden Cres NW1 10 A3
Malden Rd NW5 10 A2
Maldon Cl SE5 39 D1
Malet Pl WC1 17 D3
Malet St WC1 17 D3
Malfort Rd SE5 39 D1
Mall, The E15 13 A4
Mall, The SW1 24 C3
Mallard Cl NW6 16 B1
Mallard Path SE28 28 F1
Mallet Rd SE13 41 A4
Malling SE13 40 G3
Mallinson Rd SW11 37 F3
Mallord St SW3 30 D2
Mallory Cl SE4 40 C2
Mallory St NW8 16 F3
Mall Rd W6 29 D1
Malmesbury Rd E3 19 D2
Malmesbury Rd E16 20 B4

Malmesbury Ter E16 20 C4
Malpas Rd E8 11 G3
Malpas Rd SE4 33 D5
Maltby St SE1 25 E3
Malthouse Dr W4 29 A2
Malting Ho E14 26 D1
Maltings Pl SW6 30 C4
Malton St SE18 35 G2
Maltravers St WC2 6 H3
Malt St SE1 32 F1
Malvern Cl W10 16 A4
Malvern Ct SW7 23 E5
Malvern Pl NW6 16 A2
Malvern Rd E6 14 A5
Malvern Rd E8 11 F4
Malvern Rd NW6 16 A2
Malvern Ter N1 10 G5
Malwood Rd SW12 38 B4
Malyons Rd SE13 40 F3
Malyons Ter SE13 40 F3
Manaton Cl SE15 39 E1
Manbey Gro E15 13 B3
Manbey Pk Rd E15 13 B3
Manbey Rd E15 13 B3
Manbey St E15 13 B3
Manbre Rd W6 29 E2
Manchester Ct E16 20 E5
Manchester Dr W10 15 G3
Manchester Gro E14 33 G1
Manchester Rd E14 33 G1
Manchester Sq W1 17 A5
Manchester St W1 17 A4
Manchuria Rd SW11 38 A4
Manciple St SE1 25 B1
Mandalay Rd SW4 38 C3
Mandela Rd E16 20 D5
Mandela St NW1 10 C5
Mandela St SW9 31 G3
Mandela Way SE1 25 D5
Mandeville Pl W1 17 A5
Mandrake Way E15 13 B4
Mandrell Rd SE2 38 E3
Manette St W1 6 D2
Manfred Rd SW15 37 A3
Manger Rd N7 10 E3
Manhattan Wf E16 27 D3
Manilla St E14 26 E3
Manley St NW1 10 A5
Manor Av SE4 33 D5
Manorbrook SE3 41 D2
Manor Est SE16 25 G5
Manor Flds SW15 36 F4
Manor Gro SE15 33 A2
Manor Ho Dr NW6 8 E3
Manor La SE12 41 B2
Manor La SE13 41 B2
Manor La Ter SE13 41 B2
Manor Ms NW6 16 B2
Manor Ms SE4 33 D5
Manor Pk SE13 41 A2
Manor Pk Rd E12 13 G1
Manor Pk Rd NW10 8 B1
Manor Pl SE17 32 A1
Manor Rd E15 20 B2
Manor Rd E16 20 B2
Manor Rd SE3 41 C2
Manor Way SE3 40 A5
Manresa Rd SW3 30 F1
Mansell St E1 18 E5
Mansergh Cl SE18 35 A3
Mansfield Rd NW3 9 G2
Mansfield St W1 5 B1
Mansford St E2 18 F1
Mansion Ho EC4 7 F2
Mansion Ho Pl EC4 7 F2
Mansion Ho St EC4 7 F2
Manson Ms SW7 23 D5
Manson Pl SW7 23 E5
Manthorp Rd SE18 35 E1
Mantle Rd SE4 40 C1
Mantua St SW11 37 E1

Mantus Rd E1 19 A3
Manwood Rd SE4 40 D3
Manwood St E16 28 B2
Mapesbury Rd NW2 8 G3
Mapeshill Pl NW2 8 E3
Mape St E2 18 G3
Maple Av W3 22 A2
Maple Cl SW4 38 E4
Mapledene Rd E8 11 E4
Maplestead Rd SW2 38 F5
Mapleton Cres SW18 37 C4
Mapleton Rd SW18 37 C4
Maplin Rd E16 20 D5
Maplin St E3 19 D2
Marban Rd W9 16 A2
Marble Arch W1 23 G1
Marble Quay E1 25 F2
Marcella Rd SW9 31 G5
Marchant St SE14 33 C2
Marchbank Rd W14 30 A2
Marchmont St WC1 17 E3
Marchwood Cl SE5 32 D3
Marcia Rd SE1 25 D5
Marcilly Rd SW18 37 E3
Marcon Pl E8 11 G3
Marco Rd W6 22 E4
Marcus Ct E15 13 B5
Marcus Garvey Way SE24 38 G2
Marcus St E15 13 C5
Marcus St SW18 37 C4
Marcus Ter SW18 37 C4
Marden Sq SE16 25 G4
Maresfield Gdns NW3 9 D2
Mare St E8 11 G5
Margaret Ct W1 6 A1
Margaret St W1 17 B5
Margaretta Ter SW3 30 F2
Margery Pk Rd E7 13 D3
Margery St WC1 17 F2
Margravine Gdns W6 29 F1
Margravine Rd W6 29 F1
Marian Pl E2 18 G1
Marian Way NW10 8 A4
Maria Ter E1 19 B4
Marigold All SE1 7 B4
Marigold St SE16 25 G3
Marina Dr, Well. 35 G5
Marine Dr SE18 28 B5
Marinefield Rd SW6 30 C5
Mariners Ms E14 27 A5
Marischal Rd SE13 41 A1
Maritime Quay E14 33 E1
Maritime St E3 19 D3
Marjorie Gro SW11 37 G2
Market Ct N7 6 A1
Market Est N7 10 E3
Market Hill SE18 28 B4
Market Ms W1 24 B2
Market Pl W1 6 A1
Market Pl N7 10 E3
Market St E6 21 A1
Market St SE18 28 C5
Markham Sq SW3 30 G1
Markham St SW3 30 F1
Markland Ho W10 22 F1
Mark La EC3 7 J4
Mark St E15 13 B4
Marlborough Av E8 11 F5
Marlborough Ct W1 6 A2
Marlborough Ct W8 23 B5
Marlborough Gro SE1 32 F1

Marlborough Hill NW8 9 D5
Marlborough La SE7 34 F2
Marlborough Pl NW8 16 D1
Marlborough Rd E7 13 F4
Marlborough Rd SW1 6 B6
Marlborough Rd SW3 23 F5
Marloes Rd W8 23 C4
Marlow Ct NW6 8 B3
Marlowe Gdns SE9 42 C4
Marlowes, The NW8 9 E5
Marlow Rd E6 21 B2
Marlow Way SE16 26 B3
Marl Rd SW18 37 C2
Marmion Rd SW11 38 A2
Marmont Rd SE15 32 F4
Marmora Rd SE22 40 A4
Marne St W10 15 G2
Marney Rd SW11 38 A2
Marnham Av NW2 8 G1
Marnock Rd SE4 40 C3
Maroon St E14 19 C4
Marquess Rd N1 11 C3
Marquis Rd NW1 10 D3
Marrick Cl SW15 36 C1
Marriott Rd E15 13 B5
Marryat Sq SW6 29 G4
Marsala Rd SE13 40 F2
Marsden Rd SE15 39 E1
Marsden St NW5 10 A3
Marshall's Gro SE18 28 A5
Marshall St W1 6 B2
Marshalsea Rd SE1 25 B3
Marsham St SW1 24 D4
Marshbrook Cl SE3 41 G1
Marsh Ct E8 11 G4
Marshfield St E14 26 G4
Marshgate La E15 12 F5
Marshgate Sidings E15 12 F5
Marsh Hill E9 12 C2
Marsh Wall E14 26 E2
Marsland Cl SE17 32 A1
Martello St E8 11 G4
Martello Ter E8 11 G4
Martha Ct E2 18 G1
Martha Rd E15 13 B3
Martha St E1 18 G5
Martin Bowes Rd SE9 42 B3
Martindale Av E16 27 D1
Martindale Rd SW12 38 B5
Martineau Rd N5 11 A1
Martineau St E1 26 A1
Martin La EC4 7 G3
Martin St SE28 28 B4
Marville Rd SW6 30 A3
Mary Ann Gdns SE8 33 E2
Marybank SE18 28 B5
Mary Datchelor Cl SE5 32 C4
Mary Grn NW8 9 C5
Maryland Pk E15 13 B2
Maryland Rd E15 13 A2
Maryland Rd W9 16 B3
Maryland Sq E15 13 B2
Marylands Rd W9 16 B3
Maryland St E15 13 A2
Mary Lawrenson Pl SE3 34 C3
Marylebone High St W1 17 A4
Marylebone La W1 17 A5
Marylebone Pas W1 6 B1
Marylebone Rd NW1 16 F4
Marylebone St W1 17 A5
Marylee Way SE11 24 F5

Maryon Gro SE7 28 A5
Maryon Rd SE7 28 A5
Maryon Rd SE18 28 A5
Mary Pl W11 22 G1
Mary St N1 11 B5
Mary Ter NW1 10 B5
Masbro Rd W14 22 F4
Mascalls Rd SE7 34 F2
Mascotte Rd SW15 36 F2
Masefield Gdns E6 21 C3
Mashie Rd W3 15 A5
Maskelyne Cl SW11 30 F4
Mason Cl E16 27 D1
Masons Av EC2 7 F1
Masons Hill SE18 28 D5
Mason's Pl EC1 18 A3
Mason's St SE17 25 C5
Mason's Yd SW1 6 B5
Massey Ct E6 13 F5
Massingham St E1 19 B3
Master Gunner Pl SE18 35 A3
Masterman Ho SE5 32 C3
Masterman Rd E6 21 A2
Masters Dr SE16 32 G1
Masters St E1 19 B4
Masthouse Ter E14 26 E5
Mast Leisure Pk SE16 26 B4
Mastmaker Rd E14 26 E3
Matchless Dr SE18 35 C3
Matham Gro SE22 39 E2
Matheson Rd W14 23 A3
Mathews Av E6 21 C1
Mathews Pk Av E15 13 C3
Matilda St N1 10 F5
Matlock Cl SE24 39 B2
Matlock St E14 19 C5
Matrimony Pl SW8 31 C5
Matthew Cl W10 15 F3
Matthew Parker St SW1 24 D3
Matthews St SW11 30 G5
Matthews Yd WC2 6 E2
Matthias Rd N16 11 C2
Maud Cashmore Way SE18 28 B4
Maude Rd SE5 32 D4
Maud Gdns E13 20 C1
Maud Rd E13 20 C1
Maudslay Rd SE9 42 B1
Maud St E16 20 C4
Maud Wilkes Cl NW5 10 C2
Mauleverer Rd SW2 38 E3
Maunsel St SW1 24 D5
Maurice St W12 15 D5
Mauritius Rd SE10 27 B5
Maverton Rd E3 12 E5
Mavis Wk E6 21 A4
Mawbey Est SE1 32 E1
Mawbey Pl SE1 32 E1
Mawbey St SW8 31 E3
Maxey Rd SE18 28 E5
Maxted Rd SE15 39 E1
Maxwell Rd SW6 30 C3
Maya Cl SE15 32 G5
Mayall Rd SE24 39 A3
Maybury Gdns NW10 8 D3
Maybury Rd E13 20 F3
Mayday Gdns SE3 35 A5
Mayerne Rd SE9 41 G3
Mayfair Pl W1 24 A2
Mayfield Av W4 22 A5
Mayfield Cl SW4 38 D3
Mayfield Rd E8 11 E4
Mayfield Rd E13 20 C3
Mayfield Rd W12 22 A3
Mayflower Rd SW9 38 E1
Mayflower St SE16 26 A3
Mayford Cl SW12 37 G5
Mayford Rd SW12 38 A5
Maygood St N1 17 F1

Maygrove Rd NW6	9 A3	Melrose Rd SW13	29 B5	Micklethwaite Rd		Millwall Dock Rd
Mayhill Rd SE7	34 E2	Melrose Rd SW18	37 A4	SW6	30 B2	E14	26 E4
Mayola Rd E5	12 A1	Melrose Ter W6	22 E3	Middle Fld NW8	30 B2	Milman Rd NW6	15 G1
Mayo Rd NW10	8 A3	Melthorpe Gdns		Middle Pk Av SE9	41 G4	Milman's St SW10	30 E2
Mayplace La SE18	35 D3	SE3	35 A4	Middle Row W10	15 G3	Milne Gdns SE9	42 A3
May Rd E13	20 D1	Melton Ct SW7	23 E5	Middlesex St E1	18 D4	Milner Pl N1	10 G5
Mays Ct WC2	**6 E4**	Melton St NW1	17 D2	Middle Temple EC4	**6 J3**	Milner Rd E15	20 B2
Maysoule Rd SW11	37 E2	Melville Rd SW13	29 C4	Middle Temple La		Milner Sq N1	11 A4
Mayville Rd, Ilf.	14 F2	Memess Path		EC4	**6 J2**	Milner St SW3	23 G5
Mayville Rd E11	20 E1	SE18	35 C2	Middleton Dr SE16	26 B3	Milo Rd SE22	39 E4
Maze Hill SE3	34 B2	Memorial Av E15	20 B2	Middleton Gro N7	10 E2	**Milroy Wk SE1**	**7 B5**
Maze Hill SE10	34 B2	Mendip Rd SW11	37 D1	Middleton Rd E8	11 E4	Milson Rd W14	22 G4
Mazenod Av NW6	9 B4	Mendora Rd SW6	29 G3	Middleton St E2	18 G2	Milton Av E6	13 G4
Meadcroft Rd SE11	32 A2	Menelik Rd NW2	8 G1	Middleton Way		Milton Cl SE1	25 E5
Meadowbank NW3	9 G4	Mentmore Ter E8	11 G4	SE13	41 A4	Milton Ct Rd SE14	33 C2
Meadowbank SE3	41 C1	**Mepham St SE1**	**6 H6**	**Middle Yd SE1**	**7 G5**	Milton Gro N16	11 C1
Meadowbank		Merbury Cl SE13	40 G3	Midhurst Way E5	11 F1	Milton Rd SE24	39 A4
SW6	29 E3	Merbury Rd SE28	28 F3	Midland Rd NW1	17 D1	Milton St EC2	18 C4
Meadowcourt Rd		Mercator Rd SE13	41 A2	Midland Ter NW10	15 A3	Milverton Rd NW6	8 E4
SE3	41 C2	Merceron St E1	18 G3	Midlothian Rd E3	19 B4	Milverton St SE11	31 G1
Meadow Ms SW8	31 F2	Mercers Cl SE10	27 C5	Midship Pt E14	26 E3	Mimosa St SW6	30 A4
Meadow Pl SW8	31 F2	Mercers Pl W6	22 E5	Midstrath Rd NW10	8 A1	Minard Rd SE6	41 B5
Meadow Rd SW8	31 F2	**Mercer St WC2**	**6 E3**	Miers Cl E6	14 C5	Mina Rd SE17	32 D1
Meadow Row SE1	25 B4	Merchant St E3	19 D2	Milborne Gro		**Mincing La EC3**	**7 H3**
Meadowside SE9	41 F2	Mercia Gro SE13	40 G2	SW10	30 D2	Mineral St SE18	28 G5
Mead Pl E9	12 A3	Mercier Rd SW15	36 G3	Milborne St E9	12 A3	Minera Ms SW1	24 A5
Meadway, Ilf.	14 G1	Mercury Way SE14	33 B2	Milborough Cres		Minerva Cl SW9	31 G3
Meakin Est SE1	25 D4	Mercy Ter SE13	40 F2	SE12	41 B4	Minerva St E2	18 G1
Meanley Rd E12	14 A1	Mere Cl SW15	36 F5	Milcote St SE1	25 A3	Minet Av NW10	15 A1
Meard St W1	**6 C2**	Meredith Av NW2	8 D2	Mildenhall Rd E5	11 C3	Minet Gdns NW10	15 A1
Meath Rd E15	20 C1	Meredith St E13	20 D2	Mildmay Gro N N1	11 C2	Minet Rd SW9	32 A5
Meath St SW11	31 B4	Meredyth Rd SW13	29 C5	Mildmay Gro S N1	11 C2	Minford Gdns W14	22 F3
Mecklenburgh Pl		Meretone Cl SE4	40 C2	Mildmay Pk N1	11 C2	Ming St E14	26 E1
WC1	17 F3	Mereworth Dr SE18	35 D3	Mildmay Rd N1	11 C2	Minories EC3	18 E5
Mecklenburgh Sq		Meridian Gate E14	26 G3	Mildmay St N1	11 C2	Minson Rd E9	12 B5
WC1	17 F3	Meridian Pl E14	26 F3	Mile End Pl E1	19 B3	Minstead Gdns	
Medburn St NW1	17 D1	Meridian Rd SE7	34 G3	Mile End Rd E1	19 A4	SW15	36 B5
Medebourne Cl		Meridian Sq E15	13 A4	Mile End Rd E3	19 A4	Minster Rd NW2	8 G2
SE3	41 D1	Meridian Trd Est		Miles Dr SE28	28 F2	Mint Business Pk	
Medfield St SW15	36 D5	SE7	27 E5	Miles St SW8	31 F3	E16	20 D4
Median Rd E5	12 A2	Merifield Rd SE9	41 F2	Milfoil St W12	22 C1	Mintern St N1	18 C1
Medlar St SE5	32 C3	Merivale Rd SW15	36 G2	**Milford La WC2**	**6 H3**	Mirabel Rd SW6	30 A3
Medley Rd NW6	9 B3	Mermaid Ct SE1	25 C3	Milk St E16	28 D2	Mirfield St SE7	27 G5
Medora Rd SW2	38 F5	Mermaid Ct SE16	26 D2	**Milk St EC2**	**7 E2**	Miriam Rd SE18	35 G2
Medusa Rd SE6	40 F4	Merredene St SW2	38 F4	Milkwell Yd SE5	32 B4	Mission Pl SE15	32 F4
Medway Cl, Ilf.	14 E2	Merriam Av E9	12 E3	Milkwood Rd		Mitcham Rd E6	21 A2
Medway Rd E3	19 C1	Merrick Sq SE1	25 C4	SE24	39 A3	Mitcham Rd SW17	37 D5
Medway St SW1	24 D4	Merridale SE12	41 D3	Milk Yd E1	26 A1	Mitchell St EC1	18 B3
Medwin St SW4	38 F2	Merriman Rd SE3	34 F4	Millais Av E12	14 C1	Mitchell Wk E6	21 A4
Meerbrook Rd SE3	41 F1	Merrington Rd		Millais Rd E11	12 G1	Mitchison Rd N1	11 C3
Meeson Rd E15	13 C5	SW6	30 B2	Millbank SW1	24 E4	**Mitre Ct EC2**	**7 E1**
Meeson St E5	12 C1	Merritt Rd SE4	40 D3	Millbank Twr SW1	24 E5	**Mitre Ct EC4**	**7 A2**
Meeting Ho La		Merrow St SE17	32 B2	Millbank Way SE12	41 D3	Mitre Rd E15	20 B1
SE15	32 G4	Merryfield SE3	34 C5	Millbrook Av, Well.	42 F2	Mitre Rd SE1	24 G3
Mehetabel Rd E9	12 A3	Merryfields Way		Millbrook Rd SW9	39 A1	**Mitre Sq EC3**	**7 J2**
Melba Way SE13	33 F4	SE6	40 F5	Millender Wk SE16	26 A5	**Mitre St EC3**	**7 J2**
Melbourne Gro		Mersea Ho, Bark.	14 G3	Miller's Av E8	11 E2	Mitre Way W10	15 D3
SE22	39 D2	Merthyr Ter SW13	29 D2	Miller's Ter E8	11 E2	Moat Pl SW9	38 F1
Melbourne Ms		Merton Av W4	22 B5	Miller St NW1	17 C1	Moberley Rd SW4	38 E5
SE6	40 G5	Merton Ri NW3	9 F4	Miller Way W6	22 E5	Modder Pl SW15	36 F2
Melbourne Ms		Merton Rd SW18	37 B3	**Miller Wk SE1**	**7 A6**	Modling Ho E2	19 B1
SW9	**6 H3**	Merttins Rd SE15	40 B3	Millers Ct W4		Moira Rd SE9	42 B2
Melbourne Pl WC2	**6 H3**	Mervan Rd SW2	38 G2	Milligan St E14	26 D1	Molesford Rd SW6	30 A4
Melbourne Rd E6	14 B5	Messent Rd SE9	41 F3	Mill La NW6	9 A2	Molesworth St	
Melbury Ct W8	23 A4	Messeter Pl SE9	42 C4	Mill La SE18	35 C1	SE13	40 G1
Melbury Rd W14	23 A4	Messina Av NW6	9 B4	Millman Ms WC1	17 F3	Molly Huggins Cl	
Melcombe Pl NW1	16 G4	Meteor St SW11	38 A2	Millman St WC1	17 F3	SW12	38 C5
Melcombe St NW1	16 G3	Methley St SE11	31 G1	Millmark Gro SE14	33 C5	Molyneux St W1	16 F4
Melford Av, Bark.	14 G3	Methwold Rd W10	15 F4	Mill Pd E16		Monarch Dr E16	20 G4
Melford Rd E6	21 B3	Mews Deck E1	26 G1	Millfields Rd E5	12 A1	Mona Rd SE15	33 A5
Melford Rd E22	39 F5	Mews End E1	25 F2	Millgrove St SW11	31 A5	Mona St E16	20 C4
Melgund Rd N5	10 G2	Mexfield Rd SW15	37 B1	Millharbour E14	26 F4	Monck St SW1	24 D4
Melina Pl NW8	16 E2	**Meymott St SE1**	**7 B6**	Mill Hill Rd SW13	29 C5	Monclar Rd SE5	39 C2
Melina Rd W12	22 D3	Meynell Cres E9	12 B4	Milligan St E14	26 D1	Moncrieff St SE15	32 F5
Melior St SE1	25 C3	Meynell Gdns E9	12 B4	Mill La NW6		Monega Rd E7	13 F3
Melling St SE18	35 G2	Meynell Rd E9	12 B4	Milman Rd NW6		Monega Rd E12	13 G3
Mellish Ind Est		Meyrick Rd NW10	8 C3	Milman St SW10		Monier Rd E3	12 E4
SE18	28 A4	Meyrick Rd SW11	37 E1	Millmark Gro SE14		Monk Dr E16	20 E5
Mellish St E14	26 E4	Micawber St N1	18 B2	Mill Rd E16	27 G2	Monk St SE18	28 C5
Mellitus St W12	15 B5	Michael Rd SW6	30 C4	Mill Row N1	11 D5	Monkton St SE11	24 G5
Melody La N5	11 A2	Michaels Cl SE13	41 B2	Mill Shot Cl SW6	29 E3	Monmouth Rd E6	21 B2
Melon Rd SE15	32 F4	Micheldever Rd		Millstream Rd SE1	25 E3	Monmouth Rd W2	16 C5
Melrose Av NW2	8 D2	SE12	41 B4	Mill St SE1	25 E3	Monmouth St WC2	**6 E2**
Melrose Gdns W6	22 E4	Michigan Av E12	14 A1	**Mill St W1**	**6 A3**	Monnow Rd SE1	25 F5
						Monson Rd NW10	15 C1
						Monson Rd SE14	33 B3
						Montacute Rd SE6	40 D5

Montague Av SE4 40 D2
Montague Cl SE1 7 F5
Montague Pl WC1 17 D4
Montague Rd E8 11 F2
Montague St EC1 18 B5
Montague St WC1 17 E4
Montagu Ms N W1 16 G4
Montagu Pl W1 16 G4
Montagu Sq W1 16 G4
Montagu St W1 16 G4
Montcalm Rd SE7 34 G3
Monteagle Av,
  Bark. 14 E3
Monteagle Way
  SE15 39 G1
Montefiore St SW8 31 B5
Montem Rd SE23 40 D5
Montevetro SW11 30 E4
Montford Pl SE11 31 G1
Montgomery St
  E14 26 F2
Montholme Rd
  SW11 37 G4
Montolieu Gdns
  SW15 36 D3
Montpelier Gdns
  E6 20 G2
Montpelier Gro
  NW5 10 C2
Montpelier Pl E1 19 A5
Montpelier Pl SW7 23 F4
Montpelier Row
  SE15 32 G4
Montpelier Row
  SE3 34 C5
Montpelier Sq SW7 23 F3
Montpelier St SW7 23 F3
Montpelier Vale SE3 34 C5
Montpelier Wk SW7 23 F4
Montreal Pl WC2 6 G3
Montrose Av NW6 15 G1
Montrose Av, Well. 42 F1
Montrose Ct SW7 23 E3
Montrose Pl SW1 24 A3
Montserrat Rd
  SW15 36 G2
Monument Gdns
  SE13 40 G3
Monument St EC3 7 G3
Monza St E1 26 A1
Moodkee St SE16 26 A4
Moody Rd SE15 32 E3
Moody St E1 19 B2
Moon St N1 11 A5
Moordown SE18 35 C4
Moorehead Way
  SE3 41 E1
Moore Pk Rd SW6 30 C3
Moore St SW3 23 G5
Moorfields EC2 18 C4
Moorgate EC2 7 F1
Moorgate Pl EC2 7 F1
Moorhouse Rd W2 16 B5
Moorland Rd SW9 39 A2
Moorlands Est
  SW9 38 G2
Moor La EC2 18 C4
Moor St W1 6 D2
Morant St E14 26 E1
Mora Rd NW2 8 E1
Mora St EC1 18 B2
Morat St SW9 31 F4
Moravian St E2 19 B2
Moravian St SW9 38 F1
Morden Hill SE13 33 G5
Morden La SE13 33 G4
Morden St SE13 40 D5
Morden Rd Ms
  SE3 34 D5
Morden St SE13 33 F4
Morden Wf Rd
  SE10 27 A4
Morecambe Cl E1 19 B4
Morecambe St
  SE17 25 B5
More Cl E16 20 C5

More Cl W14 22 G5
Moreland St EC1 18 A2
Morella Rd SW12 37 G5
Morena St SE6 40 F5
Moresby Wk SW8 31 C5
Moreton Pl SW1 31 C1
Moreton St SW1 31 C1
Moreton Ter SW1 31 C1
Morgan Rd N7 10 G2
Morgan Rd W10 16 A4
Morgan St E3 19 C2
Morgan St E16 20 C4
Moriatry Cl N7 10 E1
Morie St SW18 37 C3
Morley Rd E15 20 C1
Morley Rd SE13 40 G2
Morley Rd, Bark. 14 F5
Morley St SE1 31 G5
Morna Rd SE5 32 B5
Morning La E9 12 A3
Mornington Av
  W14 23 A5
Mornington Cres
  NW1 17 C1
Mornington Gro
  E3 19 E2
Mornington Ms
  SE5 32 B4
Mornington Rd
  SE8 33 D3
Mornington St
  NW1 17 B1
Mornington Ter
  NW1 10 B5
Morocco St SE1 25 D3
Morpeth Gro E9 12 B5
Morpeth Rd E9 12 A5
Morpeth St E2 19 B2
Morpeth Ter SW1 24 C4
Morris Av E12 14 B2
Morris Gdns SW18 37 B5
Morrish Rd SW2 38 E5
Morrison St SW11 38 A1
Morris Rd E14 19 F4
Morris Rd E15 13 B5
Morse Cl E13 20 D2
Morshead Rd W9 16 B2
Morten Cl SW4 38 D4
Mortham St E15 13 A5
Mortimer Cres NW6 9 C5
Mortimer Est NW6 9 C5
Mortimer Rd E6 21 B2
Mortimer Rd N1 11 D4
Mortimer Rd NW10 15 E2
Mortimer St W1 17 C5
Mortlake Rd E16 20 E5
Mortlake Rd, Ilf. 14 E1
Morton Rd E15 13 C4
Morton Rd N1 11 B4
Morval Rd SE24 38 G3
Morville St E3 19 E1
Moscow Rd W2 23 B1
Moseley Row SE10 27 C5
Mossbury Rd SW11 37 F1
Mossford St E3 19 D3
Mossop St SW3 23 F5
Mostyn Gdns
  NW10 15 F1
Mostyn Gro E3 19 D1
Mostyn Rd SW9 31 G4
Motcomb St SW1 24 A4
Mothers' Sq E5 11 G1
Moulins Rd E9 12 A5
Mulsford Ho N7 10 D2
Mount Adon Pk
  SE22 39 F5
Mountague Pl E14 26 G1
Mount Angelus Rd
  SW15 36 B5
Mountbatten Cl
  SE18 35 G2
Mountfield Cl SE6 41 A5
Mountfield Rd E6 21 C1

Mount Pleasant
  WC1 17 G3
Mount Pleasant Rd
  NW10 8 E4
Mount Pleasant Rd
  SE13 40 F4
Mount Rd, Ilf. 14 D2
Mount Row W1 24 B1
Mountsfield Ct
  SE13 41 A4
Mounts Pond Rd
  SE3 34 A5
Mount St W1 24 A1
Mount Vernon NW3 9 D1
Movers La, Bark. 21 G1
Mowbray Rd NW6 8 G4
Mowlem St E2 18 G1
Mowll St SW9 31 G3
Moxon St W1 17 A4
Moylan Rd W6 29 G2
Mozart St W10 16 A2
Mozart Ter SW1 24 A5
Muir Dr SW18 37 E4
Muirfield W3 15 A5
Muir Rd E5 11 E5
Mulberry Cl SE22 39 F3
Mulberry Rd E8 11 E4
Mulberry Wk SW3 30 E2
Mulgrave Rd NW10 8 B1
Mulgrave Rd SE18 28 B5
Mulgrave Rd SW6 30 A2
Muller Rd SW4 38 D4
Multon Rd SW18 37 E5
Mulvaney Way SE1 25 C3
Mumford Ct EC2 7 E1
Muncaster Rd
  SW11 37 G3
Mundania Rd SE22 39 G4
Munday Rd E16 20 D5
Munden St W14 22 G5
Mund St W14 30 A1
Mundy St N1 18 D2
Munro Ms W10 15 G4
Munro Ter SW10 30 E3
Munster Rd SW6 30 A4
Munster Sq NW1 17 B2
Munton Rd SE17 25 B5
Murdock St SE15 32 G2
Muriel St N1 17 F1
Murillo Rd SE13 41 A2
Murphy St SE1 24 G3
Murray Gro N1 18 C1
Murray Ms NW1 10 D4
Murray St NW1 10 D4
Murrays Yd SE18 28 D5
Mursell Est SW8 31 F4
Musard Rd W6 29 G2
Musard Rd W14 29 G2
Musbury St E1 19 A5
Muscal W6 29 G2
Muschamp Rd
  SE15 39 E1
Muscovy St EC3 7 J4
Museum St WC1 17 E5
Musgrave Cres
  SW6 30 B4
Musgrove Rd
  SE14 33 B4
Mutrix Rd NW6 9 B5
Myatt Rd SW9 32 A4
Mycenae Rd SE3 34 D3
Myddelton Sq EC1 17 G2
Myddelton St EC1 17 G2
Myers La SE14 33 B2
Mylne St EC1 17 G2
Myrdle St E1 18 F4
Myron Pl SE13 40 G1
Myrtle Rd E6 14 A5
Myrtle Wk N1 18 D1
Mysore Rd SW11 37 G1

Nags Head Shop
  Cen N7 10 F1
Nairne Gro SE24 39 C3
Nairn St E14 19 G4
Nankin St E14 19 E5
Nansen Rd SW11 38 A1
Nantes Cl SW18 37 D2
Napier Av E14 33 E1
Napier Av SW6 37 A1
Napier Gro N1 18 B1
Napier Pl W14 23 A4
Napier Rd E6 14 C5
Napier Rd E11 13 B1
Napier Rd E15 20 B1
Napier Rd NW10 15 D2
Napier Rd W14 23 A4
Napier Ter N1 11 A4
Narbonne Av SW4 38 C3
Narborough St
  SW6 30 C5
Narcissus Rd NW6 9 B2
Narrow St E14 26 C1
Nascot St W12 15 E5
Nash Rd SE4 40 C2
Nasmyth St W6 22 D4
Nassau Rd SW13 29 B4
Nassau St W1 17 C4
Nassington Rd
  NW3 9 F1
Natal Rd, Ilf. 14 D1
Nathan Way SE28 28 G5
Naval Row E14 26 G1
Navarino Gro E8 11 F3
Navarino Rd E8 11 F3
Navarre Rd E6 21 A1
Navarre St E2 18 E3
Navy St SW4 38 D1
Naylor Rd SE15 32 G3
Nazareth Gdns
  SE15 32 G5
Nazrul St E2 18 E2
Nealden St SW9 38 F1
Neal St WC2 6 E2
Neal's Yd WC2 6 E2
Neasden Cl NW10 8 A2
Neasden La NW10 8 A1
Neate St SE5 32 D2
Neatscourt Rd E6 20 G4
Nebraska St SE1 25 C3
Neckinger SE16 25 E4
Neckinger Est SE16 25 E4
Neckinger St SE1 25 E3
Nectarine Way
  SE13 33 F5
Needleman St
  SE16 26 B3
Nelgarde Rd SE6 40 E5
Nella Rd W6 29 F2
Nelldale Rd SE16 26 A5
Nelson Cl NW6 16 B1
Nelson Gdns E2 18 F2
Nelson Mandela Rd
  SE3 41 F1
Nelson Pl N1 18 A1
Nelson Rd SE10 33 G2
Nelson Sq SE1 25 A3
Nelson's Row SW4 38 D2
Nelson St E1 18 G5
Nelson St E6 21 B1
Nelson Ter N1 18 A1
Nepaul Rd SW11 30 F5
Nepean St SW15 36 C4
Neptune St SE16 26 A4
Nesbit Rd SE9 41 G2
Nesham St E1 25 F2
Netheravon Rd
  W4 22 B5
Netheravon Rd S
  W4 29 B1
Netherby Rd SE23 40 A5
Netherfield Gdns,
  Bark. 14 F3
Netherford Rd
  SW4 31 C5
Netherhall Gdns
  NW3 9 D3

N

N1 Shop Cen N1 17 G1
Nadine St SE7 34 F1

Entry	Ref.
Netherton Gro SW10	30 D2
Netherwood Rd W14	22 F4
Netherwood St NW6	9 A4
Nettleton Rd SE14	33 B4
Nevada St SE10	33 G2
Nevern Pl SW5	23 B5
Nevern Rd SW5	23 B5
Nevern Sq SW5	23 B5
Neville Cl NW6	16 A1
Neville Cl SE15	32 F3
Neville Gill Cl SW18	37 B4
Neville Rd E7	13 D4
Neville Rd NW6	16 A1
Neville St SW7	30 E1
Neville Ter SW7	30 E1
Nevill Rd N16	11 D1
Nevinson Cl SW18	37 E4
New Acres Rd SE28	28 G2
Newark Knok E6	21 C5
Newark St E1	18 D4
New Barn St E13	20 D3
New Bond St W1	24 B1
New Br St EC4	7 B2
New Broad St EC2	18 D4
Newburgh St W1	6 A2
New Burlington Ms W1	6 A3
New Burlington Pl W1	6 A3
New Burlington St W1	6 A3
Newburn St SE11	31 F1
New Butt La SE8	33 E3
Newby Pl E14	26 G1
Newby St SW8	38 B1
New Caledonian Wf SE16	26 D4
Newcastle Cl EC4	7 B1
Newcastle Pl W2	16 E4
New Cavendish St W1	17 A4
New Change EC4	7 D2
New Ch Rd SE5	32 B3
New City Rd E13	20 F2
Newcomen Rd SW11	37 F1
Newcomen St SE1	25 C3
New Compton St WC2	6 D2
New Ct EC4	6 J3
Newcourt St NW8	16 F1
New Covent Gdn Mkt SW8	31 D3
New Cross Rd SE14	33 A4
Newell St E14	19 D5
New End NW3	9 E1
New End Sq NW3	9 E1
Newent Cl SE15	32 E3
New Ferry App SE18	28 C4
New Fetter La EC4	7 A1
Newgate St EC1	7 C1
New Globe Wk SE1	7 D6
Newham Way E6	20 F4
Newham Way E16	20 F4
Newhaven Gdns SE9	41 G2
Newhaven La E16	20 C3
Newington Butts SE1	25 A5
Newington Butts SE11	25 A5
Newington Causeway SE1	25 A4
Newington Grn N1	11 C2
Newington Grn N16	11 C2
Newington Grn Rd N1	11 C2
New Inn Pas WC2	6 H2
New Inn Yd EC2	18 D3
New Kent Rd SE1	25 B4
New Kings Rd SW6	30 A5
New King St SE8	33 E2
Newlands Ct SE9	42 C4
Newlands Quay E1	26 A1
Newland St E16	28 A1
New Lydenburg St SE7	27 F4
Newman Rd E13	20 E2
Newman's Ct EC3	7 G2
Newman St W1	17 C4
Newman Yd W1	6 C1
New Mt St E15	13 A4
New N Rd N1	18 C1
New N St WC1	17 F3
New Oxford St WC1	6 D1
New Pk Ct SW2	38 E5
New Pl Sq SE16	25 G4
New Plaistow Rd E15	13 B5
Newport Av E13	20 E3
Newport Av E14	27 A1
Newport Ct WC2	6 D3
Newport Pl WC2	6 D3
Newport Rd SW13	29 C4
Newport St SE11	24 F5
New Quebec St W1	16 G5
New Ride SW7	23 F3
New River Ct N5	11 C1
New River Wk N1	11 B3
New Rd E1	18 G4
New Row WC2	6 E3
New Sq WC2	6 H1
Newstead Rd SE12	41 B5
New St EC2	18 D4
New St Sq EC4	7 A1
Newton Gro W4	22 A5
Newton Pl E14	26 E5
Newton Rd E15	13 A2
Newton Rd W2	16 B5
Newton St WC2	6 G1
New Union Cl E14	26 G4
New Union St EC2	18 C4
New Wf Rd N1	17 E1
New Zealand Way W12	22 D1
Nicholas La EC4	7 G3
Nicholas Pas EC4	7 G3
Nicholas Rd E1	19 A3
Nicholl St E2	11 F5
Nichols Ct E2	18 E1
Nicholson St SE1	7 B6
Nickols Wk SW18	37 C2
Nicoll Rd NW10	8 A5
Nicosia Rd SW18	37 F5
Nigel Ms, Ilf.	14 D1
Nigel Rd E7	13 F2
Nigel Rd SE15	39 F1
Nigeria Rd SE7	34 F3
Nightingale Gro SE13	41 A3
Nightingale La SW4	37 G5
Nightingale La SW12	37 G5
Nightingale Pl SE18	35 C2
Nightingale Rd N1	11 B3
Nightingale Rd NW10	15 B1
Nightingale Sq SW12	38 A5
Nightingale Vale SE18	35 C2
Nightingale Wk SW4	38 B4
Nightingale Way E6	21 A4
Nile Rd E13	20 F1
Nile St N1	18 C2
Nile Ter SE15	32 E1
Nimegen Way SE22	39 D3
Nine Acres Cl E12	14 A2
Nine Elms La SW8	31 C2
Niton St SW6	29 F3
Noble St EC2	7 D1
Noel Rd E6	21 A3
Noel Rd N1	18 A1
Noel St W1	6 B2
Nolan Way E5	11 F1
Norbiton Rd E14	19 D5
Norbroke St W12	22 B1
Norcroft Gdns SE22	39 F5
Norfolk Cres W2	16 F5
Norfolk Cres, Sid.	42 G5
Norfolk Ho SE3	34 B2
Norfolk Pl W2	16 E5
Norfolk Rd E6	14 B5
Norfolk Rd NW8	9 E5
Norfolk Rd NW10	8 A4
Norfolk Rd, Bark.	14 G4
Norfolk Sq W2	16 E5
Norfolk St E7	13 D1
Norgrove St SW12	38 A5
Norland Ho W11	22 F2
Norland Pl W11	22 G2
Norland Rd W11	22 F2
Normanby Rd NW10	8 B1
Normand Rd W14	30 A2
Normandy Rd SW9	31 G4
Normandy Ter E16	20 E5
Norman Gro E3	19 C1
Norman Rd E6	21 B3
Norman Rd SE10	33 F3
Norman Rd, Ilf.	14 D5
Norris St SW1	6 C4
Norroy Rd SW15	36 F2
Northampton Gro N1	11 C2
Northampton Pk N1	11 B3
Northampton Rd EC1	17 G3
Northampton Sq EC1	18 A2
North Access Rd E17	11 B4
North Audley St W1	17 A5
North Bk NW8	16 F3
Northbourne Rd SW4	38 D2
Northbrook Rd SE13	41 A3
Northburgh St EC1	18 A3
North Carriage Dr W2	23 E1
Northchurch Rd N1	11 D4
Northchurch Ter N1	11 D4
North Circular Rd (A406) E6	21 D1
North Circular Rd (A406) E12	14 C2
North Circular Rd (A406), Bark.	21 D1
North Colonnade E14	26 E2
Northcote Rd NW10	8 A4
Northcote Rd SW11	37 F2
North Cres E16	20 A3
North Cres WC1	17 D4
North Cross Rd SE22	39 E3
Northdown St N1	17 F1
North End Cres W14	23 A5
North End Ho W14	22 G5
North End Rd SW6	30 A2
North End Rd W14	22 G5
Northey St E14	26 C1
Northfield Rd E6	14 B4
Northfields SW18	37 B2
North Gower St NW1	17 C2
Northiam St E9	11 G5
Northington St WC1	17 F3
Northlands St SE5	32 B5
North Ms WC1	17 F3
Northolme Rd N5	11 B1
North Pk SE9	42 B4
North Pas SW18	37 B2
North Peckham Est SE15	32 E3
North Pole Rd W10	15 E4
Northport St N1	11 C5
North Ride W2	23 F1
North Rd N7	10 E3
North Rd SE18	28 G5
North Row W1	23 G1
North Side Wandsworth Common	37 E3
North St E13	20 D1
North St SW4	14 D3
North St Pas E13	20 E1
North Tenter St E1	18 E5
North Ter SW3	23 F4
Northumberland All EC3	7 J2
Northumberland Av WC2	6 E5
Northumberland Av, Well.	42 F2
Northumberland Pl W2	16 B5
Northumberland St EC6	21 A5
Northumberland St WC2	6 E5
Northumbria St E14	19 E5
Northview Cres NW10	8 B1
North Vil NW1	10 D3
North Way SE5	39 B1
North Wf Rd W2	16 E4
Northwick Ter NW8	16 E3
North Woolwich Rd E16	27 D2
Norton Folgate E1	18 D4
Norway Gate SE16	26 C4
Norway St SE10	33 F2
Norwich Rd E7	13 D2
Norwich St EC4	6 J1
Notley St SE5	32 C3
Notre Dame Est SW4	38 C2
Notting Barn Rd W10	15 F3
Nottingham Av E16	20 F4
Nottingham Ct WC2	6 E2
Nottingham Pl W1	17 A3
Nottingham St W1	17 A4
Notting Hill Gate W11	23 B2
Novello St SW6	30 B4
Nowell Rd SW13	29 C2
Nuding Cl SE13	40 E1
Nugent Ter NW8	16 E1
Nun Ct EC2	7 F1
Nunhead Cres SE15	39 G1
Nunhead Grn SE15	39 G2
Nunhead Gro SE15	39 G1
Nunhead La SE15	39 G1
Nursery Cl SE4	33 D5
Nursery Cl SW15	36 F2
Nursery La E2	11 F5
Nursery La E7	13 D3
Nursery La W10	15 E4
Nursery Rd SW9	38 F2
Nursery Row SE17	25 C5
Nursery St N16	11 C2
Nutbourne St W10	15 G2
Nutbrook St SE15	39 F1

Nutcroft Rd SE15 28 G3
Nutfield Rd E15 12 G1
Nutfield Rd SE22 35 E5
Nutford Pl W1 16 G5
Nuthatch Gdns
SE28 28 F3
Nutley Ter NW3 9 D3
Nutmeg La E14 20 A5
Nuttall St N1 18 D1
Nutt St SE15 32 E3
Nyanza St SE18 35 F2
Nynehead St SE14 33 C3

O

Oakbank Gro SE24 39 B3
Oakbury Rd SW6 30 C5
Oak Cres E16 20 B4
Oakcroft Rd SE13 34 A6
Oakdale Rd E7 13 E4
Oakdale Rd SE15 40 A1
Oakden St SE11 24 G5
Oake Ct SW15 36 G3
Oakey La SE1 24 G4
Oakfield Rd E6 14 A5
Oakfield Rd SW10 30 D2
Oakford Rd NW5 10 C1
Oak Gro NW2 8 G1
Oakhill Av NW3 9 C1
Oak Hill Pk NW3 9 C1
Oak Hill Pk Ms NW3 9 D1
Oakhill Rd SW15 37 A3
Oak Hill Way NW3 9 D1
Oakhurst Gro SE22 29 F5
Oakington Rd W9 16 B3
Oakland Rd E15 12 G1
Oaklands Est SW4 38 C4
Oaklands Gro W12 22 C2
Oaklands Rd NW2 8 F1
Oak La E14 26 D1
Oakley Dr SE13 41 A4
Oakley Gdns SW3 30 F2
Oakley Pl SE1 32 E1
Oakley Rd N1 11 C4
Oakley Sq NW1 17 C1
Oakley St SW3 30 F2
Oakley Wk W6 29 F2
Oak Pk Gdns SW19 36 F5
Oaks, The SE18 35 E1
Oakshaw Rd SW18 37 C5
Oaktree Gro, Ilf. 14 F2
Oak Tree Rd NW8 16 F2
Oak Village NW5 10 A1
Oak Way W3 22 A2
Oakways SE9 42 D4
Oakwood Ct W14 23 A4
Oakwood La W14 23 A4
Oakworth Rd W10 15 E4
Oat La EC2 7 D1
Oban Cl E13 20 F3
Oban Rd E13 20 F2
Oban St E14 20 A5
Oberstein Rd
SW11 37 E2
Oborne Cl SE24 39 A3
Observatory Gdns
W8 23 B3
Occupation La
SE18 35 D4
Occupation Rd
SE17 32 B1
Ocean Est E1 19 B4
Ocean St E1 19 B4
Ocean Wf E14 19 B2
Ockendon Rd N1 11 C3
Octavia St SW11 30 G4
Octavius St SE8 33 E3
Odessa Rd NW10 15 C1
Odessa St SE16 26 D3
Odger St SW11 30 G5
Odhams Wk WC2 6 E2
Offenbach Ho E2 19 B1
Offerton Rd SW4 38 C1
Offley Rd SW9 31 G3
Offord Rd N1 10 F4
Offord St N1 10 F4

Ogilby St SE18 28 B5
Oglander Rd SE15 39 E2
Ogle St W1 17 C4
Ohio Rd E13 20 C3
Oil Mill La W6 29 C1
Okehampton Rd
NW10 8 E5
Olaf St W11 22 F1
Old Bailey EC4 7 C2
Old Bellgate Pl
E14 26 E4
Old Bethnal Grn Rd
E2 18 F2
Old Bond St W1 6 A4
Old Brewers Yd WC2 6 E2
Old Broad St EC2 7 G2
Old Brompton Rd
SW5 30 B1
Old Brompton Rd
SW7 30 B1
Old Bldgs WC2 6 J1
Old Burlington St
W1 6 A3
Oldbury Pl W1 17 A3
Old Castle St E1 18 E4
Old Cavendish St
W1 17 B5
Old Ch Rd E1 19 B5
Old Ch St SW3 30 E1
Old Compton St W1 6 C3
Old Ct Pl W8 23 C3
Old Devonshire Rd
SW12 38 B5
Old Dover Rd SE3 34 D3
Oldfield Gro SE16 26 B5
Oldfield Rd NW10 8 B4
Old Fish St Hill EC4 7 D3
Old Fleet La EC4 7 B1
Old Ford Rd E2 19 A1
Old Ford Rd E3 19 C1
Old Gloucester St
WC1 17 E4
Old Jamaica Rd
SE16 25 F4
Old James St
SE15 39 G1
Old Jewry EC2 7 F2
Old Kent Rd SE1 25 D5
Old Kent Rd SE15 25 D5
Old Marylebone Rd
NW1 16 F4
Old Mill Rd SE18 35 F2
Old Montague St
E1 18 F4
Old Nichol St E2 18 E3
Old Oak Common La
NW10 15 A3
Old Oak Common La
W3 15 A4
Old Oak La NW10 15 A2
Old Oak Rd W3 22 B1
Old Palace Yd SW1 24 E4
Old Paradise St
SE11 24 F5
Old Pk Av SW12 38 A4
Old Pk La W1 24 A2
Old Pye St SW1 24 D4
Old Quebec St W1 16 G5
Old Queen St SW1 24 D3
Oldridge Rd SW12 38 A5
Old River Lea Towpath
E15 12 F4
Old Rd SE13 41 B2
Old Royal Free Sq
N1 10 G5
Old Sch Cl SE10 27 B4
Old Sch Cres E7 13 C3
Orlop St SE10 34 B1
Old Seacoal La EC4 7 B1
Old S Lambeth Rd
SW8 31 E3
Old Spitalfields Mkt
E1 18 E4
Old Sq WC2 6 H1
Old St E13 20 E1
Old St EC1 18 B3
Old Town SW4 38 C1

Old Woolwich Rd
SE10 34 A2
Old York Rd SW18 37 C3
O'Leary Sq E1 19 A4
Oliphant St W10 15 F2
Oliver Gdns E6 21 A5
Oliver-Goldsmith Est
SE15 32 F4
Oliver Ms SE15 32 F5
Olive Rd E13 20 F2
Olive Rd NW2 8 E1
Olivette St SW11 36 F1
Ollerton Grn E3 12 D5
Ollgar Cl W12 22 B2
Olliffe St E14 26 G4
Olmar St SE1 32 F2
Olney Rd SE17 31 G3
Olven Rd SE18 35 E3
Olympia Way W14 22 G4
Oman Av NW2 8 E1
O'Meara St SE1 7 E6
Omega St SE14 33 E4
Ommaney Rd
SE14 33 B4
Ondine Rd SE15 39 E2
Onega Gate SE16 26 C4
One Tree Cl SE23 40 A4
Ongar Rd SW6 30 B2
Onslow Gdns SW7 30 E1
Onslow Sq SW7 23 F6
Ontario St SE1 25 A4
Ontario Way E14 26 E1
Opal Cl E16 20 G5
Opal St SE11 25 A5
Ophir Ter SE15 32 F4
Oppenheim Rd
SE13 33 G5
Oppidans Rd NW3 9 G4
Orangery La SE9 42 B3
Orange St WC2 6 C4
Orange Yd W1 6 D2
Oransay Rd N1 11 B3
Orbain Rd SW6 30 A4
Orbel St SW11 30 F4
Orb St SE17 25 C5
Orchard, The SE3 34 A5
Orchard Cl W10 15 G4
Orchard Pl E5 11 G2
Orchard Pl E14 27 B1
Orchard Ri W, Sid. 42 G3
Orchard Rd SE3 34 B5
Orchard Rd SE18 28 F5
Orchardson St
NW8 16 E3
Orchard St W1 17 A5
Orchid Cl E6 21 A4
Orchid St W12 22 C1
Ordell Rd E3 19 D1
Ordnance Cres
SE10 27 A3
Ordnance Hill NW8 9 E5
Ordnance Rd E16 20 C4
Ordnance Rd SE18 35 D2
Oregano Dr E14 20 A5
Oregon Av E13 14 B1
Oriel Dr SW13 29 D2
Oriel Rd E9 12 B3
Oriental Rd E16 27 G2
Orissa Rd SE18 35 G1
Orkney St SW11 31 A5
Orlando Rd SW4 38 C1
Orleston Ms N7 10 G3
Orleston Rd N7 10 G3
Orlop St SE10 34 B1
Orme Ct W2 23 C1
Orme La W2 23 C1
Ormiston Gro W12 22 D2
Ormiston Rd SE10 34 D1
Ormonde Gate
SW3 30 G1
Ormonde Ter NW8 9 G5
Ormond Yd SW1 6 B5
Ormsby St E2 18 E1
Ormside St SE15 33 A2

Ornan Rd NW3 9 F2
Orpheus St SE5 32 C4
Orsett St SE11 31 F1
Orsett Ter W2 16 D5
Orsman Rd N1 11 D5
Orville Rd SW11 30 E5
Orwell Ct N5 11 B1
Orwell Rd E13 20 F1
Osberton Rd SE12 41 D3
Osborn Cl E8 11 F5
Osborne Rd E7 13 F2
Osborne Rd E9 12 D3
Osborne Rd NW2 8 D3
Osborn La SE23 40 C5
Osborn St E1 18 E4
Oscar St SE8 33 E4
Oseney Cres NW5 10 C3
Osier La SE10 27 C4
Osier Ms W4 29 B2
Osiers Rd SW18 37 B2
Osier St E1 19 A3
Oslo Sq SE16 26 C4
Osnaburgh St NW1 17 B3
Osnaburgh St
(north section)
NW1 17 B2
Ospringe Rd NW5 10 C1
Osric Path N1 18 D1
Ossington St W2 23 C1
Ossory Rd SE1 32 F1
Ossulston St NW1 17 D2
Ostade Rd SW2 38 F5
Osterley Rd N16 11 D1
Oswell Ho E1 25 G2
Oswin St SE11 25 A5
Oswyth Rd SE5 32 D5
Otford Cres SE4 40 D1
Otis St E3 19 G2
Otley Rd E16 20 F5
Otterburn Ho SE5 32 B3
Otter Cl E15 12 G5
Otto St SE17 32 A2
Outer Circle NW1 17 B1
Outgate Rd NW10 8 B5
Outram Pl N1 10 E5
Outram Rd E6 14 A5
Outwich St EC3 7 J1
Oval, The E2 18 G1
Oval Pl SW8 31 F3
Oval Rd NW1 10 B5
Oval Way SE11 31 F1
Overbury St E5 12 B1
Overcliff Rd SE13 40 E1
Overhill Rd SE22 39 F5
Overmead, St. 42 F5
Oversley Ho W2 16 B4
Overstone Rd W6 22 E4
Overton Rd SW9 31 G5
Ovex Cl E14 26 G3
Ovington Gdns
SW3 23 F4
Ovington Ms SW3 23 F4
Ovington Sq SW3 23 F4
Ovington St SW3 23 F4
Owens Way SE23 40 C5
Oxberry Av SW6 29 G5
Oxendon St SW1 6 C4
Oxenford St SE15 39 E1
Oxenholme NW1 17 C1
Oxestalls Rd SE8 33 C1
Oxford Circ Av W1 6 A2
Oxford Ct EC4 7 F3
Oxford Dr SE1 7 H6
Oxford Gdns W10 15 G5
Oxford Gate W6 22 F5
Oxford Rd E15 13 A3
Oxford Rd NW6 16 B1
Oxford Rd SW15 36 G2
Oxford Rd, Ilf. 14 E1
Oxford Sq W2 16 F5
Oxford St W1 17 B5
Oxleas E6 21 D5
Oxleas Cl, Well. 35 F5
Oxley Cl SE1 32 E1
Oxonian St SE22 39 E3
Oxo Twr Wf SE1 7 A4

Ozolins Way E16	20 D5	

P

Pacific Rd E16	20 D5
Packington Sq N1	11 B5
Packington St N1	11 A5
Packmores Rd SE9	42 F3
Padbury SE17	32 D1
Padbury Ct E2	19 B1
Paddenswick Rd W6	22 C4
Paddington Grn W2	16 E4
Paddington St W1	17 A4
Paddock Cl SE3	34 D5
Paddock Way SW15	36 E5
Padfield Rd SE5	39 B1
Pagden St SW8	31 B4
Pageantmaster Ct EC4	7 B2
Page St SW1	24 D5
Pages Wk SE1	32 D1
Paget Ri SE18	35 C3
Paget Rd, Ilf.	14 D1
Paget Ter SE18	35 C2
Pagnell St SE14	33 C3
Pagoda Gdns SE3	33 B5
Pakenham St WC1	17 F2
Palace Av W8	23 C2
Palace Ct W3	9 C2
Palace St W2	23 C1
Palace Gdns Ms W8	23 B2
Palace Gdns Ter W8	23 B2
Palace Gate W8	23 D3
Palace Grn W8	23 C3
Palace St SW1	24 C4
Palatine Rd N16	11 D1
Palermo Rd NW10	15 C1
Palfrey Pl SW8	31 F3
Palgrave Gdns NW1	16 F3
Palgrave Rd W12	22 B4
Pallet Way SE18	35 A4
Palliser Rd W14	29 C1
Pall Mall SW1	6 B6
Pall Mall E SW1	6 D5
Palmer Pl N7	10 G2
Palmer Rd E13	20 E3
Palmers Rd E2	19 B1
Palmerston Cres SE18	35 E2
Palmerston Rd E7	13 E2
Palmerston Rd NW6	9 B4
Palmer St SW1	24 D4
Pancras La EC4	7 E2
Pancras Rd NW1	17 D1
Pandora Rd NW6	9 B3
Pangbourne Av W10	15 E4
Pangbourne Ho N7	10 E2
Panmure Cl N5	11 A1
Pansy Gdns W12	22 C1
Panton St SW1	6 C4
Panyer All EC4	7 C2
Papillons Wk SE3	34 D5
Papworth Way SW2	38 G5
Parade, The SW11	30 G3
Paradise Pas N7	10 G2
Paradise Rd SW4	31 E5
Paradise Rd SE16	26 G3
Paradise Wk SW3	30 G2
Paragon, The SE3	34 C5
Paragon Cl E16	20 D5
Paragon Pl SE3	34 C5
Paragon Rd E9	12 A3
Pardoner St SE23	40 F4
Pardoner St SE1	25 C4
Parfett St E1	18 F4
Parfrey St W6	29 E2
Paris Gdn SE1	7 B5

Parish Gate Dr, Sid.	42 G4
Park Av E6	14 C5
Park Av, Bark.	14 E3
Park Av NW2	8 D3
Park Av N NW10	8 D2
Park Cl E9	12 A5
Park Cl SW1	23 G3
Park Cl W14	23 A4
Park Cres W1	17 B3
Park Dr SE7	35 A2
Park Dr NW11	8 C1
Park Dr SW14	36 A3
Parker Cl E16	28 A1
Parker Ms WC2	6 F1
Parke Rd SW13	29 C4
Parker Rd E16	28 A2
Parker St WC2	6 F1
Parkfield Av SW14	36 A2
Parkfield Rd NW10	8 D3
Parkfield Rd SE14	33 D4
Parkfields SW15	36 E2
Parkgate SE3	41 C1
Parkgate Rd SW11	30 F3
Park Gro E15	13 D5
Park Hall Rd W3	9 G2
Parkhill Rd NW3	9 G2
Parkhill Wk NW3	9 G2
Parkholme Rd E8	11 G3
Parkhouse St SE5	32 C3
Parkhurst Rd E12	14 C1
Parkhurst Rd N7	10 E1
Park La W1	24 A1
Parkmead SW15	36 D4
Park Par NW10	15 B1
Park Pl E14	26 E2
Park Pl SW1	6 A6
Park Pl Vil W2	16 D4
Park Rd E6	13 F5
Park Rd NW1	16 F2
Park Rd NW8	16 F2
Park Rd NW10	8 A5
Park Rd Row SE10	34 A2
Parkside SE3	34 C4
Parkside Rd SW11	31 A4
Parkside SE10	34 B1
Park Sq E NW1	17 B3
Park Sq Ms NW1	17 B3
Park Sq W NW1	17 B3
Parkstead Rd SW15	36 C3
Park St SE1	7 D5
Parkthorne Rd SW12	38 D5
Park Vw East E2	19 B1
Park Vw Est N5	11 B1
Park Vw Ms SW9	31 F5
Park Vw Rd NW10	8 B1
Park Village E NW1	17 B1
Park Village W NW1	17 B1
Parkville Rd SW6	30 A3
Park Vista SE10	34 A2
Park Wk SW10	30 D2
Parkway NW1	10 B5
Parliament Hill NW3	9 F1
Parliament Sq SW1	24 E3
Parliament St SW1	24 E3
Parliament Vw Apartments SE1	24 F5
Parma Cres SW11	37 G2
Parmiter St E2	18 G1
Parnell Cl W12	22 D4
Parnell Rd E3	12 D5
Parr Rd E6	13 G5
Parr St N1	18 C1
Parry Av E6	21 B5
Parry St SE18	28 D5
Parry Rd W10	15 G2
Parry St SW8	31 E2
Parsifal Rd NW6	9 B2

Parsonage St E14	26 G5
Parsons Grn SW6	30 B4
Parsons Grn La SW6	30 B4
Parson's Ho W2	16 E3
Parthenia Rd SW6	30 B4
Parvin St SW8	31 D4
Pascal St SW8	31 D3
Pascoe Rd SE13	41 A3
Passey Pl SE9	42 B4
Passmore St SW1	24 A5
Paston Cres SE12	41 E5
Pastor St SE11	25 A5
Patcham Ter SW8	31 B4
Patemoster Row EC4	7 D2
Patemoster Sq EC4	7 C1
Pater St W8	23 B4
Patience Rd SW11	30 F5
Patio Cl SW4	38 D4
Patmore Est SW8	31 C4
Patmore Rd SW8	31 C4
Patmos Rd SW9	32 A3
Paton Cl E3	19 E2
Patrick Rd E13	20 F2
Patriot Sq E2	19 A1
Patrol Pl SE6	40 F4
Patshull Rd NW5	10 C2
Patten Rd SW18	37 F5
Patterdale Rd SE15	33 A3
Pattina Wk SE16	26 D2
Pattison Wk SE18	35 E1
Paul Cl E15	13 B5
Paulet Rd SE5	32 A5
Paul Julius Cl E14	27 A1
Paul St E15	13 A5
Paul St EC2	18 C3
Paul's Wk EC4	7 C3
Paultons Sq SW3	30 E2
Paultons St SW3	30 E2
Paveley Dr SW11	30 F3
Paveley St NW8	16 F3
Pavement, The SW4	38 C2
Pavilion Rd SW1	23 G3
Paxton Rd W4	29 A2
Paxton Ter SW1	31 B2
Payne Cl, Bark.	14 G5
Payne Rd E3	19 F1
Payne St SE8	33 D2
Paynes Wk W6	29 G2
Peabody Est SE1	7 A6
Peabody Est SE24	39 B5
Peabody Est SW10	15 E4
Peabody Hill Est SE21	39 A5
Peabody Sq SE1	25 A3
Peach Rd W10	15 F2
Peachum Rd SE3	34 C2
Peacock Wk E16	20 E5
Peardon St SW8	31 B4
Pearl Cl E6	21 C5
Pearman St SE1	24 G3
Pearscroft Ct SW6	30 C4
Pearscroft Rd SW6	30 C4
Pearson St E2	18 D1
Pear Tree Cl E2	11 E1
Pear Tree Ct EC1	17 G3
Pear Tree St EC1	18 A3
Peartree Way SE10	27 D5
Peckford Pl SW9	31 G5
Peckham Gro SE15	32 D3
Peckham High St SE15	32 F4
Peckham Hill St SE15	32 F3
Peckham Pk Rd SE15	32 F3
Peckham Rd SE5	32 D4
Peckham Rd SE15	32 D4
Peckham Rye SE15	39 F1
Peckham Rye SE22	39 F2
Peckwater St NW5	10 C2
Pedlars Wk N7	10 E3

Pedley St E1	18 E3
Peel Gro E2	19 A1
Peel Prec NW6	16 B1
Peel Rd NW6	16 A2
Peel St W8	23 B2
Peerless St EC1	18 C2
Pegwell St SE18	35 G3
Pekin St E14	19 E5
Pelham Cl SE5	32 D5
Pelham Cres SW7	23 F5
Pelham Pl SW7	23 F5
Pelham St SW7	23 F5
Pelican Est SE15	32 E4
Pellant Rd SW6	29 G3
Pellatt Rd SE22	39 E3
Pellerin Rd N16	11 D2
Pelling St E14	19 E5
Pelly Rd E13	20 D1
Pelter St E2	18 E2
Pelton Rd SE10	34 B1
Pember Rd NW10	15 F2
Pembroke Row EC4	7 A1
Pembridge Cres W11	23 B1
Pembridge Gdns W2	23 B1
Pembridge Ms W11	23 B1
Pembridge Pl SW15	37 B3
Pembridge Pl W2	23 B1
Pembridge Rd W11	23 B1
Pembridge Sq W2	23 B1
Pembridge Vil W2	23 B1
Pembridge Vil W11	23 B1
Pembroke Av N1	10 E5
Pembroke Cl SW1	24 A3
Pembroke Gdns W8	23 A5
Pembroke Gdns Cl W8	23 B4
Pembroke Pl W8	23 B4
Pembroke Rd E6	21 B4
Pembroke Rd W8	23 B5
Pembroke Rd N1	10 E4
Pembroke Studios W8	23 A4
Pembroke Vil W8	23 B5
Pembroke Wk W8	23 B5
Pembry Cl SW9	31 G4
Pembury Pl E5	11 G2
Pembury Rd E5	11 G2
Penang St E1	25 G2
Penarth St SE15	33 A2
Pencraig Way SE15	32 G2
Penderyn Way N7	10 D1
Pendrell Rd SE4	33 C5
Pendrell St SE18	35 F3
Penfold Pl NW1	16 F4
Penfold St NW1	16 F3
Penfold St NW8	16 E3
Penfold Gdns SE9	41 G1
Penford St SE5	32 A5
Penge Rd E13	13 F4
Penhall Rd SE7	27 G5
Peninsular Pk Rd SE7	27 D5
Pennack Rd SE15	32 E2
Pennant Ms W8	23 C5
Pennard Rd W12	22 E3
Pennethorne Rd SE15	32 G3
Pennington St E1	25 F1
Penn Rd N7	10 E2
Penn St N1	11 C5
Pennyfields E14	26 E1
Pennyroyal Av E6	21 C5
Penpoll Rd E8	11 G3
Penrith Cl SW15	36 G3
Penrose Gro SE17	32 B1
Penrose Ho SE17	32 B1
Penrose St SE17	32 B1

Penryn St NW1	17	D1
Pensbury Pl SW8	31	C5
Pensbury St SW8	31	C5
Penshurst Rd E9	12	B4
Pentland St SW18	27	D4
Pentlow St SW15	36	E1
Penton Pl SE17	32	A1
Penton Ri WC1	17	F2
Penton St N1	17	G1
Pentonville Rd N1	17	F1
Pentridge St SE15	32	E3
Penywern Rd SW5	30	B1
Penzance Pl W11	22	G2
Penzance St W11	22	G2
Peony Gdns W12	22	C1
Peploe Rd NW6	15	F1
Pepper Cl E6	21	B5
Pepys St EC3	**7**	**J3**
Perceval Av NW3	3	F5
Perch St E8	11	E1
Percival St EC1	18	A3
Percy Rd E16	20	B4
Percy Rd W12	22	C3
Percy St W1	17	D2
Peregrine Ho EC1	18	A2
Perham Rd W14	29	G1
Peridot St E6	21	A4
Periton Rd SE9	41	G2
Perkin's Rents SW1	24	D4
Perkins Sq SE1	**7**	**E5**
Perpins Rd SE9	42	G4
Perrers Rd W6	22	D5
Perrins La NW3	9	D1
Perrin's Wk NW3	9	D1
Perrott St SE18	28	E5
Perryman Ho, Bark.	14	E5
Perrymead St SW6	30	B4
Perrys Pl W1	**6**	**C1**
Perseverance Pl		
SW9	31	G3
Perth Rd E13	20	D1
Perth Rd, Bark.	21	F1
Peter Av NW10	8	D4
Peterborough Ms		
SW6	30	B5
Peterborough Rd		
SW6	30	B5
Peterborough Vil		
SW6	30	C4
Petergate SW11	37	D2
Peters Cl, Well.	35	G5
Petersham La SW7	23	D4
Petersham Ms SW7	23	D4
Petersham Pl SW7	23	D4
Peters Hill EC4	**7**	**D3**
Peter St W1	**6**	**B3**
Petherton Rd N5	11	B2
Petley Rd W6	29	E2
Peto Pl NW1	16	E3
Petrie Cl NW2	8	G3
Petticoat La E1	18	D4
Petticoat Sq E1	18	E5
Pettiward Cl SW15	36	E2
Pettman Cres SE28	28	F4
Pett St SE18	28	A5
Petty France SW1	24	C4
Petworth St SW11	30	F4
Petyward SW3	23	F5
Pevensey Rd E7	13	C1
Peyton Pl SE10	33	G3
Phelp St SE17	32	C2
Phene St SW3	30	F2
Philbeach Gdns		
SW5	30	B1
Philimore Cl SE18	35	G1
Philpot Path SE9	42	B4
Philippa Gdns SE9	41	G3
Philip St E13	20	D3
Philip Wk SE15	39	F1
Phillimore Gdns		
NW10	8	E5
Phillimore Gdns		
W8	23	B3
Phillimore Pl W8	23	B3
Phillimore Wk W8	23	B4
Phillipp St N1	11	D5
Philpot La EC3	**7**	**H3**
Philpot St E1	18	G5
Phineas Pett Rd SE9	42	A1
Phipp St EC2	18	D3
Phoebeth Rd SE4	40	E3
Phoenix Pl WC1	17	F3
Phoenix Rd NW1	17	D2
Phoenix St WC2	**6**	**D2**
Phoenix Wf SE10	27	C3
Piccadilly W1	24	B2
Piccadilly Arc SW1	**6**	**A5**
Piccadilly Circ W1	**6**	**C4**
Piccadilly Pl W1	**6**	**B4**
Pickering Av E6	21	C1
Pickering Pl SW1	**6**	**B6**
Pickets St SW12	38	B5
Pickfords Wf N1	18	B1
Pickwick Rd SE21	39	C5
Picton St SE5	32	C3
Piedmont Rd SE18	35	F1
Pier Head E1	25	G2
Pier Rd E16	28	B3
Pier St E14	26	G5
Pier Way SE28	28	E1
Pigott St E14	19	E5
Pilgrimage St SE1	25	C3
Pilgrims Ct SE3	34	D4
Pilgrim's La NW3	9	E1
Pilgrim St EC4	**7**	**B2**
Pilkington Rd SE15	32	G5
Pilot Cl SE8	33	D2
Pilton Pl SE17	32	B1
Pimlico Rd SW1	31	A1
Pinchin St E1	25	F1
Pincott Pl SE4	40	B2
Pindar St EC2	18	D4
Pine Av E15	13	A2
Pinefield Cl E14	26	E1
Pine Rd NW2	8	E1
Pine St EC1	17	G3
Pinnell Rd SE9	41	G2
Pinto Way SE3	41	E4
Pioneer St SE15	32	F4
Piper Cl N7	10	F3
Pirie St E16	27	E2
Pitchford St E15	13	A4
Pitfield Est N1	18	C2
Pitfield St N1	18	D2
Pitfold Cl SE12	41	D4
Pitfold Rd SE12	41	D4
Pitsea St E1	19	B5
Pittman Gdns, Ilf.	14	E2
Pitt's Head Ms W1	24	A2
Pitt St W8	23	B3
Pixley St E14	19	D5
Plaistow Gro E15	13	C5
Plaistow Pk Rd E13	20	E1
Plaistow Rd E13	13	C5
Plaistow Rd E15	13	C5
Plantation, The SE3	34	D5
Plantation Wf SW11	37	D1
Plashet Gro E6	13	F5
Plashet Rd E13	13	D5
Plassy Rd SE6	40	F5
Plato Rd SW2	38	E2
Platt, The SW15	36	F1
Platt's La NW3	9	B1
Platt St NW1	17	D1
Playfield Cres		
SE22	39	E3
Playhouse Yd EC4	**7**	**B2**
Plaza Shop Cen, The		
W1	**6**	**B1**
Pleasance, The		
SW15	36	D2
Pleasance Rd		
SW15	36	D3
Pleasant Pl N1	11	A4
Pleasant Row NW1	10	B5
Plender St NW1	10	C5
Pleshey Rd N7	10	D1
Plevna St E14	26	G4
Pleydell Av W6	22	B5
Pleydell Ct EC4	**7**	**A2**
Pleydell St EC4	**7**	**A2**
Plough Ct EC3	**7**	**G3**
Plough La SE22	39	E4
Plough Pl EC4	**7**	**A1**
Plough Rd SW11	37	E1
Plough Ter SW11	37	E2
Plough Way SE16	26	B5
Plough Yd EC2	18	D3
Plover Way SE16	26	C4
Plumbers Row E1	18	F4
Plum La SE18	35	D3
Plummer Rd SW4	38	D5
Plumstead Common		
Rd SE18	35	D2
Plumstead High St		
SE18	28	G5
Plumstead Rd		
SE18	28	D5
Plumtree Ct EC4	**7**	**A1**
Plymouth Rd E16	20	D4
Plymouth Wf E14	27	A5
Plympton Av NW6	9	A4
Plympton Rd NW6	9	A4
Plympton St NW8	16	B3
Pocock St SE1	25	A3
Podmore Rd SW18	37	D2
Poets Rd N5	11	C2
Pointers Cl E14	33	F1
Point Hill SE10	33	G3
Point Pleasant		
SW18	37	B2
Poland Ho E15	13	A5
Poland St W1	**6**	**B2**
Polebrook Rd SE3	41	F1
Polesworth Ho W2	16	B4
Pollard Cl E16	27	D1
Pollard Cl N7	10	F2
Pollard Row E2	18	F2
Pollard St E2	18	F2
Polsted Rd SE6	40	D5
Polthorne Est		
SE18	28	F5
Polthorne Gro		
SE18	28	E5
Polygon Rd NW1	17	D1
Polytechnic St		
SE18	28	C5
Pomeroy St SE14	33	A4
Pond Cl SE3	34	C5
Pond Mead SE21	39	C4
Pond Pl SW3	23	F5
Pond Rd E15	20	B1
Pond Rd SE3	34	C5
Pond St NW3	9	F2
Ponler St E1	18	G5
Ponsard Rd NW10	15	D2
Ponsford St E9	12	A3
Ponsonby Pl SW1	31	D1
Ponsonby Rd		
SW15	36	D5
Ponton Rd SW8	31	D2
Pont St SW1	23	G4
Pont St Ms SW1	23	G4
Poole Rd E9	12	B3
Poole St N1	11	C5
Poolmans St SE16	26	B3
Popes Rd SW9	38	G1
Pope St SE1	25	D3
Popham Rd N1	11	B5
Popham St N1	11	A5
Poplar Business Pk		
E14	26	G1
Poplar Gro W6	22	E3
Poplar High St E14	26	E1
Poplar Pl W2	23	C1
Poplar Rd SE24	39	B2
Poplars Av NW10	8	E3
Poplar Wk SE24	39	B2
Poppins Ct EC4	**7**	**B2**
Porchester Cl SE5	39	B2
Porchester Gdns		
W2	23	C1
Porchester Ms W2	16	C5
Porchester Pl W2	16	F5
Porchester Rd W2	16	C4
Porchester Sq W2	16	C5
Porchester Ter W2	23	D1
Porchester Ter N		
W2	16	C5
Porden Rd SW2	38	F2
Porlock St SE1	25	C3
Porlet Rd E1	19	B2
Porten Rd W14	22	G4
Porter Rd E6	21	B5
Porter St SE1	**7**	**E5**
Porteus Rd W2	16	D4
Portia Way E3	19	D3
Portinscale Rd		
SW15	36	G3
Portland Gro SW8	31	F4
Portland Ms W1	**6**	**B2**
Portland Pl W1	17	B4
Portland Rd W11	22	G1
Portland St SE17	32	C1
Portman Cl W1	16	G5
Portman Ms S W1	17	A5
Portman Pl E2	19	A2
Portman Sq W1	16	G5
Portman St W1	17	A5
Portnall Rd W9	16	A1
Portobello Rd W10	16	A5
Portobello Rd W11	16	A5
Portpool La EC1	17	G4
Portree St E14	20	A5
Portslade Rd SW8	31	C5
Portsmouth Rd		
SW15	36	D5
Portsmouth St		
WC2	**6**	**G2**
Portsoken St E1	25	E1
Portugal St WC2	**6**	**G2**
Portway E15	13	C5
Post Office App E7	13	E2
Post Office Ct EC3	**7**	**G2**
Post Office Way		
SW8	31	D3
Potier St SE1	25	C4
Potterne Cl SW19	36	F5
Potters Flds SE1	**7**	**J6**
Potters Rd SW6	30	D5
Pottery St SE16	25	G3
Pott St E2	18	G2
Poulett Rd E6	21	B1
Poultry EC2	**7**	**F2**
Pound La NW10	8	C3
Pound Pk Rd SE7	27	G5
Pound Pl SE9	42	C4
Pountney Rd SW11	38	A1
Powell's Wk W4	29	A2
Powerscroft Rd E5	12	A1
Powis Gdns NW11	16	A5
Powis Gdns W11	17	E3
Powis Ms W11	19	F2
Powis Sq W11	16	A5
Powis St SE18	28	C4
Powis Ter W11	16	A5
Pownall Rd E8	11	E5
Poynders Gdns		
SW4	38	C5
Poynders Rd		
SW4	38	C4
Poynter Ho W11	22	F2
Poyntz Rd SW11	30	G5
Poyser St E2	18	G1
Praed St W2	16	E5
Pragel St E13	20	E2
Prague Pl SW2	38	E3
Prairie St SW8	30	G5
Pratt St NW1	10	C5
Pratt Wk SE11	24	F5
Prebend Gdns W4	22	B4
Prebend Gdns W6	22	B4
Prebend St N1	11	B5
Prendergast Rd		
SE3	41	B1

Name	Ref
Prentiss Ct SE7	27 G5
Prescot St E1	25 E1
Prescott Pl SW4	38 D1
Prestage Way E14	26 G1
Prestbury Rd E7	13 F4
Preston Pl NW2	8 C3
Prestons Rd E14	26 G3
Pretoria Rd E16	20 C2
Pretoria Rd, Ilf.	14 D2
Price's Ct SW11	37 E1
Price's St SE1	7 C6
Prices Yd N1	10 F5
Prideaux Pl WC1	17 F2
Prideaux Rd SW9	38 D1
Priest Ct EC2	7 D1
Priests Br SW14	36 A1
Priests Br SW15	36 A1
Prima Rd SW9	31 G3
Primrose Gdns NW3	9 F3
Primrose Hill EC4	7 A2
Primrose Hill Ct NW3	9 G4
Primrose Hill Rd NW3	9 F4
Primrose Ms SE3	34 E3
Primrose Sq E9	12 A4
Primrose St EC2	18 D4
Primula St W12	15 C5
Prince Albert Rd NW1	16 F1
Prince Albert Rd NW8	16 F1
Prince Arthur Rd NW3	9 D2
Prince Charles Rd SE3	34 C4
Prince Consort Rd SW7	23 D4
Princedale Rd W11	22 G2
Prince Edwards Rd E9	12 D3
Prince George Rd N16	11 D1
Prince Henry Rd SE7	34 G3
Prince Imperial Rd SE18	35 B4
Prince John Rd SE9	42 A3
Princelet St E1	18 E4
Prince of Wales Dr SW8	31 B3
Prince of Wales Dr SW11	30 G4
Prince of Wales Gate SW7	23 F3
Prince of Wales Rd NW5	10 A3
Prince of Wales Rd SE3	34 C4
Prince of Wales Ter W4	29 A1
Prince Regent La E13	20 E2
Prince Regent La E16	20 E2
Prince Rupert Rd SE9	42 B2
Prince's Arc SW1	6 B5
Princes Ct E1	25 G1
Princes Ct SE16	26 D4
Princes Gdns SW7	23 E4
Princes Gate SW7	23 F3
Princes Gate Ms SW7	23 E4
Princes Pl SW1	6 B5
Princes Pl W11	22 G2
Princes Ri SE13	33 G5
Princes Riverside Rd SE16	26 B2
Princess Alice Way SE28	28 F3
Princess May Rd N16	11 D1
Princes Sq W2	23 C1
Princess Rd NW1	10 A5
Princess Rd NW6	16 B1
Princess St SE1	25 A4
Princes St EC2	7 F2
Princes St W1	17 B5
Princes Ter E13	13 E5
Prince St SE8	33 D2
Princes Way SW19	36 F5
Princethorpe Ho W2	16 C4
Princes St WC1	17 F4
Printers Inn Ct EC4	6 J1
Printers Ms E3	12 C5
Printer St EC4	7 A1
Priolo Rd SE7	34 F1
Prior Bolton St N1	11 A3
Prioress St SE1	25 C4
Prior St SE10	33 G3
Priory Av W4	22 A5
Priory Ct SW8	31 D4
Priory Gdns SW13	36 B1
Priory Gdns W4	22 A5
Priory Grn Est N1	17 F1
Priory Gro SW8	31 D4
Priory La SW15	36 A4
Priory Ms SW8	31 D4
Priory Pk Rd NW6	9 A5
Priory Rd E6	13 G5
Priory Rd NW6	9 C5
Priory Rd, Bark.	14 F4
Priory Ter NW6	9 C5
Priory Wk SW10	30 D1
Pritchard's Rd E2	11 F5
Priter Rd SE16	25 F4
Probert Rd SW2	38 G3
Procter St WC1	17 F4
Promenade, The W4	29 A4
Promenade App Rd W4	29 A4
Prospect Pl E1	26 A2
Prospect Quay SW18	37 B2
Prospect Vale SE18	28 A5
Prothero Rd SW6	29 G3
Prout Gro NW10	8 A1
Providence Ct W1	24 A1
Provost Est N1	18 C1
Provost Rd NW3	9 F3
Provost St N1	18 C2
Prudent Pas EC2	7 E1
Prusom St E1	25 G2
Pudding La EC3	7 G4
Pudding Mill La E15	12 F5
Puddle Dock EC4	7 C3
Pulborough Rd SW18	37 A5
Pulleyns Av E6	21 A2
Pullman Gdns SW15	36 E4
Pullman Pl SE9	42 A3
Pulross Rd SW9	38 F1
Pulteney Cl E3	12 D5
Pulteney Ter N1	10 F5
Pulton Pl SW6	30 B3
Pump Ct EC4	6 J2
Pumping Sta Rd W4	29 A3
Pump La SE14	33 A3
Pundersons Gdns E2	18 G2
Purbrook St SE1	25 D4
Purcell Cres SW6	29 G3
Purcell St N1	18 D1
Purchese St NW1	17 D1
Purdy St E3	19 F3
Purelake Ms SE13	41 A1
Purneys Rd SE9	41 G2
Purser's Cross Rd SW6	30 A4
Purves Rd NW10	15 E1
Puteaux Ho E2	19 B1
Putney Br SW6	36 G1
Putney Br SW15	36 G1
Putney Br App SW6	36 G1
Putney Br Rd SW15	36 G2
Putney Br Rd SW18	36 G2
Putney Common SW15	36 E1
Putney Ex Shop Cen SW15	36 F2
Putney Heath SW15	36 F4
Putney Heath La SW15	36 E4
Putney High St SW15	36 F2
Putney Hill SW15	36 F4
Putney Pk Av SW15	36 C2
Putney Pk La SW15	36 D2
Putney Wf Twr SW15	36 G1
Pyrland Rd N5	11 C2
Pytchley Rd SE22	39 D1

Q

Name	Ref
Quadrant Arc W1	6 B4
Quadrant Gro NW5	9 G2
Quaggy Wk SE3	41 D2
Quaker's Pl E7	13 G2
Quaker St E1	18 E3
Quality Ct WC2	6 J1
Quarrendon St SW6	30 B5
Quarry Rd SW18	37 D4
Quarterdeck, The E14	26 D4
Quarter Mile La E10	12 F1
Quebec Way SE16	26 B3
Queen Anne Rd E9	12 B3
Queen Anne's Gdns W4	22 A4
Queen Anne's Gate SW1	24 D3
Queen Anne's Gro W4	22 A4
Queen Anne St W1	17 B5
Queen Caroline Est W6	29 E1
Queen Caroline St W6	22 E5
Queen Elizabeth St SE1	25 E3
Queen Elizabeth Wk SW13	29 D4
Queenhithe EC4	7 E3
Queen Margaret's Gro N1	11 D2
Queen of Denmark Ct SE16	26 D3
Queensberry Pl E12	13 G2
Queensberry Pl SW7	23 E5
Queensborough Ter W2	23 C1
Queensbridge Rd E2	11 E4
Queensbridge Rd E8	11 E4
Queensbury St N1	11 B4
Queens Club Gdns W14	29 G2
Queen's Cres NW5	10 A3
Queenscroft Rd SE9	41 G3
Queensdale Cres W11	22 F2
Queensdale Pl W11	22 G2
Queensdale Rd W11	22 F2
Queensdale Wk W11	22 G2
Queensdown Rd E5	11 G1
Queens Gdns SW7	23 D1
Queen's Gate SW7	23 E5
Queen's Gate Gdns SW7	23 D4
Queen's Gate Ms SW7	23 D3
Queensgate Pl NW6	9 B4
Queen's Gate Pl SW7	23 D4
Queen's Gate Pl Ms SW7	23 D4
Queen's Gate Ter SW7	23 D4
Queen's Gro NW8	9 E5
Queen's Gro Ms NW8	9 E5
Queen's Head Pas EC4	7 D1
Queen's Head St N1	11 A5
Queens Head Yd SE1	7 F6
Queensland Rd N7	10 G1
Queensmead NW8	9 E5
Queens Ms W2	23 C1
Queensmill Rd SW6	29 F3
Queens Pk Ct W10	15 F2
Queen Sq WC1	17 E3
Queens Ride SW13	36 C1
Queens Ride SW15	36 C1
Queens Rd E13	13 E5
Queens Rd SE14	32 G4
Queens Rd SE15	32 G4
Queens Rd, Bark.	14 E4
Queens Rd W E13	20 D1
Queen's Row SE17	32 C2
Queens Ter E13	13 E5
Queen's Ter NW8	16 E1
Queenstown Rd SW8	31 B2
Queen St EC4	7 E3
Queen St W1	24 B2
Queen St Pl EC4	7 E4
Queensville Rd SW12	38 D5
Queen's Wk SE1	6 G6
Queen's Wk SW1	6 A6
Queensway W2	16 C5
Queen Victoria St EC4	7 C3
Quemerford Rd N7	10 F2
Quentin Pl SE13	41 B1
Quentin Rd SE13	41 B1
Querrin St SW6	30 D5
Quex Rd NW6	9 B5
Quick Rd W4	29 A1
Quick St N1	18 A1
Quill La SW15	36 F2
Quilter St E2	18 F2
Quince Rd SE13	33 F5
Quixley St E14	27 A1
Quorn Rd SE22	39 D2

R

Name	Ref
Rabbits Rd E12	14 A1
Racton Rd SW6	30 B2
Radbourne Rd SW12	38 C5
Radcliffe Av NW10	15 C1
Radcliffe Sq SW15	36 F4
Radcot St SE11	31 G1
Raddington Rd W10	15 G4
Radfield Way, Sid.	42 F5
Radford Rd SE13	40 G4
Radipole Rd SW6	30 A4
Radland Rd E16	20 C5
Radlett Cl E7	13 C3
Radlett Pl NW8	9 F5
Radley Ms W8	23 B4
Radnor Pl W2	16 F5
Radnor Rd NW6	8 G5
Radnor Rd SE15	32 F3
Radnor St EC1	18 B2
Radnor Ter W14	23 A5
Radnor Wk SW3	30 F1
Radstock St SW11	30 F3
Raeburn Rd, Sid.	42 G4
Raeburn St SW2	38 E2
Raglan Ct SE12	41 D3

Raglan Rd SE18 35 E1
Raglan St NW5 10 B3
Railey Ms NW5 10 C2
Railton Rd SE24 38 G2
Railway App SE1 7 G5
Railway Av SE16 26 A3
Railway Side SW13 36 A1
Railway St N1 33 F1
Rainbow Av E14 33 F1
Rainbow Quay
SE16 26 C4
Rainton St SE5 32 D3
Raine St E1 25 G2
Rainham Cl SE9 42 F4
Rainham Cl SW11 37 G4
Rainham Rd NW10 15 E2
Rainhill Way E3 19 E2
Rainsborough Av
SE8 26 C5
Rainton Rd SE7 34 D1
Rainville Rd W6 29 E2
Raleana Rd E14 26 D4
Raleigh St N1 11 A5
Ramac Way SE7 27 E5
Ramilles Cl SW2 38 E4
Ramillies Pl W1 6 A2
Ramillies St W1 6 A2
Rampayne St SW1 31 D1
Ramsay Rd E7 13 B1
Ramsden Rd SW12 38 F1
Ramsey St E2 18 F3
Ramsey Wk N1 11 C3
Ram St SW18 37 C3
Rancliffe Gdns SE9 42 A2
Rancliffe Rd E6 21 A1
Randall Cl SW11 30 F4
Randall Pl SE10 33 G3
Randall Rd SE11 24 F5
Randell's Rd N1 10 E5
Randolph App E16 20 G5
Randolph Av W9 16 D3
Randolph Cres W9 16 D3
Randolph Gdns
NW6 16 C1
Randolph Ms W9 16 D3
Randolph Rd W9 16 D3
Randolph St NW1 10 C4
Ranelagh Av SW6 37 A1
Ranelagh Av SW13 29 C5
Ranelagh Gdns
SW6 36 G2
Ranelagh Gdns W6 22 B4
Ranelagh Gro SW1 31 A1
Ranelagh Rd E6 14 C5
Ranelagh Rd E11 13 B1
Ranelagh Rd E15 13 B5
Ranelagh Rd NW10 15 B3
Rangers Sq SE10 34 A4
Rannoch Rd W6 29 E2
Ranulf Rd NW2 9 A1
Ranwell St E3 12 D5
Raphael St SW7 23 G3
Ratcliffe Cl SE12 41 D5
Ratcliffe Cross St E1 19 B5
Ratcliffe La E14 19 B5
Ratcliffe Orchard E1 26 B1
Ratcliff Rd E7 13 F2
Rathbone Pl W1 6 C1
Rathbone St E16 20 D5
Rathbone St W1 17 C4
Rathmell Dr SW4 38 D4
Rathmore Rd SE7 34 E1
Rattray Rd SW2 38 G2
Raul Rd SE15 32 F4
Raveley St NW5 10 C1
Ravenhill Rd E13 20 F1
Ravenna Rd SW15 36 F3
Raven Row E1 18 F4
Ravensbourne Pk
SE6 40 E5
Ravensbourne Pk Cres
SE6 40 D5
Ravensbourne Pl
SE13 33 F5
Ravensbourne Rd
SE6 40 D5

Ravenscourt Av W6 22 C5
Ravenscourt Gdns
W6 22 C5
Ravenscourt Pk W6 22 C4
Ravenscourt Pl W6 22 D5
Ravenscourt Rd W6 22 D5
Ravenscourt Sq W6 22 C4
Ravenscroft Cl E16 20 D4
Ravenscroft Rd E16 20 D4
Ravenscroft St E1 31 G1
Ravenshaw St NW6 9 A2
Ravenslea Rd SW12 37 G5
Ravensmede Way
W4 22 B5
Ravenstone SE17 32 D1
Ravens Way SE12 41 G3
Ravenswood Rd
SW12 38 B5
Ravensworth Rd
NW10 15 D2
Ravine Gro SE18 35 G2
Rawlings St SW3 23 G5
Rawstone Wk E13 20 D1
Rawstorne St EC1 18 A2
Rayford Av SE12 41 C5
Rayleas Cl SE18 35 D4
Rayleigh Rd E16 27 E2
Raymere Gdns
SE18 35 F3
Raymond Rd E13 13 F4
Raymouth Rd SE16 25 G5
Rayners Rd SW15 36 G3
Raynham Rd W6 22 D5
Ray St EC1 17 G3
Reading La E8 11 G3
Reardon Path E1 25 G2
Reardon St E1 25 G2
Reaston St SE14 33 A3
Reckitt Rd W4 29 A1
Record St SE15 33 A2
Rector St N1 11 B5
Rectory Fld Cres
SE7 34 E3
Rectory Gro SW4 38 C1
Rectory Pl SE18 28 C5
Rectory Rd E12 14 B2
Rectory Rd SW13 29 C5
Rectory Sq E1 19 B4
Reculver Rd SE16 33 B1
Redan Pl W2 16 C5
Redan St W14 22 F4
Red Barracks Rd
SE18 28 B5
Redbridge Gdns
SE5 32 D3
Redburn St SW3 30 G2
Redcar St SE5 32 B3
Redcastle Cl E1 26 A1
Redchurch St E2 18 E3
Redcliffe Gdns
SW5 30 C1
Redcliffe Gdns
SW10 30 C1
Redcliffe Ms SW10 30 C1
Redcliffe Pl SW10 30 D2
Redcliffe Rd SW10 30 D1
Redcliffe Sq SW10 30 C1
Redcliffe St SW10 30 C2
Redclyffe Rd E6 13 F5
Redcross Way SE1 25 B3
Reddins Rd SE15 32 F2
Redesdale St SW3 30 G2
Redfern Rd NW10 8 A4
Redfern Rd SE6 40 G5
Redfield La SW5 23 B5
Redgrave Rd SW15 36 F1
Redhill St NW1 17 B1
Redington Gdns
NW3 9 C1
Redington Rd NW3 9 C1
Redlands Way SW2 38 F5
Red Lion Ct EC4 7 A1
Red Lion La SE18 35 C3
Red Lion Row SE17 32 B2
Red Lion Sq WC1 17 F1

Red Lion St WC1 17 F4
Redman's Rd E1 19 A4
Redmore Rd W6 22 D5
Red Path E9 12 D3
Red Post Hill SE21 39 C3
Red Post Hill SE24 39 C2
Redriffe Rd E13 13 C5
Redriff Est SE16 26 B5
Redriff Rd SE16 26 B5
Redruth Rd E9 12 B5
Redward Rd E5 12 B1
Redwing Path
SE28 28 F3
Redwood Cl E3 19 E1
Redwood Cl SE16 26 C2
Reece Ms SW7 23 E5
Reed Cl E16 20 D5
Reed Cl SE12 41 D3
Reedham St SE15 32 F5
Reedworth St SE11 24 G5
Reesland Cl E12 14 C3
Rees Ms N1 11 B5
Rees Rd E3 19 F3
Reeves Rd SE18 35 D2
Reform St SW11 30 G5
Regan Way N1 18 D1
Regency St SW1 24 D5
Regent Pl W1 6 B3
Regent Pl SE24 39 A4
Regents Br Gdns
SW8 31 E3
Regent's Pk NW1 17 A1
Regents Pk Rd NW1 9 G5
Regent's Pl SE3 34 D5
Regent Sq E3 19 F2
Regent Sq WC1 17 F2
Regents Row E8 11 F5
Regent St W1 6 C4
Regent St W1 17 B5
Reginald Rd E7 13 E2
Reginald Rd SE8 33 E3
Reginald Sq SE8 33 E3
Regis Pl SW2 38 F2
Regis Rd NW5 10 B2
Reidhaven Rd
SE18 28 G5
Reinickendorf Av
SE9 42 E3
Relay Rd W12 22 E1
Relf Rd SE15 39 F1
Rembrandt Cl E14 27 A4
Rembrandt Rd
SE13 41 B2
Remington Rd E6 21 A5
Remington St N1 18 A1
Remnant St WC2 6 G1
Rendlesham Rd E5 11 F1
Renforth St SE16 26 A3
Renfrew Cl E6 28 C1
Renfrew Rd SE11 25 A5
Rennell St SE13 40 G1
Rennets Cl SE9 42 G3
Rennets Wd Rd
SE9 42 F3
Rennie St SE16 25 G5
Rennie St SE1 7 B5
Reporton Rd SW6 29 G4
Repository Rd
SE18 35 B2
Reservoir Rd SE4 33 C5
Resolution Wk
SE18 28 B4
Restell Cl SE3 34 B2
Restons Cres SE9 42 E3
Retreat Pl E9 12 A3
Revelon Rd SE4 40 C2
Reverdy Rd SE1 25 F5
Rewell St SW6 30 D3
Rexford Av E12 14 C2
Reynolds Pl SE3 34 E3
Reynolds Rd SE15 39 G3
Rheidol Ter N1 18 A1
Rhodesia Rd SW9 31 E5
Rhodeswell Rd E14 19 D5

Rhondda Gro E3 19 C2
Rhyl St NW5 10 A3
Ricardo St E14 19 F5
Richard Cl SE18 28 A5
Richard Ho Dr E16 20 G5
Richardson Rd E15 20 B1
Richborne Ter SW8 31 F3
Richborough Rd
NW2 8 F1
Richford Rd E15 13 C5
Richford St W6 22 E3
Richmond Av N1 10 F5
Richmond Av NW10 8 E3
Richmond Bldgs W1 6 C2
Richmond Cres N1 10 F5
Richmond Gro N1 11 A4
Richmond Ms W1 6 C2
Richmond Pl SE18 28 E5
Richmond Rd E7 13 E2
Richmond Rd E8 11 E4
Richmond Rd E13 20 D1
Richmond Ter SW1 24 E3
Richmond Way W12 22 F3
Richmond Way W14 22 F4
Richmount Gdns
SE3 41 D1
Rich St E14 26 D1
Rickett St SW6 30 B2
Rick Roberts Way
E15 12 G5
Rickyard Path SE9 42 A2
Rideout St SE18 28 B5
Rider Cl, Sid. 42 G4
Ridgdale St E3 19 F1
Ridgebrook Rd
SE3 41 F1
Ridge Cl SE28 28 F3
Ridgeway Rd SW9 39 A1
Ridgeway W, Sid. 42 G3
Ridgmount Rd
SW18 37 C3
Ridgwell Rd E16 20 G4
Riding Ho St W1 17 B4
Ridley Rd E7 13 F1
Ridley Rd E8 11 E2
Ridley Rd NW10 15 C1
Riefield Rd SE9 42 E2
Riffel Rd NW2 8 E2
Rifle Pl SE11 19 F4
Rifle St E14 19 F4
Rigault Rd SW6 29 G5
Rigden St E14 19 F5
Rigeley Rd NW10 15 C2
Rigge Pl SW4 38 D2
Riley Rd SE1 25 E4
Riley St SW10 30 E2
Rinaldo Rd SW12 38 B5
Ring, The W2 23 E1
Ringcroft St N7 10 G2
Ringford Rd SW18 37 A3
Ringlet Cl E16 20 E4
Ringmer Av SW6 29 G4
Ringmore Ri SE23 39 G5
Ring Rd W12 22 E2
Ringstead Rd SE6 40 F5
Ripley Rd E16 20 F5
Ripon Rd SE18 35 D2
Ripple Rd, Bark. 14 E4
Ripplevale Gro N1 10 F4
Risdon St SE16 26 A3
Riseldine Rd SE23 40 A4
Risinghill St N1 17 F1
Rita Rd SW8 31 F3
Ritchie St N1 17 G1
Ritson Rd E8 11 F3
Ritter St SE18 35 C2
Rivaz Pl E9 12 A3
Rivercourt Rd W6 22 D5
Rivermead Ct SW6 37 A1
River Pl N1 11 B4
River Rd, Bark. 21 G1
Riverside SE7 27 E4
Riverside Cl SW8 31 D3
Riverside Gdns W6 29 D1
Riverside Rd E15 19 G1
Riverside Twr SW6 30 E3

River St EC1 17 G2
Riverton Cl W9 16 A2
Riverview Gdns SW13 29 D2
Rivington Ct NW10 8 C5
Rivington St EC2 18 D2
Rixsen Rd E12 12 E4
Roach Rd E3 12 C4
Roan St SE10 33 G2
Robert Adam St W1 17 A5
Roberta St E2 18 F2
Robert Dashwood Way SE17 25 B5
Robert Lowe Cl SE14 33 B3
Robert Owen Ho SW6 29 F4
Roberts Cl SE16 26 B3
Robertson Rd E15 12 G5
Robertson St SW8 38 B1
Robert St E16 28 D2
Robert St NW1 17 B2
Robert St SE18 28 G5
Robert St WC2 6 F4
Robin Cl SE16 25 F5
Robin Cres E6 20 G4
Robin Hood La E14 26 G1
Robinson Rd E2 19 A1
Robsart St SW9 31 F5
Robson Av NW10 8 C5
Rochelle Cl SW11 37 E2
Rochester Av E13 13 F5
Rochester Ms NW1 10 C4
Rochester Pl NW1 10 C3
Rochester Rd NW1 10 C3
Rochester Row SW1 24 C5
Rochester Sq NW1 10 C4
Rochester St SW1 24 D4
Rochester Ter NW1 10 C3
Rochester Wk SE1 7 F5
Rochester Way SE3 34 E4
Rochester Way SE9 42 B1
Rochester Way Relief Rd SE3 34 E4
Rochester Way Relief Rd SE9 42 A2
Rochford St NW5 9 F2
Rockells Pl SE22 39 G4
Rockhall Rd NW2 8 F1
Rockingham Cl SW15 36 B2
Rockingham Est SE1 25 B4
Rockingham St SE1 25 B4
Rockland Rd SW15 36 B2
Rockley Rd W14 22 F3
Rocks La SW13 29 C4
Rockwood Pl W12 22 F2
Rocombe Cres SE23 40 A5
Rocque La SE3 41 C1
Rodenhurst Rd SW4 38 C4
Roderick Rd NW3 9 G1
Roding Rd E5 12 B1
Roding Rd E6 21 D4
Roding Trd Est, Bark. 14 D4
Rodmarton St W1 16 G4
Rodmill La SW2 38 E5
Rodney Pl SE17 25 B5
Rodney Rd SE17 25 B5
Rodney St N1 17 F1
Rodway Rd SW15 36 C5
Rodwell Rd SE22 39 E4
Roebourne Way E16 28 C3
Roedean Cres SW15 36 A4
Roehampton Cl SW15 36 C2
Roehampton Gate SW15 36 A4

Roehampton High St SW15 36 D5
Roehampton La SW15 36 C2
Roffey St E14 26 G3
Roger Dowley Ct E2 19 A1
Rogers Rd E16 19 G5
Roger St WC1 17 F3
Rokeby Rd SE4 33 D5
Rokeby St E15 12 G5
Rokesby Cl, Well. 35 F5
Roland Gdns SW7 30 D1
Roland Way SE17 32 C1
Rollins St SE15 33 A2
Rolls Bldgs EC4 6 J1
Rollscourt Av SE24 39 B3
Rolls Pas EC4 6 J1
Rolt St SE8 33 C2
Romanfield Rd SW2 38 F5
Roman Rd E2 19 A2
Roman Rd E3 19 C1
Roman Rd E6 21 A3
Roman Rd W4 22 B5
Roman Rd, Ilf. 14 D3
Roman Way N7 10 F3
Romborough Gdns SE13 40 G3
Romborough Way SE13 40 G3
Romero Sq SE3 41 F2
Romford Rd E7 13 E2
Romford Rd E12 14 A1
Romford Rd E15 13 B4
Romford St E1 18 F4
Romilly St W1 6 C3
Romney Rd SE10 33 G2
Romney St SW1 24 E4
Ronald Av E15 20 B2
Ronalds Rd N5 10 G2
Ronaldstone Rd, Sid. 42 G5
Rona Rd NW3 10 A1
Rondu Rd NW2 8 G2
Ron Leighton Way E6 14 A5
Ronver Rd SE12 41 C5
Rood La EC3 7 H3
Rookery Rd SW4 38 C2
Rooke Way SE10 34 C1
Rootes Dr W10 15 F3
Ropemaker Rd SE16 26 C4
Ropemaker St EC2 18 C4
Roper St SE9 42 B4
Ropery St E3 19 D3
Rope St SE16 26 C5
Rope Yd Rails SE18 28 D4
Ropley St E2 18 F1
Rosaline Rd SW6 29 G3
Rosary Gdns SW7 23 D5
Rosaville Rd SW6 30 A3
Rose All SE1 7 E5
Rose & Crown Ct EC2 7 D1
Rose & Crown Yd SW1 6 B5
Rosebank Gdns E3 19 E1
Roseberry Pl E8 11 E3
Roseberry St SE16 25 G5
Rosebery Av E12 14 A3
Rosebery Av EC1 17 G3
Rosebery Av, Sid. 42 G4
Rosebery Rd SW2 38 E4
Rosebury Rd SW6 30 C5
Rosedale Ct N5 11 A1
Rosedale Rd E7 13 F2
Rosedene NW6 8 F5
Rosedew Rd W6 29 F2
Rosefield Gdns E14 26 E1
Roseford Ct W12 22 F3
Rosehill Rd SW18 37 D4
Roseleigh Av N5 11 A1

Rosemary Dr E14 20 A5
Rosemary Rd SE15 32 E3
Rosemary Rd NW3 8 B3
Rosemoor St SW3 23 G5
Rosenau Cres SW11 30 F4
Rosenau Rd SW11 30 F4
Rosendale Rd SE21 39 B5
Rosendale Rd SE24 39 B5
Roseneath Rd SW11 38 A4
Rosenthal Rd SE6 40 F4
Rosenthorpe Rd SE15 40 B3
Roserton St E14 26 G3
Rose Sq SW3 30 E1
Rose St EC4 7 D1
Rose St WC2 6 E3
Rosethorn Cl SW12 38 C5
Rosetta Cl SW8 31 E3
Rose Way SE12 41 D3
Roseway SE21 39 C4
Rosher Cl E15 13 A4
Rosina St E9 12 B2
Roskell Rd SW15 36 F1
Rosmead Rd W11 22 G1
Rosoman St EC1 17 G2
Ross Ct SW15 36 F5
Rossdale Rd SW15 36 E2
Rosse Ms SE3 34 E4
Rossendale Way NW1 10 C4
Rossetti Rd SE16 32 G1
Rosslyn Av SW13 36 A1
Rosslyn Hill NW3 9 E1
Rosslyn Rd, Bark. 14 F4
Rossmore Rd NW1 16 F3
Rostella Rd SW17 42 A1
Rostrevor Ms SW6 30 A4
Rostrevor Rd SW6 30 A4
Rothbury Rd E9 12 D4
Rotherfield St N1 11 B4
Rotherham Wk SE1 7 B6
Rotherhithe New Rd SE16 32 F1
Rotherhithe Old Rd SE16 26 B5
Rotherhithe St SE16 26 A3
Rotherhithe Tunnel E14 26 A2
Rotherhithe Tunnel App E14 26 C1
Rotherhithe Tunnel App SE16 26 A3
Rotherwood Rd SW15 36 F1
Rothery Ter SW9 32 A3
Rothsay Rd E7 13 F3
Rothsay St SE1 25 D4
Rothwell St NW1 9 G5
Rotten Row SW1 23 G3
Rotten Row SW7 23 F3
Rotterdam Dr E14 26 G4
Rouel Rd SE16 25 F4
Roundwood Rd NW10 8 B3
Rounton Rd E3 19 E3
Roupell St SE1 7 A6
Rousden St NW1 10 C4
Routemaster Cl E13 20 E2
Routh Rd SW18 37 F5
Routh St E6 21 B4
Rowallan Rd SW6 29 G3
Rowan Cl, Ilf. 14 F2
Rowan Rd W6 22 F5
Rowberry Cl SW6 29 E3
Rowcross St SE1 32 E1
Rowditch La SW11 31 A5
Rowdon Av NW10 8 D4
Rowe La E9 12 A2
Rowena Cres SW11 30 F5
Rowhill Rd E5 11 G1
Rowington Cl W2 16 C4
Rowland Ct E16 20 C3
Rowland Hill St NW3 9 F2

Rowley Way NW8 9 C5
Rowse Cl E15 12 G4
Rowstock Gdns N7 10 D2
Rowton Rd SE18 35 E3
Roxby Pl SW6 30 B2
Roxley Rd SE13 40 F4
Roxwell Rd W12 22 C3
Royal Albert Dock E16 28 B1
Royal Albert Way E16 27 G1
Royal Arc W1 6 A4
Royal Av SW3 30 G1
Royal Cl SE8 33 D2
Royal Coll St NW1 10 C4
Royal Cl SE16 26 D4
Royal Cres W11 22 F2
Royal Docks Rd E6 21 D5
Royal Ex EC3 7 G2
Royal Ex Av EC3 7 G2
Royal Ex Bldgs EC3 7 G2
Royal Herbert Pavilions SE18 35 B4
Royal Hill SE10 33 G3
Royal Hosp Rd SW3 30 G2
Royal Mint, The SW1 24 B4
Royal Mint Ct EC3 25 E1
Royal Mint St E1 25 E1
Royal Naval Pl SE14 33 D3
Royal Oak Pl SE22 39 G4
Royal Oak Rd E8 11 G3
Royal Opera Arc SW1 6 C5
Royal Orchard Cl SW18 36 G5
Royal Par SE3 34 B5
Royal Pl SE10 33 G3
Royal Rd E16 20 G5
Royal Rd SE17 32 A2
Royal St SE1 24 F4
Royalty Ms W1 6 C2
Royal Victoria Dock E16 27 E1
Royal Victor Pl E3 19 B1
Roydene Rd SE18 35 G2
Royston St E2 19 A1
Rozel Ct N1 11 D5
Rozel Rd SW4 31 C5
Ruby St SE15 32 G2
Ruckholt Rd E10 12 E1
Rucklidge Av NW10 15 B1
Ruddington Cl E5 12 C1
Ruddstreet Cl SE18 28 D5
Rudloe Rd SW12 38 C5
Rudolph Ct SE22 39 F5
Rudolph Rd E13 20 C1
Rudolph Rd NW6 16 B1
Rufford St N1 10 E5
Rugby Rd W4 22 A3
Rugby St WC1 17 F3
Rugg St E14 26 E1
Rumbold Rd SW6 30 C3
Rum Cl E1 26 A1
Rumsey Rd SW9 38 F1
Runcorn Pl W11 22 G1
Rupert Ct W1 6 C3
Rupert Gdns SW9 32 A5
Rupert Rd NW6 16 A1
Rupert Rd W4 22 A3
Rupert St W1 6 C3
Ruscoe Rd E16 20 C5
Rusham Rd SW12 37 G4
Rush Common Ms SW2 38 F5
Rushcroft Rd SW2 38 G2
Rushey Grn SE6 40 F5
Rushey Mead SE4 40 E3
Rushford Rd SE4 40 D4
Rush Gro St SE18 28 B5
Rush Hill Rd SW11 38 A1
Rushmore Rd E5 12 A1
Rusholme Rd SW15 36 F4
Rushton St N1 18 C1
Rushworth St SE1 25 A3

Ruskin Av E12 14 A3
Ruskin Pk Ho SE5 39 C1
Ruskin Wk SE24 39 B3
Russell Cl SE7 34 F3
Russell Cl W4 29 B2
Russell St SW1 6 B6
Russell Gdns W14 22 G4
Russell Gdns Ms
W14 22 G4
Russell Gro SW9 31 G3
Russell Rd E16 20 D5
Russell Rd W14 22 G4
Russell Sq WC1 17 D4
Russell St WC2 6 F3
Russia Ct EC2 7 E1
Russia Dock Rd
SE16 26 C2
Russia La E2 18 G1
Russia Row EC2 7 E2
Russia Wk SE16 26 C3
Ruston Rd SE18 28 A4
Ruston St E3 12 D5
Rust Sq SE5 32 C3
Rutherford St SW1 24 D5
Ruthin Rd SE3 34 C5
Rutland Gdns SW7 23 F3
Rutland Gate SW7 23 F3
Rutland Gro W6 29 D1
Rutland Pk NW2 8 E3
Rutland Rd E7 13 G4
Rutland Rd E9 12 A5
Rutland Rd, Ilf. 14 D1
Rutland St SW7 23 F4
Rutts Ter SE14 33 B4
Ruvigny Gdns
SW15 36 F1
Ryan Cl SE3 41 F2
Rycuff Sq SE3 34 C5
Ryder Ct SW1 6 B5
Ryder Dr SE16 32 G1
Ryder St SW1 6 B5
Ryder Yd SW1 6 B5
Rydons Cl SE9 42 A1
Rycroft Rd SE13 40 G3
Rycroft St SW6 30 B2
Ryedale SE22 39 G4
Rye Hill Pk SE15 40 A2
Ryelands Cres SE12 41 F4
Rye La SE15 32 F4
Rye Pas SE15 39 F1
Rye Rd SE15 40 B1
Ryland Rd NW5 10 B3
Rylett Cres W12 22 B4
Rylett Rd W12 22 B3
Rylston Rd SW6 30 A2
Rymer St SE24 39 A4
Rymill St E16 28 C2
Rysbrack St SW3 23 G4

S

Sabine Rd SW11 37 G1
Sackville St W1 6 B4
Saffron Av E14 27 A1
Saffron Hill EC1 17 G3
Sail St SE11 24 E5
St. Agnes Pl SE11 31 G2
St. Aidan's Rd SE22 39 G4
St. Albans Av E6 21 B2
St. Albans Ct EC2 7 D1
St. Albans Gro W8 23 A4
St. Alban's Pl N1 11 A5
St. Alban's Rd NW10 8 A5
St. Albans St W1 6 C4
St. Alfege Pas SE10 33 G2
St. Alfege Rd SE7 34 G2
St. Alphonsus Rd
SW4 38 C2
**St. Andrew's Hill
EC4** 7 C3
St. Andrews Pl
NW1 17 B3
St. Andrews Rd
E13 20 E2
St. Andrews Rd
NW10 8 D3

St. Andrews Rd
W3 22 A1
St. Andrews Rd
W14 29 G2
St. Andrew St EC4 29 G2
St. Andrews Way E3 19 F3
St. Anne's Ct W1 6 C2
St. Ann's, Bark. 14 E5
St. Ann's Cres
SW18 37 D4
St. Ann's Hill SW18 37 C3
St. Ann's Pk Rd
SW18 37 D4
St. Ann's Pas SW13 36 A1
St. Ann's Rd SW13 29 B5
St. Anns Rd W11 22 F1
St. Ann's St SW1 24 D4
St. Ann's Ter NW8 16 E1
St. Anns Vil W11 22 F2
St. Anthonys Cl E1 25 F2
St. Antony's Rd E7 13 E4
St. Asaph Rd SE4 40 B1
St. Augustines Rd
NW1 10 D4
St. Austell Rd SE13 33 G5
St. Barnabas St
SW1 31 A1
St. Barnabas Ter E9 12 B2
St. Barnabas Vil
SW8 31 E4
St. Bartholomew's Rd
E6 14 A5
St. Benet's Pl EC3 7 G3
St. Bernard's Rd E6 13 G5
St. Botolph St EC3 18 E5
St. Brides Av EC4 7 B2
St. Bride's Pas EC4 7 B2
St. Bride St EC4 7 B1
St. Chad's Pl WC1 17 E2
St. Chad's St WC1 17 E2
St. Charles Sq W10 15 G4
St. Clair Rd E13 20 E1
**St. Clement's La
WC2** 6 H2
St. Clements St N7 10 G3
St. Crispins Cl NW3 9 F1
St. Cross St EC1 17 G4
St. Cuthberts Rd
NW2 9 A3
St. Davids Sq E14 33 F1
St. Dionis Rd SW6 30 A5
St. Donatts Rd
SE14 33 D4
**St. Dunstan's All
EC3** 7 H3
**St. Dunstan's Hill
EC3** 7 H4
**St. Dunstan's La
EC3** 7 H4
St. Dunstan's Rd E7 13 F3
St. Dunstans Rd W6 29 F1
St. Edmunds Sq
SW13 29 E2
St. Edmunds Ter
NW8 9 F5
St. Elmo Rd W12 22 B2
St. Elmos Rd SE16 26 C3
St. Erkenwald Rd,
Bark. 14 F5
St. Ervans Rd W10 15 G4
St. Francis Rd SE22 39 D2
St. Francis Way, Ilf. 14 G1
St. Gabriels Rd
NW2 8 F2
St. Georges Av E7 13 E4
St. Georges Av N7 10 D1
St. Georges Circ
SE1 25 A4
St. Georges Ct E6 21 B3
**St. George's Dr
SW1** 24 B5
St. Georges Flds
W2 16 F5

St. Georges La EC3 7 H3
St. Georges Rd E7 13 E3
St. Georges Rd SE1 24 G4
St. Georges Rd W4 22 A3
St. Georges Sq E7 13 E3
St. Georges Sq SE8 26 D5
St. George's Sq
SW1 31 D1
St. George's Sq Ms
SW1 31 D1
St. George St W1 17 B5
St. Georges Way
SE15 32 D2
St. George Wf SE8 31 E1
St. Gerards Cl SW4 38 C3
St. German's Pl SE3 34 D4
**St. Giles High St
WC2** 6 D1
St. Giles Pas WC2 6 D1
St. Giles Rd SE5 32 D3
St. Gilles Ho E2 19 B1
St. Helena Rd
SE16 26 B5
St. Helens Gdns
W10 15 F5
St. Helen's Pl EC3 7 H1
St. Hildas Cl NW6 8 F4
St. Hilda's Rd SW13 29 D2
St. James Ms E14 33 C2
St. James Rd E15 13 C2
St. James's SE14 33 C4
St. James's Av E3 19 A1
St. James's Cl SW1 24 C4
St. James's Cres
SW9 38 G1
**St. James's Mkt
SW1** 6 C4
St. James's Palace
SW1 24 C2
St. James's Pk SW1 24 D3
St. James's Pl SW1 6 A6
St. James's Rd SE1 32 F1
St. James's Rd
SE16 25 F4
St. James's Sq SW1 6 B5
St. James's St SW1 6 A5
St. James's Ter Ms
NW8 9 G5
St. James St W6 29 E1
St. James's Wk EC1 18 A3
St. John's Av NW10 8 B5
St. John's Av SW15 36 F3
St. John's Ch Rd E9 12 B2
St. John's Cres
SW9 38 G1
St. John's Est N1 18 C1
St. John's Gdns
W11 23 A1
St. John's Hill
SW11 37 E2
St. John's Hill Gro
SW11 37 E2
St. John's La EC1 18 A3
St. John's Pk SE3 34 C3
St. John's Rd E16 20 D5
St. John's Rd SW11 37 F2
St. John's Rd, Bark. 14 G5
St. Johns Ter E7 13 E3
St. Johns Ter SE18 35 E2
St. John St EC1 33 E5
St. Johns Vale SE8 33 E5
St. John's Wd High St
NW8 16 E1
St. John's Wd Pk
NW8 9 E5
St. John's Wd Rd
NW8 16 E3
St. John's Wd Ter
NW8 16 E1
St. Joseph's Cl SE7 34 E2
St. Joseph's Vale
SE3 34 A5
St. Jude's Rd E2 18 G1

St. Jude St N16 11 D2
St. Julian's Rd NW6 9 A4
**St. Katharine's Way
E1** 25 E2
**St. Katherine's Row
EC3** 7 J2
St. Laurence Cl NW6 8 F5
St. Lawrence St
E14 26 G2
St. Lawrence Ter
W10 15 G4
St. Lawrence Way
SW9 31 G4
St. Leonards Ct N1 18 C2
St. Leonards Gdns,
Ilf. 14 E2
St. Leonards Rd E14 19 F4
St. Leonards Sq
NW5 10 A3
St. Leonards St E3 19 F2
St. Leonard's Ter
SW3 30 G1
St. Loo Av SW3 30 F2
St. Lucia Dr E15 13 C5
St. Luke's Av SW4 38 D2
St. Luke's Av, Ilf. 14 D2
St. Luke's Cl EC1 18 B3
St. Luke's Est EC1 18 C2
St. Lukes Rd W11 16 A4
St. Lukes Sq E16 20 C5
St. Luke's St SW3 30 F1
St. Luke's Yd W9 16 A1
St. Margarets, Bark. 14 F5
**St. Margaret's Ct
SE1** 7 E6
St. Margaret's Cres
SW15 36 D3
St. Margaret's Gro
SE18 35 E2
St. Margarets La W8 23 C4
St. Margarets Path
SE18 35 E1
St. Margaret's Rd
NW10 15 E2
St. Margaret's Rd
SE4 40 D2
St. Margaret's St
SW1 24 E3
St. Margaret's Ter
SE18 35 E2
St. Marks Cres NW1 10 A5
St. Mark's Gro
SW10 30 C2
St. Marks Pl W11 15 G5
St. Marks Ri E8 11 E2
St. Marks Rd W10 15 F5
St. Marks Rd W11 15 G5
St. Mark St E1 10 A5
St. Mark St E1 18 E6
St. Martins Av E6 20 G1
St. Martin's CI NW1 10 C5
St. Martin's La WC2 6 E3
**St. Martin's-le-Grand
EC1** 7 D1
St. Martin's Ms WC2 6 E4
St. Martin's PI WC2 6 E4
St. Martin's Rd SW9 31 F5
St. Martin's St WC2 6 E4
St. Mary Abbots Pl
W8 23 A4
St. Mary at Hill EC3 7 H4
St. Mary Axe EC3 7 H2
St. Marychurch St
SE16 26 A3
St. Marys, Bark. 14 F5
St. Marys App E12 14 B2
St. Marys Ct E6 21 B3
St. Mary's Ct SE7 34 G3
St. Mary's Gdns
SE11 24 G5
St. Mary's Gate W8 23 C4
St. Mary's Gro N1 11 A3
St. Mary's Gro
SW13 36 D1
St. Marys Mans W2 16 D4
St. Marys Path N1 11 A5

St. Mary's Pl W8 23 C4
St. Marys Rd E13 20 E1
St. Maur Rd NW10 8 A5
St. Marys Rd SW15 33 A4
St. Marys Sq W2 16 E4
St. Mary Ter W2 16 E4
St. Mary St SE18 28 B5
St. Mary's Wk SE11 24 G5
St. Matthew's Rd SW2 38 F2
St. Matthew's Row E2 18 F2
St. Maur Rd SW6 30 A4
St. Merryn Cl SE18 35 F3
St. Michael's All EC3 7 G2
St. Michaels Rd NW2 8 E1
St. Michael's Rd SW9 31 F5
St. Michaels St W2 16 E5
St. Mildreds Rd SE12 41 B5
St. Norbert Grn SE4 40 C2
St. Norbert Rd SE4 40 C2
St. Olaf's Rd SW6 29 G3
St. Olaves St EC2 7 F2
St. Olaves Rd E6 14 C5
St. Olav's Sq SE16 26 A4
St. Oswald's Pl SE11 31 F1
St. Pancras Way NW1 10 C4
St. Paul's Av NW2 8 D3
St. Pauls Av SE16 26 B2
St. Paul's Chyd EC4 7 A2
St. Paul's Cl SE7 34 G1
St. Pauls Cres NW1 10 D4
St. Pauls Dr E15 13 A2
St. Paul's Pl N1 11 A3
St. Paul's Rd N1 11 A3
St. Paul's Rd, Bark. 14 G4
St. Paul's Shrubbery N1 11 C3
St. Paul St N1 11 B5
St. Pauls Way E3 19 D4
St. Pauls Way E14 19 D4
St. Peter's All EC3 7 G2
St. Petersburgh Ms W2 23 C1
St. Petersburgh Pl W2 23 C1
St. Peter's Cl E2 18 F1
St. Peters Gro W6 22 E5
St. Peter's Rd W6 29 C1
St. Peters Sq N1 11 A5
St. Peters Ter SW6 29 G3
St. Peter's Vil W6 22 E5
St. Peter's Way N1 11 D4
St. Philip Sq SW8 31 B5
St. Philip's Rd E8 11 F3
St. Philip St SW8 31 B5
St. Quintin Av W10 15 E4
St. Quintin Gdns W10 15 D4
St. Quintin Rd E13 20 E1
St. Rule St SW8 31 C5
St. Saviour's Est SE1 25 E4
St. Saviour's Rd SW2 38 F3
Saints Dr E7 13 G2
St. Silas Pl NW5 10 A3
St. Silas St Est NW5 10 A3
St. Simon's Av SW15 36 E3
St. Stephens Av W12 22 D3
St. Stephens Cres W2 16 B5
St. Stephens Gdns W2 16 B5
St. Stephens Gro SE13 40 G1
St. Stephen's Rd E3 19 D1
St. Stephens Rd E6 13 F4
St. Stephens Row EC4 7 F2
St. Stephens Ter SW8 31 F3
St. Stephen's Wk SW7 23 D5
St. Swithin's La EC4 7 F3
St. Swithun's Rd SE13 41 A3
St. Thomas Gdns, Ilf.
St. Thomas Rd E16 20 D5
St. Thomas's Pl E9 12 A4
St. Thomas's Rd NW10 8 A5
St. Thomas's Sq E9 11 G4
St. Thomas St SE1 7 F6
St. Thomas's Way SW6 30 A3
St. Winefride's Av E12 14 B2
Salamanca St SE1 24 E5
Salcombe Rd N16 11 D2
Salcott Rd SW11 37 F3
Salehurst Rd SE4 40 D4
Salem Rd W2 23 C1
Sale Pl W2 16 F4
Salisbury Av, Bark. 14 G4
Salisbury Ct EC4 7 B2
Salisbury Pl SW9 32 A3
Salisbury Pl W1 16 G4
Salisbury Rd E7 13 D3
Salisbury Rd E12 14 G3
Salisbury Sq EC4 7 A2
Salisbury St NW8 16 F3
Salisbury Ter SE15 40 A1
Salmen Rd E13 20 C1
Salmon La E14 19 C5
Saltcoats Rd W4 22 A3
Salter Rd SE16 26 B2
Salters Hall Ct EC4 7 F3
Salters Rd E10 15 F3
Salter St E14 26 E1
Salter St NW10 15 C2
Saltoun Rd SW2 38 G2
Saltram Cres W9 16 A2
Saltwell St E14 26 E1
Salusbury Rd NW6 9 A5
Salutation Rd SE10 27 B5
Salvin Rd SW15 36 F1
Sam Bartram Cl SE7 34 F1
Samford St NW8 16 F3
Sampson St E1 25 F2
Samson St E13 20 F1
Samuel Cl SE14 33 B2
Samuel Cl SE18 28 A5
Samuel Lewis Trust Dws SW6 30 B3
Samuel St SE15 32 E3
Samuel St SE18 28 B5
Sancroft St SE11 31 F1
Sandall Rd NW5 10 C3
Sandal St E15 13 B1
Sandbach Pl SE18 28 E5
Sandbourne Rd SE4 33 C5
Sandby Grn SE9 42 A1
Sanderson Cl NW5 10 B1
Sandford Cl E6 21 A3
Sandford Rd E6 21 A3
Sandgate St SE15 32 G2
Sandilands Rd SW6 30 C4
Sandison St SE15 39 G1
Sandland St WC1 17 A3
Sandmere Rd SW4 38 E2
Sandpiper Cl SE16 26 D3
Sandpit Pl SE7 35 A1
Sandringham Dr, Well. 35 G5
Sandringham Rd E7 13 D2
Sandringham Rd E8 11 E2
Sandringham Rd NW2 8 D5
Sandrock Rd SE13 40 E1
Sand's End La SW6 30 C4
Sandstone La E16 27 E1
Sandtoft Rd SE7 34 E2
Sandwell Cres NW6 9 B3
Sandwich St WC1 17 F2
Sandy Hill Av SE18 35 D1
Sandy Hill Rd SE18 35 D1
Sandyhill Rd, Ilf. 14 D1
Sandy's Row E1 18 D4
Sanford St SE14 33 C2
Sangley Rd SE6 40 F5
Sangora Rd SW11 37 E2
Sansom St SE5 32 C3
Sans Wk EC1 17 G3
Santley St SW4 38 F2
Santos Rd SW18 37 B3
Sapcote Ter Cen NW10 8 B2
Saperton Wk SE11 24 F5
Sapphire Cl E6 21 C5
Sapphire Rd SE8 33 C4
Saracen St E14 19 E5
Sarah Ho SW15 36 E2
Saratoga Rd E5 12 A1
Sardinia St WC2 6 G2
Sark Wk E16 20 E5
Sarre Rd NW2 9 A2
Sartor Rd SE15 40 B2
Satchwell Rd E2 18 F2
Saunders Ness Rd E14 33 G1
Saunders St SE11 24 G5
Savage Gdns E6 21 B5
Savage Gdns EC3 7 J3
Savernake Rd NW3 9 G1
Savile Row W1 6 A3
Saville Rd E16 28 A2
Savona Est SW8 31 C3
Savona St SW8 31 C3
Savoy Bldgs WC2 6 G4
Savoy Hill WC2 6 F4
Savoy Pl WC2 6 F4
Savoy Row WC2 6 G3
Savoy St WC2 6 G3
Savoy Way WC2 6 G4
Sawley Rd W12 22 B2
Sawmill Yd E3 12 C5
Sawyer St SE1 25 B3
Saxby Rd SW2 38 E3
Saxham Rd, Bark. 21 G1
Saxonfield Cl SW2 38 F5
Saxon Rd E3 19 D1
Saxon Rd E6 21 B3
Saxon Rd, Ilf. 14 D3
Saxton Cl SE13 41 A1
Sayes Ct St SE8 33 D2
Scala St W1 17 C4
Scampston Ms W10 15 F5
Scandrett St E1 25 G2
Scarsbrook Rd SE3 41 G1
Scarsdale Vil W8 23 B4
Scawfell St E2 18 E1
Sceaux Est SE5 32 D4
Sceptre Rd E2 19 A2
Schoolbank Rd SE10 27 C5
Schoolhouse La E1 26 B1
Schooner Cl E14 27 A4
Schubert Rd SW15 37 A3
Sclater St E1 18 E3
Scoresby St SE1 7 B6
Scotia Rd SW2 38 G3
Scotland Pl SW1 6 E5
Scotsdale Rd SE12 41 E3
Scott Ellis Gdns NW8 16 E2
Scott Lidgett Cres SE16 25 F3
Scotts Rd W12 22 D3
Scott St E1 18 G3
Scoulding Rd E16 20 D5
Scout App NW10 8 A1
Scriven St E8 11 E5
Scrooby St SE6 40 F4
Scrubs La NW10 15 C2
Scrubs La W10 15 C2
Scrutton Cl SW12 38 D5
Scrutton St EC2 18 C3
Scutari Rd SE22 40 A3
Scylla Rd SE15 39 G1
Seaford St WC1 17 F2
Seaforth Cres N5 11 B2
Seagrave Rd SW6 30 B2
Seagull La E16 27 D1
Seal St E8 11 E1
Searles Cl SW11 30 F3
Searles Dr E6 21 D4
Searles Rd SE1 25 C5
Sears St SE5 32 C3
Seaton Av, Ilf. 14 F2
Seaton Pt E5 11 G1
Sebastian St EC1 18 A2
Sebbon St N1 11 A4
Sebert Rd E7 13 E2
Secker St SE1 6 J6
Second Av E12 14 A1
Second Av E13 20 D2
Second Av SW14 36 A1
Second Av W3 22 B2
Second Av W10 15 G3
Sedding St SW1 24 A5
Sedgebrook Rd SE3 34 G5
Sedgeford Rd W12 22 B2
Sedgmoor Pl SE5 32 D3
Sedgwick St E9 12 B2
Sedleigh Rd SW18 37 A4
Sedlescombe Rd SW6 30 A2
Seething La EC3 7 J4
Sefton St SW15 29 E5
Segal Cl SE23 40 C5
Sekforde St EC1 18 A3
Selbie Av NW10 8 B2
Selby Rd E13 20 E4
Selby St E1 18 F3
Selden Rd SE15 32 G5
Sellons Av NW10 8 B5
Selsdon Rd E13 13 F5
Selsdon Way E14 26 F4
Selsey St E14 19 E4
Selwood Pl SW7 30 E1
Selworthy Ho SW11 30 E5
Selwyn Ct SE3 41 B1
Selwyn Rd E3 19 D1
Selwyn Rd E13 13 E5
Semley Pl SW1 24 A5
Senate St SE15 33 A5
Sendall Cl SW11 37 E1
Senior St W2 16 C4
Senrab St E1 19 B5
Serenaders Rd SW9 31 G5
Serjeants Inn EC4 7 A2
Serle St WC2 6 H1
Sermon La EC4 7 D2
Serpentine Rd W2 23 G2
Settles St E1 18 F4
Settrington Rd SW6 30 C5
Sevenoaks Rd SE4 40 C4
Seventh Av E12 14 B1
Severnake Cl E14 26 E5
Severn Way NW10 8 B2
Severus Rd SW11 37 F2
Seville Ms N1 11 D4
Seville St SW1 23 G3
Sevington St W9 16 C3
Seward St EC1 18 B2
Sewardstone Rd E2 19 A1
Sewell St E13 20 D2
Sextant Av E14 27 A5
Seymour Gdns SE4 40 C1
Seymour Ms W1 17 A5
Seymour Pl W1 16 F4
Seymour Rd E6 20 G1
Seymour Rd SW18 37 A5
Seymour St SE18 28 E4
Seymour St W1 16 G5
Seymour St W2 16 G5
Seymour Wk SW10 30 D2
Seyssel St E14 26 G5

Shackleton Ct W12	22 D3	Sherard Rd SE9	42 A3	Sidbury St SW6	29 G4	Slippers Pl SE16	25 G4
Shacklewell Grn E8	11 E1	Sheraton St W1	6 C2	Sidcup Rd SE9	41 G5	Sloane Av SW3	23 F5
Shacklewell La E8	11 E2	Sherborne La EC4	7 F3	Sidcup Rd SE12	41 E3	Sloane Ct W SW3	31 A1
Shacklewell Rd N16	11 E1	Sherborne St N1	11 C5	Sidmouth Rd NW2	8 E4	Sloane Gdns SW1	24 A5
Shacklewell Row E8	11 E1	Sherbrooke Rd SW6	30 A3	Sidmouth St WC1	17 E2	Sloane Sq SW1	23 G5
Shacklewell St E2	18 E3	Sherfield Gdns		Sidney Rd SW9	31 F5	Sloane St SW1	23 G3
Shad Thames SE1	25 E2	SW15	36 B4	Sidney Sq E1	19 A5	Sloane Ter SW1	23 G5
Shaftesbury Av W1	6 C3	Sheridan Rd E12	14 A2	Sidney St E1	18 G4	Smart's Pl WC2	6 F1
Shaftesbury Av WC2	6 C3	Sheringham Av E12	14 B1	Sidworth St E8	11 G4	Smart St E2	19 B2
Shaftesbury Gdns		Sheringham Av E12	14 B1	Sidworth St E8	11 G4	Smeaton Rd SW18	37 B5
NW10	15 A3	Sherington Rd SE7	34 E2	Siemens Rd SE18	27 G4	Smeaton St E1	25 G2
Shaftesbury Rd E7	13 F4	Sherrard Rd E7	10 F3	Sigdon Rd E8	11 F2	Smedley St SW4	31 D5
Shaftesburys, The,		Sherrard Rd E12	13 G3	Silchester Rd W10	15 F5	Smedley St SW8	31 D5
Bark.	14 E5	Sherrick Grn Rd		Silex St SE1	25 A3	Smeed Rd E3	12 E4
Shaftesbury St N1	18 B1	NW10	8 D2	Silk Cl SE12	41 D3	Smiles Pl SE13	33 G5
Shafton Rd E9	12 B5	Sherriff Rd NW6	9 B3	Silk Mills Pas SE13	33 F5	Smith Cl SE16	26 B2
Shakespeare Cres		Sherrin Rd E10	12 E1	Silk Mills Sq E9	12 D3	Smithies Ct E15	12 G2
E12	13 F4	Sherwin Rd SE14	33 B4	Silk St EC2	18 B4	Smith's Ct W1	6 B3
Shakespeare Rd		Sherwood Gdns		Silver Birch Gdns		Smith Sq SW1	24 E4
SE24	39 A3	E14	26 E5	E6	21 B3	Smith St SW3	30 G1
Shakspeare Wk N16	11 D1	Sherwood Gdns		Silverland St E16	28 B2	Smith Ter SW3	30 G1
Shalbourne Sq E9	12 D2	SE16	32 F1	Silvermere Rd SE6	40 F4	Smithy St E1	19 A4
Shalcomb St SW10	30 D2	Sherwood Gdns,		Silver Pl W1	6 B3	Smokehouse Yd	
Shallfleet Dr W10	22 F1	Bark.	14 F4	Silver Rd SE13	40 F1	EC1	18 A4
Shamrock St SW4	38 D1	Sherwood Rd, Well.	35 G5	Silver Rd W12	22 F1	Smugglers Way	
Shandon Rd SW4	38 C4	Sherwood St W1	6 B3	Silverthorne Rd		SW18	37 C2
Shand St SE1	25 D3	Shetland Rd E3	19 D1	SW8	31 B5	Smyrks Rd SE17	32 D1
Shandy St E1	19 A4	Shinfield St W12	15 E5	Silverton Rd W6	29 F2	Smyrna Rd NW6	9 B4
Shannon Gro SW9	38 F2	Shipman Rd E16	20 E5	Silvertown Way		Smythe St E14	26 F1
Shardcroft Av SE24	39 A3	Ship St SE8	33 E4	E16	20 C5	Snarsgate St W10	15 E4
Shardeloes Rd SE4	40 D1	Ship Tavern Pas EC3	7 H3	Silver Wk SE16	26 D2	Sneyd Rd NW2	8 E1
Shardeloes Rd SE14	40 D1	Shipton St E2	18 E2	Silvester Rd SE22	39 E3	Snowberry Cl E15	13 A1
Sharon Gdns E9	12 A5	Shipwright Rd SE16	26 C3	Silvocea Way E14	20 A5	Snowbury Rd SW6	30 C5
Sharpleshall St NW1	9 G4	Shipwright Yd SE1	7 H6	Silwood St SE16	26 A5	Snowden St EC2	18 D3
Sharratt St SE15	33 A5	Shirbutt St E14	26 F1	Silwood St SE16	26 A5	Snow Hill EC1	18 A4
Sharsted St SE17	32 A1	Shirebrook Rd SE3	41 G1	Simmons Rd SE18	35 D1	Snow Hill Ct EC1	7 C1
Shavers Pl SW1	6 C4	Shirland Ms W9	16 A2	Simms Rd SE1	25 F5	Snowman Rd NW6	9 C5
Shawbrooke Rd SE9	41 F3	Shirland Rd W9	16 B2	Simnel Rd SE12	41 E5	Snowsfields SE1	25 C3
Shawbury Rd SE22	39 E3	Shirley Gdns, Bark.	14 G3	Simpsons Rd E14	26 F1	Snowshill Rd E12	14 A2
Shaw Ct SW11	37 E1	Shirley Gro SW11	38 A1	Simpson St SW11	30 F5	Soames St SE15	39 E1
Shawfield St SW3	30 F1	Shirley Ho Dr SE7	34 F3	Sims Wk SE3	41 C2	Soho Sq W1	6 C1
Shawford Ct SW15	36 C5	Shirley Rd E15	13 B1	Sinclair Gdns W14	22 F3	Soho St W1	6 C1
Shaw Rd SE22	39 D2	Shirley St E16	20 C5	Sinclair Pl SE4	40 E4	Solebay St E1	19 C3
Shearling Way N7	10 E3	Shirlock Rd NW3	9 G1	Sinclair Rd W14	22 F3	Solent Rd E13	20 D2
Shearman Rd SE3	41 C2	Shoebury Rd E6	14 B4	Sir Alexander Cl W3	22 B2	Solent Rd NW6	9 B2
Sheepcote La SW11	30 G5	Shoe La EC4	6 G1	Sir Alexander Rd		Solna Av SW15	36 E3
Sheep La E8	11 G5			W3	22 B2	Solomon's Pas	
Sheerness Ms E16	28 D3	Shooter's Hill SE18	35 C4	Sirdar Rd W11	22 F1	SE15	39 G2
Sheerwater Rd E16	10 G4	Shooter's Hill, Well.	35 C4	Sirinham Pt SW8	31 F2	Solon New Rd SW4	38 E2
Sheffield St WC2	6 G2	Shooter's Hill Rd		Sise La EC4	7 F2	Solon Rd SW2	38 E2
Sheffield Ter W8	23 B2	SE3	34 C4	Sisley Rd, Bark.	14 G5	Solway Rd SE22	39 F2
Shelburne Rd N7	10 F1	Shooter's Hill Rd		Sispara Gdns		Somali Rd NW2	9 A1
Shelbury Rd SE22	39 G3	SE10	34 A4	SW18	37 A4	Somerby Rd, Bark.	14 F4
Sheldon Cl SE12	41 E3	Shooter's Hill Rd		Sissulo Ct E6	13 F5	Somerfield Rd N4	11 E1
Sheldon Rd NW2	8 F1	SE18	34 E3	Sisters Av SW11	37 G2	Somerford St E1	18 G3
Sheldon Sq W2	16 D4	Shoot Up Hill NW2	8 G1	Sisulu Pl SW9	38 G1	Somerford Way	
Sheldrake Cl E16	28 B2	Shoreditch High St		Sivill Ho E2	18 E2	SE16	26 C3
Sheldrake Pl W8	23 A3	E1	18 D3			Somerleyton Pas	
Shelduck Ct E15	13 C2	Shore Pl E9	12 A4	Six Bridges Trd Est		SW9	39 A2
Shelgate Rd SW11	37 F3	Shore Rd E9	12 A4	SE1	32 F1	Somerleyton Rd	
Shelley Av E12	14 A3	Shorncliffe Rd SE1	32 E1	Sixth Av E12	14 B1	SW9	38 G2
Shelley Cl SE15	32 G5	Shorrolds Rd SW6	30 A3	Sixth Av W10	15 G2	Somers Cres W2	16 F5
Shelley Dr, Well.	35 G4	Shorter St E1	25 E1	Skardu Rd NW2	8 G2	Somerset Est SW11	30 E4
Shellgrove Est N16	11 D2	Shortlands W6	22 F5	Skeena Hill SW18	36 G5	Somerset Gdns	
Shellness Rd E5	11 G2	Short Rd E15	13 A5	Skeffington Rd E6	14 A5	SE13	33 F5
Shell Rd SE13	40 F1	Short Rd W4	29 A2	Skeffington St SE18	28 E5	Somerset Rd SW19	36 G5
Shellwood Rd		Shorts Gdns WC2	6 E2	Skelgill Rd SW15	37 A2	Somerset Rd SW19	36 G5
SW11	30 G5	Short Wall E15	19 G2	Skelley Rd E15	13 C4	Somers Pl SW2	38 F4
Shelmerdine Cl E3	19 E4	Short Way SE9	42 A1	Skelton Rd E7	13 D3	Somers Rd SW2	38 F4
Shelton St WC2	6 E2	Shottendane Rd		Skelwith Rd W6	29 E2	Somerton Rd SE15	39 G2
Shenfield St N1	18 D1	SW6	30 B4	Sketchley Gdns		Somerville Av	
Shenley Rd SE5	32 D4	Shottfield Av SW14	36 A2	SE16	33 B1	SW13	29 D2
Shepherdess Wk N1	18 B1	Shouldham St W1	16 F4	Skiers St E15	13 B5	Sondes St SE17	32 C2
Shepherds Bush Grn		Shrapnel Cl SE18	35 A3	Skinners La EC4	7 E3	Sonia Gdns NW10	8 B1
W12	22 E3	Shrapnel Rd SE9	42 B1	Skinner St EC1	17 G2	Sophia Rd E10	12 B2
Shepherds Bush Mkt		Shrewsbury La		Skipsey Av E6	21 B2	Sopwith Way SW8	31 B3
W12	22 E3	SE18	35 D4	Skipworth Rd E9	12 A5	Sorrel Gdns E6	21 A4
Shepherds Bush Pl		Shrewsbury Rd E7	13 G2	Skylines Village		Sorrel La E14	20 A5
W12	22 F3	Shrewsbury Rd W2	16 B5	E14	26 G3	Sotheran Cl E8	11 F5
Shepherds Bush Rd		Shrewsbury St W10	15 E3	Slade, The SE18	35 G2	Sotheron Rd SW6	30 C3
W6	22 E5	Shroton St NW1	16 F4	Sladebrook Rd SE3	41 G1	Soudan Rd SW11	30 G4
Shepherds La E9	12 B2	Shrubland Rd E8	11 F5	Sladedale Rd SE18	35 G1	Souldern Rd W14	22 F4
Shepherds Wk NW3	9 E2	Shuttleworth Rd		Slagrove Pl SE13	40 E3	South Africa Rd	
Sheppard Dr SE16	32 G1	SW11	30 F5	Slaidburn St SW10	30 D2	W12	22 D2
Sheppard St E16	20 C3	Sibella Rd SW4	31 D5	Slaithwaite Rd SE13	40 G2	Southall Rd E15	25 C3
Shepperton Rd N1	11 B5	Sibley Gro E12	14 A4	Sleaford St SW8	31 C3	Southampton Bldgs	
		Sibthorpe Rd SE12	41 E4	Slingsby Pl WC2	6 E3	WC2	6 J1

Southampton Pl WC1
Southampton Rd NW5 17 E4
Southampton Rd NW5 9 G2
Southampton Row WC1 17 E4
Southampton St WC2 **6 E3**
Southampton Way SE5 32 C3
Southam St W10 15 G3
South Audley St W1 24 A1
Southbank Business Cen SW8 31 D2
South Black Lion La W6 29 C1
South Bolton Gdns SW5 30 C1
Southborough Rd E9 12 A5
Southbourne Gdns SE12 41 E3
Southbourne Gdns, Ilf. 14 E2
Southbrook Ms SE12 41 C4
Southbrook Rd SE12 41 C4
South Carriage Dr SW1 23 F3
South Carriage Dr SW7 23 F3
Southchurch Rd E6 21 B1
South Circular Rd (A205) SE6 41 A5
South Circular Rd (A205) SE9 42 B1
South Circular Rd (A205) SE12 41 E4
South Circular Rd (A205) SW4 38 A3
South Circular Rd (A3) SW11 37 F3
South Circular Rd (A205) SW14 36 A2
South Circular Rd (A205) SW15 36 E2
South Circular Rd (A3) SW18 37 F3
South Colonnade E14 26 E2
Southcombe St W14 22 G5
Southcote Rd N19 10 C1
South Cres E16 20 A3
South Cres WC1 17 D4
Southcroft Av, Well. 42 G1
South Eaton Pl SW1 24 A5
South Edwardes Sq W8 23 A4
South End Cl NW3 9 F1
Southend Cl SE9 42 D4
Southend Cres SE9 42 D4
Southend Rd E6 14 B4
South End Rd NW3 9 F1
South End Row NW8 23 C4
Southernagate Way SE14 33 C3
Southern Gro E3 19 D2
Southern Rd E13 20 D1
Southern Row W10 15 G3
Southern St N1 17 F1
Southern Way SE10 27 C5
Southerton Rd W6 22 E4
South Esk Rd E7 13 F3
Southey Rd SW9 31 G4
Southfield Rd W4 22 A4
Southfields Pas SW18 37 B4
Southfields Rd SW18 37 B4
Southgate Gro N1 11 C5
Southgate Rd N1 11 C5
South Hill Pk NW3 9 F1

South Hill Pk Gdns NW3 9 F1
South Island Pl SW9 31 F3
South Lambeth Pl SW8 31 E2
South Lambeth Rd SW8 31 E2
South Molton La W1 17 B5
South Molton Rd E16 20 D5
South Molton St W1 17 B5
Southmoor Way E9 12 D3
Southolm St SW11 31 B4
South Par SW3 30 E1
South Pk Rd W6 30 B5
South Pk Dr, Bark. 14 G1
South Pk Dr, Ilf. 14 G1
South Pk Ms SW6 37 C1
South Pl EC2 18 B3
South Ri Way SE18 35 F1
South Row SE3 34 C5
South Sea St SE16 26 D4
South Side W6 22 A4
Southspring, Sid. 42 F5
South St W1 23 F2
South Tenter St E1 25 E1
South Ter SW7 23 F6
Southvale Rd SE3 34 B5
Southview Av NW10 8 B2
South Vil NW1 10 D3
Southville SW8 31 D4
Southwark Br EC4 **7 E5**
Southwark Br SE1 **7 E5**
Southwark Br Rd SE1 25 A4
Southwark Pk Est SE16 25 G5
Southwark Pk Rd SE16 25 E5
Southwark St SE1 **7 C5**
Southwater Cl E14 19 D5
Southwell Gdns SW7 23 D5
Southwell Rd SE5 39 B5
South Wf Rd W2 16 E5
Southwick Pl W2 16 F5
Southwick St W2 16 F5
South Worple Av SW14 36 A1
Sovereign Cl E1 25 G1
Sowerby Cl SE9 42 A3
Spa Grn Est EC1 17 G2
Spanby Rd E3 19 E3
Spanish Pl W1 17 A5
Spanish Rd SW18 37 D3
Sparkford Ho SW11 30 D4
Spa Rd SE16 25 E4
Sparrows La SE9 42 D5
Sparsholt Rd, Bark. 14 G5
Sparta St SE10 33 F4
Spearman St SE18 35 C2
Spear Ms SW5 23 B5
Speke Ho SE5 32 B3
Speldhurst Rd E9 12 B4
Spelman St E1 18 F4
Spencer Gdns SE9 42 B3
Spencer Pk SW18 37 E3
Spencer Ri NW5 10 B1
Spencer Rd E6 13 G5
Spencer Rd SW18 37 E2
Spencer St EC1 18 A2
Spencer Wk NW3 9 F1
Spencer Wk SW15 36 F2
Spenser Gro N16 11 D1
Spenser Rd SE24 38 C3
Spenser St SW1 24 C4
Spert St E14 26 E1
Spey St E14 19 G4
Spezia Rd NW10 15 C1
Spicer Cl SW9 32 A5
Spindle Cl SE18 28 A4
Spindrift Av E14 26 E5
Spital Sq E1 18 D4
Spital St E1 18 F3

Sporle Ct SW11 37 E1
Sportsbank St SE6 40 G5
Spray St SE18 28 D5
Sprimont Pl SW3 30 G1
Springall St SE15 32 G3
Springbank Rd SE13 41 A4
Springdale Rd N16 11 C1
Springfield Gro SE7 34 F2
Springfield La NW6 9 C5
Springfield Rd E6 14 B4
Springfield Rd E15 20 B2
Springfield Rd NW8 9 D5
Springfield Rd NW6 11 C1
Spring Gdns SW1 **6 D5**
Springhill Cl SE5 39 C1
Spring Path NW3 9 E2
Springrice Rd SE13 40 G4
Spring St W2 16 E5
Springvale Ter W14 22 F4
Springwater Cl SE18 35 C4
Springwell Av NW10 8 B5
Sprowston Ms E7 13 D3
Sprowston Rd E7 13 D3
Sprules Rd SE4 33 C5
Spurgeon St SE1 25 C4
Spurling Rd SE22 39 E2
Spur Rd SE1 24 G3
Spur Rd SW1 24 C3
Spur Rd, Bark. 21 E2
Spurstowe Ter E8 11 G2
Square, The W6 29 E1
Squirries St E2 18 F2
Stables Way SE11 31 G1
Stable Yd Rd SW1 **6 A6**
Stacey St WC2 **6 D2**
Stadium Rd SE18 35 A3
Stadium St SW10 30 D3
Stafford Cl NW6 16 B2
Stafford Ct W8 23 B4
Stafford Pl SW1 24 C4
Stafford Rd E3 19 D1
Stafford Rd E7 13 F4
Stafford Rd NW6 16 B2
Staffordshire St SE15 32 F4
Stafford St W1 **6 A5**
Stafford Ter W8 23 B4
Stag Pl SW1 24 C4
Stainer St SE1 **7 G6**
Staines Rd, Ilf. 14 E1
Staining La EC2 **7 E1**
Stainsby Rd E14 19 E5
Stainton Rd SE6 41 A4
Stalham St SE16 25 G4
Stamford Brook Av W6 22 B4
Stamford Brook Rd W6 22 B4
Stamford Rd E6 14 A5
Stamford Rd N1 11 D4
Stamford St SE1 **6 J6**
Stamp Pl E2 18 E2
Stanbridge Rd SW15 36 E1
Stanbury Rd SE15 32 G4
Standard Ind Est E16 28 B3
Standen Rd SW18 37 A5
Standish Rd W6 22 C5
Stane Way SE18 34 G3
Stanfield Rd E3 19 C1
Stanford Rd W8 23 C4
Stanhope Gdns SW7 23 D5
Stanhope Gate W1 24 A2
Stanhope Ms E SW7 23 D5
Stanhope Ms W SW7 23 D5
Stanhope Pl W2 16 G5
Stanhope St NW1 17 C2

Stanhope Ter W2 23 E4
Stanlake Ms W12 22 E2
Stanlake Rd W12 22 D2
Stanlake Vil W12 22 D2
Stanley Cl SW8 31 F2
Stanley Cres W11 23 A1
Stanley Gdns NW2 8 E2
Stanley Gdns W3 23 A1
Stanley Gdns W11 23 A1
Stanley Gdns SW8 31 A5
Stanley Rd E12 14 A2
Stanley Rd E15 13 A5
Stanley St SE8 33 D4
Stanmer St SW11 30 F4
Stannard Ms E8 11 F3
Stannard Rd E8 11 F3
Stannary Pl SE11 31 G1
Stannary St SE11 31 G2
Stansfeld Rd E6 20 G4
Stansfield Rd SW9 38 F1
Stanswood Gdns SE5 32 D3
Stanton Rd SW13 29 B5
Stanway St N1 18 D1
Stanwick Rd W14 23 A5
Stanworth St SE1 25 E3
Stapleford Cl SW19 36 G5
Staplehurst Rd SE13 41 B3
Staple Inn Bldgs WC1 17 G4
Staples Cl SE16 26 C2
Staple St SE1 25 C3
Star All EC3 **7 J3**
Starboard Way E14 26 E4
Starcross St NW1 17 C2
Starfield Rd W12 22 C3
Star La E16 20 B3
Star Rd W14 30 A2
Star St E16 20 C4
Star St W2 16 F5
Star Yd WC2 **6 J1**
Station App SE1 24 G3
Station App SW6 36 G1
Station App Path SE9 42 B3
Station Cres SE3 34 D1
Station Par NW2 8 E3
Station Par, Bark. 14 E4
Station Pas SE15 32 G4
Station Rd E7 13 D1
Station Rd E12 13 G1
Station Rd NW10 15 B1
Station Rd SE13 40 G1
Station Rd SW13 29 B5
Station Rd E15 13 A4
Station Rd SE16 28 D2
Station Rd NW10 15 F1
Station Ter SE5 32 B4
Staunton St SE8 33 D2
Staverton Rd NW2 8 E4
Stave Yd Rd SE16 26 B2
Stavordale Rd N5 11 A1
Stayner's Rd E1 19 B3
Stead St SE17 25 C5
Stean St E8 11 E5
Stebbing Ho W11 22 F2
Stebondale St E14 33 G1
Stedham Pl WC1 **6 E1**
Steele Rd E11 13 B1
Steeles Rd NW3 9 G3
Steeple Cl SW6 29 G5
Steers Way SE16 26 C3
Stephan Cl E8 11 F5
Stephendale Rd SW6 30 C5
Stephenson St E16 20 B3
Stephenson St NW10 15 A2
Stephenson Way NW1 17 C3
Stephen's Rd E15 13 B5
Stephen St W1 17 D4
Stepney Causeway E1 19 B5
Stepney Grn E1 19 A4

Stepney High St E1 19 B4
Stepney Way E1 18 G4
Sterling Cl NW10 8 C3
Sterling Gdns SE14 33 C2
Sterndale Rd W14 22 F4
Sterne St W12 23 B2
Sternhall La SE15 39 F1
Sterry St SE1 15 B5
Steucers La SE23 40 C5
Stevenage Rd E6 14 C3
Stevenage Rd SW6 29 F3
Stevens Av E9 12 A3
Stevenson Cres
SE16 32 F1
Steventon Rd W12 22 B1
Steward St E1 18 D4
Stewart Rainbird Ho
E12 14 C2
Stewart Rd E15 12 G1
Stewart's Gro SW3 23 E5
Stewart's Rd SW8 31 C3
Stewart St E14 26 G3
Stew La EC4 7 D3
Stillingfleet Rd
SW13 29 C2
Stillington St SW1 24 C5
Stillness Rd SE4 40 C4
Stirling Rd E13 20 E1
Stirling Rd SW9 31 E5
Stockholm Ho E1 25 F1
Stockholm Rd SE16 33 A1
Stockholm Way E1 25 F2
Stockhurst Cl SW15 29 E5
Stock Orchard Cres
N7 10 F2
Stock Orchard St N7 10 F2
Stock St E13 20 D1
Stockwell Av SW9 38 F1
Stockwell Gdns
SW9 31 F5
Stockwell Gdns Est
SW9 31 E5
Stockwell Grn SW9 31 E5
Stockwell La SW9 31 F5
Stockwell Pk Cres
SW9 31 F4
Stockwell Pk Est
SW9 31 G5
Stockwell Pk Rd
SW9 31 F4
Stockwell Pk Wk
SW9 38 F1
Stockwell Rd SW9 31 F5
Stockwell St SE10 33 G2
Stockwell Ter SW9 31 F4
Stoford Cl SW19 36 G5
Stokenchurch St
SW6 30 C4
Stoke Newington Rd
N16 11 E2
Stoke Pl NW10 15 B2
Stokesley St W12 15 B5
Stokes Rd E6 21 A3
Stondon Pk SE23 40 C5
Stondon Wk E6 20 G1
Stone Bldgs WC2 17 F4
Stonecutter St EC4 7 B1
Stonefield St N1 10 G5
Stone Ho EC2 7 F1
Stone Lake Retail Pk
SE7 27 E5
Stoneleigh Pl W11 22 F1
Stoneleigh St W11 22 F1
Stones End St SE1 25 B3
Stonewall E6 21 C4
Stoney All SE18 35 C5
Stoneycroft Cl
SE12 41 C5
Stoney La E1 7 J1
Stoney St SE1 7 F5
Stonhouse St SW4 38 D1
Stonor Rd W14 23 A5
Stopes St SE15 32 E3
Stopford Rd E13 13 D5
Stopford Rd SE17 32 A1
Store Rd E16 28 C3

Storers Quay E14 27 A5
Store St WC1 13 A2
Store St W15 13 A2
Store St WC1 17 C5
Storey's Gate SW1 24 D3
Storey St E16 28 C5
Stories Ms SE5 32 D5
Stories Rd SE5 39 D1
Stork Rd E7 13 C3
Storks Rd SE16 25 F4
Stormont Rd SW11 38 A1
Stott Cl SW18 37 E4
Stourcliffe St W1 16 G5
Stour Rd E3 12 E4
Stowage SE8 33 E2
Stowe Rd W12 22 D3
Stracey Rd E7 13 D1
Stradbroke Rd N5 11 B1
Stradella Rd SE24 39 B4
Strafford St E14 26 E3
Strahan Rd E3 19 C2
Straightsmouth
SE10 33 G3
Strait Rd E6 28 A1
Straker's Rd SE22 39 G2
Strand WC2 6 E4
Strand WC2 6 H3
Strandfield Cl SE18 35 G1
Strand La WC2 6 H3
Stranraer Way N1 10 E1
Strasburg Rd SW11 31 B4
Stratford Cen, The
E15 13 A4
Stratford Gro
SW15 36 F2
Stratford Pl W1 17 B5
Stratford Rd E13 13 C5
Stratford Rd W8 23 B4
Stratford Vil NW1 10 C4
Strathan Cl SW14 36 G4
Strathaven Rd
SE12 41 E4
Strathblaine Rd
SW11 37 E2
Strathearn Pl W2 23 F1
Strathleden Rd SE3 34 D4
Strathfield Gdns,
Bark. 14 F3
Strathleven Rd
SW2 38 E3
Strathnairn St SE1 25 F5
Strathray Gdns NW3 9 F3
Strath Ter SW11 37 F1
Strattondale St E14 26 G4
Stratton St W1 24 B2
Streatfield Av E6 14 B5
Streatham Pl SW2 38 E5
Streatham St WC1 6 D1
Streatley Rd NW6 9 A4
Streetfield Ms SE3 41 D1
Streimer Rd E15 19 G1
Strelley Way W3 22 A1
Strickland Row
SW18 37 E5
Strickland St SE8 33 E5
Stride Rd E13 20 C1
Strode Rd E7 13 B2
Strode Rd NW10 8 C3
Strode Rd SW6 29 F3
Strone Rd E7 13 F3
Strone Rd E12 13 G3
Strongbow Cres
SE9 42 B3
Strongbow Rd SE9 42 B3
Stronsa Rd W12 22 B3
Stroudley Wk E3 19 F2
Strutton Grd SW1 24 D4
Stuart Rd NW6 16 B2
Stuart Rd SE15 40 A4
Stuart Twr W9 16 D2
Stubbs Dr SE16 32 G1
Stubbs Pt E13 20 E3
Studdridge St SW6 30 B3
Studd St N1 11 A5
Studholme Ct NW3 9 B1
Studholme St SE15 32 G3
Studland St W6 22 D5
Studley Cl E5 12 C2

Studley Est SW4 31 E4
Studley Rd E7 13 E3
Studley Rd SW4 31 E4
Studley Rd E7 13 E4
Stukeley Rd E7 13 E4
Stukeley St WC2 6 F1
Sturdy Rd SE15 32 G5
Sturgeon Rd SE17 32 B1
Sturmer Way N7 10 F3
Sturry St E14 19 F5
Sturt St N1 18 B1
Stutfield St E1 18 F5
Styles Gdns SW9 39 A1
Sudbourne Rd SW2 38 E3
Sudbrooke Rd
SW12 37 G4
Sudeley St N1 18 A1
Sudlow Rd SW18 37 B5
Suffolk La EC4 7 F3
Suffolk Pl SW1 6 D5
Suffolk Rd E13 20 C2
Suffolk Rd NW10 8 A4
Suffolk Rd SW13 29 B3
Suffolk Rd, Bark. 14 F4
Suffolk St SW1 6 D5
Sugar Ho La E15 19 G1
Sugar Quay Wk EC3 7 J4
Sugden Rd SW11 38 A1
Sulgrave Rd W6 22 E3
Sulina Rd SW2 38 E5
Sulivan Ct SW6 30 B5
Sulivan Rd SW6 37 B1
Sullivan Av E16 20 G4
Sullivan Cl SW11 37 F1
Sullivan Rd SW11 25 A5
Sultan St SE5 32 B3
Sumatra Rd NW6 9 B2
Sumburgh Rd
SW12 38 A4
Summercourt Rd
E1 19 A5
Summerfield Av
NW6 15 G1
Summerfield St
SE12 41 C5
Summit Cl NW2 8 G2
Sumner Est SE15 32 E3
Sumner Pl SW7 23 E5
Sumner Pl Ms SW7 23 E5
Sumner Rd SE15 32 E3
Sumner St SE1 7 C5
Sunbeam Cres W10 15 E3
Sunbury La SW11 30 E4
Sunbury St SE18 28 B4
Sun Ct EC3 7 G2
Sunderland Ct
SE22 39 F5
Sunderland Ter W2 16 C5
Sundew Av W12 22 C1
Sundorne Rd SE7 35 F5
Sundridge Av, Well. 35 F5
Sunfields Pl SE3 34 E3
Sun La SE3 34 E3
Sunlight Sq E2 18 G2
Sunningdale Av W3 22 A1
Sunningdale Av,
Bark. 14 F5
Sunningdale Cl E6 21 B2
Sunninghill Rd
SE13 33 F5
Sunnydale Rd SE12 41 E3
Sunnyhill Cl E5 12 C1
Sunnymead Rd
SW15 36 D3
Sunray Av SE24 39 C2
Sun Rd W14 30 A1
Sunset Rd SE5 39 B2
Sun St EC2 7 G1
Surma Cl E1 18 G3
Surrendale Pl W9 16 B3
Surrey Canal Rd
SE14 33 A2
Surrey Canal Rd
SE15 33 A2
Surrey La SW11 30 F4
Surrey La Est SW11 30 F4

Surrey Quays Retail
Cen SE16 26 B4
Surrey Quays Rd
SE16 26 B3
Surrey Rd SE15 40 B3
Surrey Rd, Bark. 14 G5
Surrey Row SE1 25 A3
Surrey Sq SE17 32 D1
Surrey St E13 20 E2
Surrey St WC2 6 H3
Surrey Ter SE17 32 D1
Surrey Water Rd
SE16 26 B2
Surr St N7 10 E2
Susannah St E14 19 F5
Susan Rd SE3 34 E5
Sussex Gdns W2 16 E5
Sussex Pl NW1 16 G2
Sussex Pl W2 16 E5
Sussex Pl W6 29 E1
Sussex Pl SW7 14 C5
Sussex Sq W2 23 E1
Sussex St E13 20 E2
Sussex St SW1 31 B1
Sutcliffe Rd SE18 35 G2
Sutherland Av W9 16 D2
Sutherland Av,
Well. 42 G2
Sutherland Gdns
SW14 36 A1
Sutherland Gro
SW18 36 G4
Sutherland Pl W2 16 B5
Sutherland Rd W4 29 A2
Sutherland Row
SW1 31 B1
Sutherland Sq SE17 32 B1
Sutherland St SW1 31 B1
Sutherland Wk SE17 32 B1
Sutlej Rd SE7 34 F3
Sutterton St N7 10 F3
Sutton Ct Rd E13 20 F2
Sutton Est SW3 30 F1
Sutton Est W10 15 E4
Sutton Est, The N1 11 A4
Sutton Pl E9 12 A2
Sutton Rd E13 20 C3
Sutton Rd, Bark. 21 G1
Sutton Row W1 6 D1
Sutton Wk SE1 6 H6
Sutton Way W10 15 E4
Swaffield Rd SW18 37 C5
Swain Rd SW18 37 C5
Swainson Rd W3 22 B3
Swain St NW8 16 F3
Swallow Cl SE14 33 A4
Swallowfield Rd
SE7 34 E1
Swallow St E6 21 A4
Swallow St W1 6 B4
Swanage Rd SW18 37 D4
Swan App E6 21 A4
Swandon Way
SW18 37 C2
Swanfield St E2 18 E2
Swan La EC4 7 F4
Swan Mead SE1 25 D5
Swan Pl SW13 29 B5
Swan Rd SE16 26 A3
Swan Rd SE18 27 G4
Swanscombe Rd
W4 29 A1
Swanscombe Rd
W11 22 F2
Swan St SE1 25 B4
Swan Wk SW3 30 G2
Swanwick Cl SW15 36 B5
Swaton Rd E3 19 E3
Swedenborg Gdns
E1 25 F1
Sweden Gate SE16 26 C4
Sweeney Cres SE1 25 E5
Swete St E13 20 D1
Sweyn Pl SE3 34 D5
Swift St SW6 30 A4
Swinbrook Rd W10 15 G4

Swinburne Rd SW15	36 C2	Tasker Rd NW3	9 G2	Testerton Wk W11	22 F1	Thornton Av W4	22 A5
Swindon St W12	22 D2	Tasman Rd SW9	38 E1	Tetcott Rd SW10	30 D3	Thornton PI W1	16 G4
Swinford Gdns SW9	39 A1	Tasso Rd W6	29 G2	Teversham La SW8	31 E4	Thornton Rd SW12	38 D5
Swingate La SE12	35 G2	Tate & Lyle Jetty E16	28 A3	Teviot St E14	19 G1	Thornton Rd, Ilf.	31 G5
Swinnerton St E9	12 C2	Tatnell Rd SE23	40 C4	Tewson Rd SE18	35 G1	Thornton Rd SW19	41 D5
Swinton PI WC1	17 F2	Tattersall CI SE9	42 A3	Thackeray Rd E6	29 B2	Thorntree Rd SE7	34 G1
Swinton St WC1	17 F2	Taunton PI NW1	16 G3	Thackeray Rd SW8	31 B5	Thornville St SE8	33 E4
Swiss Ct W1	**6 D4**	Taunton Rd SE12	41 B3	Thackeray St W8	23 C3	Thornwood Rd SE13	41 B3
Swiss Ter NW3	9 E4	Tavern La SW9	31 G5	Thalia CI SE10	34 A2	Thorogood Gdns E15	13 B2
Sybil Phoenix CI SE8	33 B1	Tavistock Cres W11	16 A4	Thame Rd SE16	26 B3	Thorparch Rd SW8	31 D4
		Tavistock Gdns, Ilf.	14 G1	Thameside Ind Est E16	28 A3	Thorpebank Rd W12	22 C2
Sycamore Av E3	12 D5	Tavistock PI WC1	17 D3	Thames PI SW15	36 F1	Thorpe Rd E6	14 B4
Sycamore Gdns W6	22 D5	Tavistock Rd E7	13 C1	Thames Rd E16	27 G2	Thorpe Rd E7	13 C1
Sycamore Gro SE6	40 G4	Tavistock Rd E15	13 C3	Thames St SE10	33 F2	Thorpe Rd, Bark.	14 F4
Sycamore Ms SW4	38 C1	Tavistock Rd NW10	15 B1	Thames Wf E16	27 C2	Thoydon Rd E3	19 C1
Sydmons CI SE23	40 A5	Tavistock Rd W11	16 A5	Thanet St WC1	17 D2		
Sydner Rd N16	11 E1	Tavistock Sq WC1	17 D3	Thanington Ct SE9	42 G4	**Thrale St SE1**	**7 E6**
Sydney CI SW3	23 E5	**Tavistock St WC2**	**6 F3**	**Thavies Inn EC1**	**7 A1**	Thrawl St E1	18 E4
Sydney Ms SW3	23 E5	Taviton St WC1	17 D3	Thaxton Rd W14	30 A2	**Threadneedle St EC2**	**7 G2**
Sydney PI SW7	23 E5	Tavy CI SE11	31 G1	Thayer St W1	17 A4		
Sydney St SW3	23 E5	Tawny Way SE16	26 B5	Theatre St SW11	37 G1	**Three Barrels Wk EC4**	**7 E3**
Sylvan Gro NW2	8 F1	Taybridge Rd SW11	38 A1	Theberton St N1	10 G5		
Sylvan Gro SE15	32 G3	Tayburn CI E14	19 G5			Three Colts La E2	18 G3
Sylvan Rd E7	13 D3	Taylor CI SE8	33 D2	**Theed St SE1**	**6 J6**	Three Colt St E14	26 D1
Sylvester Rd E8	11 G3	Taylors La NW10	8 A4	Thelma Gdns SE3	34 G4	Three Kings Yd W1	24 B3
Symons St SW3	23 G5	Tayport St N1	10 E4	Theobald's Rd WC1	17 F4	Three Mill La E3	19 G2
		Teak CI SE16	26 C4	Theodore Rd SE13	40 G4	**Three Quays Wk EC3**	**7 J4**
T		Teale St E2	18 F1	Therapia Rd SE22	40 A4	Threshers PI W11	22 G1
		Teal St SE10	27 C4	Theresa Rd W6	22 C5	Throckmorten Rd E16	20 E5
Tabard Gdn Est SE1	25 C3	Teasel Cres SE28	28 G2	Thermopylae Gate E14	26 F4		
Tabard St SE1	25 C2	Teasel Way E15	20 B2	Thessaly Rd SW8	31 C3	**Throgmorton Av EC2**	**7 G1**
Tabernacle St EC2	18 C3	Tedworth Sq SW3	30 G1	Third Av E13	14 A1	**Throgmorton St EC2**	**7 G1**
Tableer Av SW4	38 D3	Tee, The W3	15 A1	Third Av E13	20 D2	Thurland Rd SE16	25 F4
Tabley Rd N7	10 E1	Teesdale CI E2	18 G1	Third Av W10	22 B2	Thurleigh Av SW12	38 A4
Tabor Rd W6	22 D4	Teesdale St E2	18 G1	Third Av W10	15 G2	Thurleigh Rd SW12	38 A4
Tachbrook Est SW1	31 D1	Teignmouth CI SW12	38 D2	Thirleby Rd SW1	24 C4	Thurloe CI SW7	23 F4
Tachbrook St SW1	24 C5	Teignmouth Rd NW2	8 F2	Thirsk Rd SW11	38 A1	Thurloe PI SW7	23 E5
Tack Ms SE4	40 E1	Telegraph PI E14	26 F5	Thistle Gro SW10	30 D1	Thurloe Sq SW7	23 E5
Tadema Rd SW10	30 D3	Telegraph Rd SW15	36 D5			Thurloe St SW7	23 E5
Tadmor St W12	22 F2	**Telegraph St EC2**	**7 F1**	Thomas Baines Rd SW11	37 E1	Thurlow Rd NW3	9 E2
Taeping St E14	26 F5	Telemann Sq SE3	41 E1			Thurlow St SE17	32 C1
Talacre Rd NW5	10 A3	Telford Rd W10	15 G4	Thomas Cribb Ms E6	21 B5	Thurlow Ter NW5	10 A2
Talbot Ct EC3	**7 G3**	Telford Ter SW1	31 C2	Thomas Darby Ct W11	22 G1	Thurston Rd SE13	33 F5
Talbot PI SE3	34 B5	Telford Way W3	15 A4			Thurtle Rd E2	11 E5
Talbot Rd E6	21 C1	Telham Rd E6	21 C1	Thomas Doyle St SE1	25 A4	Tibbatts Rd E3	19 F3
Talbot Rd E7	13 D1	Tell Gro SE22	39 E2			Tibbenham Wk E13	20 C1
Talbot Rd SE22	39 D2	Tellson Av SE18	35 A4	Thomas La SE6	40 E6	Tibbet's Cor SW15	36 F5
Talbot Rd W2	16 A5	Temperley Rd SW12	38 A5	Thomas More St E1	25 F1	Tibbet's Ride SW15	36 F6
Talbot Rd W11	16 A5	Templar St SE5	32 A5	Thomas Rd E14	19 D5	Tidal Basin Rd E16	27 C1
Talbot Sq W2	16 E5	Temple EC4	24 G1	Thomas St SE18	28 D5	Tideswell Rd SW15	36 E3
Talbot Wk W11	15 G5	**Temple Av EC4**	**7 A3**	Thompson Rd SE22	39 E4	Tideway Ind Est SW8	31 C2
Talbot Yd SE1	**7 F6**	Temple CI SE28	28 E4			Tideway Wk SW8	31 C2
Talfourd PI SE15	32 E4	Templecombe Rd E9	12 A5	Thompson's Av SE5	39 E5	Tidey St E3	19 E4
Talfourd Rd SE15	32 E4	**Temple La EC4**	**7 A2**	Thorburn Sq SE1	25 F5	Tidy St E3	19 E3
Talgarth Rd W6	29 G1	Templemead CI W3	15 A5	Thornbury Rd SW2	38 E4	Tiepolo Rd E5	11 G1
Talgarth Rd W14	29 G1	Temple Mill La E15	12 F5	Thorncliffe Rd SW2	38 E4	Tilbrook Rd SE3	41 F1
Tallis CI E16	20 E5	**Temple PI WC2**	**6 H3**	Thorncombe Rd SE22	39 D3	Tilbury Rd E6	21 B1
Tallis Gro SE7	34 E2	Temple Rd E6	14 A5			Tildesley Rd SW15	36 E4
Tallis St EC4	**7 A3**	Temple Rd NW2	8 E1	Thorncroft St SW8	31 E3	Tileyard Rd N7	10 E4
Talma Rd SW2	38 G2	Temple Rd W4	22 A4	Thorndike CI SW10	30 D3	Tiller Rd E14	26 E4
Talwin St E3	19 F2	Temple Sq E8	18 G1	Thorndike Rd N1	11 B3	Tilney Gdns N1	11 C3
Tamarisk Sq W12	22 B1	Templeton PI SW5	23 B5	Thorndike St SW1	24 D5	Tilney St W1	24 A2
Tamworth St SW6	30 B2	Temple W Ms SE11	25 A4	Thorne CI E11	13 B1	Tilson Gdns SW2	38 E5
Tanfield Av NW2	8 A1	Tench St E1	25 G2	Thorne CI E16	20 D5	Tilton St SW6	30 A2
Tangley Gro SW15	36 B4	**Tenison Ct W1**	**6 A3**	Thorne Pas SW13	29 A5	Tilt Yd App SE9	42 B4
Tanners Hill SE8	33 D4	Tennis St SE1	25 C3	Thorne Rd SW8	31 E3		
Tanner St SE1	25 D3	Tennyson Av E12	14 A4	Thorne St SW13	36 A1	Timbercroft La SE18	35 G2
Tanner St, Bark.	14 E3	Tennyson Av, Well.	35 G4	Thorney Cres SW11	30 E3	Timberland Rd E1	18 G5
Tansy CI E6	21 C5	Tennyson Rd E15	13 B4	Thorney St SW1	24 E5	Timber Mill Way SW4	38 D1
Tant Av E16	20 C5	Tennyson Rd NW6	9 A5	Thornfield Rd W12	22 D3		
Tanza Rd NW3	9 G1	Tennyson Rd SW8	31 B5	Thornford Rd SE13	40 G3	Timber Pond Rd SE16	26 B3
Taplow NW3	9 E4	Tenterden St W1	17 B5	Thorngate Rd W9	16 B3		
Taplow St N1	18 B1	Tenter St E1	18 G3	Thorngrove Rd E13	13 E5	Time Sq E8	11 E2
Tappesfield Rd SE15	40 A1	Teredo St SE16	26 B4	Thornham Gro E15	13 A2	Timothy Rd E3	19 D4
Tapp St E1	18 G3	Terminus PI SW1	24 B4	Thornham St SE10	33 E2	Tindal St SW9	32 A4
Tarbert Rd SE22	39 D3	Terrace, The NW6	9 A5	Thornhaugh St WC1	17 D3	Tinsley Rd E1	19 A4
Tariff Cres SE8	26 D5	Terrace, The SW13	29 A5	Thornhill Av SE18	35 G3	Tintagel Cres SE22	39 E2
Tarling Rd E16	20 C5	Terrace Gdns SW13	29 B5	Thornhill Cres N1	10 F4	Tintern CI SW15	36 G3
Tarling St E1	18 G5	Terrace Rd E9	12 A4			Tintern St SW4	38 E2
Tarling St Est E1	19 A5	Terrace Rd E13	15 D5	Thornhill Gdns, Bark.	14 G4	Tinto Rd E16	20 D3
Tarragon CI SE14	33 C3	Terrick St W12	15 D5			Tinworth St SE11	31 F1
Tarrant PI W1	16 G4	Tessa Sanderson PI SW8	38 B1	Thornhill Rd N1	10 F4	Tipthorpe Rd SW11	38 A1
Tarver Rd SE17	32 A1			Thornhill Sq N1	10 F4	Tisdall PI SE17	25 C5
Tarves Way SE10	33 F3						

Titchfield St NW8 9 G5
Titchwell Rd SW18 37 E5
Tite St SW3 30 G1
Tiverton Rd NW10 8 F5
Tiverton St SE1 25 B4
Tivoli Ct SE16 26 G2
Tivoli Gdns SE18 28 A5
Tobacco Dock E1 25 G1
Tobin Cl NW3 9 F4
Toby La E1 19 C3
Tokenhouse Yd EC2 7 F1
Toland Sq SW15 36 C3
Tollet St E1 19 C1
Tollgate Gdns NW6 16 C1
Tollgate Rd E6 20 G4
Tollgate Rd E16 20 F4
Tollington Rd N7 10 F1
Tolpuddle St N1 18 A3
Tolsford Rd E5 11 G2
Tom Cribb Rd SE28 28 E4
Tom Jenkinson Rd E16 27 D2
Tomlins Gro E3 19 E2
Tomlinson Cl E2 18 E2
Tomlins Orchard, Bark. 14 E5
Tom Mann Cl, Bark. 14 F4
Tom Nolan Cl E15 20 B1
Tonbridge St WC1 17 E2
Tonsley Hill SW18 37 C3
Tonsley Pl SW18 37 C3
Tonsley Rd SW18 37 C3
Tonsley St SW18 37 C3
Took's Ct EC4 6 J1
Tooley St SE1 7 G5
Topley St SE9 41 G2
Topmast Pt E14 26 F3
Tor Gdns W8 9 A4
Tor Gro SE28 28 G2
Tormount Rd SE18 35 G2
Toronto Av E12 14 B1
Toronto Rd E11 13 A1
Torrance Ct SE7 34 G4
Torrens Rd E11 13 C3
Torrens Rd SW2 38 F3
Torrens Sq E15 13 B3
Torrens St EC1 17 G1
Torriano Av NW5 10 D2
Torridge Gdns SE15 40 A2
Torridon Rd SE13 41 A5
Torrington Pl E1 25 F3
Torrington Pl WC1 17 D4
Torrington Sq WC1 17 D3
Torwood Rd SW15 36 C3
Tothill St SW1 6 D7
Tottan Ter E1 19 B5
Tottenham Ct Rd W1 17 C3
Tottenham Rd N1 11 D3
Tottenham St W1 17 C4
Totteridge Ho SW11 30 E5
Toulmin St SE1 25 B3
Toulon St SE5 32 B3
Tournay Rd SW6 30 A3
Tours Pas SW11 37 C2
Towcester Rd E3 19 F3
Tower 42 EC2 7 H1
Tower Br E1 25 E2
Tower Br SE1 25 E2
Tower Br App E1 25 E2
Tower Br Rd SE1 25 D4
Tower Br Wf E1 25 F2
Tower Ct WC2 6 E2
Tower Hamlets Rd E7 13 C1
Tower Hill EC3 7 J4
Tower Millennium Pier EC3 7 J5
Tower Pl EC3 7 J4
Tower Rd NW10 8 C4
Tower Royal EC4 7 F2
Tower St WC2 6 D2
Town Hall Rd SW11 37 G1
Townley Ct E15 13 C3

Townley Rd SE22 39 D3
Townmead Rd SW6 30 D5
Town Quay, Bark. 14 D5
Townsend St SE17 25 D5
Townshend Est NW8 16 F1
Towpath Wlk E9 12 F3
Toynbee St E1 18 E4
Tracey Av NW2 8 E2
Trader Rd E6 21 D5
Tradescant Rd SW8 31 E3
Trafalgar Av SE15 32 E1
Trafalgar Gdns E1 19 C1
Trafalgar Gro SE10 34 A2
Trafalgar Ms E9 12 D3
Trafalgar Rd SE10 34 A2
Trafalgar Sq SW1 6 D5
Trafalgar Sq WC2 6 D5
Trafalgar St SE17 32 C1
Trafalgar Way E14 26 G2
Trafford Cl E15 12 F3
Tramway Av E15 13 B4
Tranquil Vale SE3 34 B5
Transept St NW1 16 F4
Transom Sq E14 26 F5
Tranton Rd SE16 25 F4
Treadgold St W11 22 F1
Treadway St E2 18 G1
Treaty St N1 10 F5
Trebovir Rd SW5 29 E1
Treby St E3 19 D1
Tredegar Rd E3 19 D1
Tredegar Sq E3 19 D2
Tredegar Ter E3 19 D2
Trederwen Rd E8 11 F5
Treen Av SW13 36 B1
Tree Rd E16 20 F5
Trefil Wlk N7 10 E1
Trefoil Rd SW18 37 D3
Tregarvon Rd SW11 38 A2
Trego Rd E9 12 E4
Tregothnan Rd SW9 38 E1
Tregunter Rd SW10 29 D2
Trehurst St E5 12 C2
Trelawney Est E9 12 A3
Trelawn Rd SW2 38 G3
Trellis Twr W10 16 A3
Tremadoc Rd SW4 38 D2
Tremaine Cl SE4 33 D2
Trenchard St SE10 34 A1
Trenchold St SW8 31 E2
Trenmar Gdns NW10 15 D2
Trent Rd SW2 38 F3
Treport St SW18 37 C5
Tresco Rd SE15 39 G2
Tresham Cres NW8 16 F6
Tressillian Cres SE4 40 E1
Tressillian Rd SE4 40 D2
Trevanion Rd W14 29 G1
Trevelyan Av E12 14 B1
Trevelyan Gdns NW10 8 E5
Trevelyan Rd E15 13 C1
Treverton St W10 15 F3
Treville St SW15 36 D5
Trevithick St SE8 33 E1
Trevor Pl SW7 23 F3
Trevor Sq SW7 23 G3
Trevor St SW7 23 F3
Triangle Pl SW4 38 D2
Triangle Rd E8 11 G5
Trident St SE16 26 B5
Trig La EC4 7 D3
Trigon Rd SW8 31 F3
Trim St SE14 33 D2
Trinidad St E14 26 D1
Trinity Buoy Wf E14 27 C1
Trinity Ch Pas SW13 29 D2
Trinity Ch Rd SW13 29 D2

Trinity Ch Sq SE1 25 B4
Trinity Cl E8 11 E3
Trinity Gdns SW9 38 F2
Trinity Gro SE10 33 G4
Trinity Rd SW18 37 E3
Trinity Sq EC3 7 J4
Trinity St SE1 25 B3
Trinity Wk NW3 9 F3
Trinity Way W3 22 A1
Trio Pl SE1 25 B3
Triton Sq NW1 17 C3
Trocadero Shop Cen W1 6 C4
Troon St E1 19 C5
Trossachs Rd SE22 39 C3
Trott St SW11 30 F4
Troughton Rd SE7 34 E1
Troutbeck Rd SE14 33 C4
Trouville Rd SW4 38 C4
Trowbridge Rd E9 12 D3
Troy Ct SE18 28 F5
Troy Town SE15 39 F1
Truesdale Rd E6 21 B5
Truman's Rd N16 11 D2
Trumpington Rd E7 13 C1
Trump St EC2 7 E2
Trundleys Rd SE8 33 B1
Trundleys Ter SE8 26 B5
Truro Rd N5 10 G1
Truro St NW5 10 A3
Trussley Rd W6 22 E4
Tryon Cres E9 12 A5
Tryon St SW3 30 G1
Tuam Rd SE18 35 F2
Tubbs Rd NW10 15 B1
Tudor Cl NW3 9 F2
Tudor Cl SW2 38 F4
Tudor Gro E9 12 A4
Tudor Rd E6 13 F5
Tudor Rd E9 11 G5
Tudor St EC4 7 A3
Tudway Rd SE3 41 E1
Tufnell Pk Rd N7 10 C1
Tufnell Pk Rd N19 10 C1
Tufton St SW1 24 D4
Tugboat St SE28 28 G3
Tuilerie St E2 18 F1
Tulip Gdns, Ilf. 14 D3
Tulse Hill SW2 38 G4
Tulse Hill Est SW2 38 G4
Tunis Rd W12 22 D2
Tunley Rd NW10 15 A1
Tunmarsh La E13 20 F2
Tunnan Leys E6 21 C5
Tunnel Av SE10 27 A3
Tunnel Rd SE16 26 A3
Tunstall Rd SW9 38 G2
Tunworth Cres SW15 36 B4
Tuppy St SE28 28 E4
Turenne Cl SW18 37 D2
Turin St E2 18 F2
Turks Row SW3 30 G1
Turley Cl E15 13 B5
Turnagain La EC4 7 B1
Turner Cl SW9 32 A4
Turners Rd E3 19 D4
Turner St E1 18 G4
Turner St E16 20 C5
Turneville Rd W14 30 A2
Turney Rd SE21 39 C5
Turnham Grn Ter W4 29 C5
Turnham Rd SE4 40 C3
Turnmill St EC1 17 G3
Turnpike Ho EC1 18 A2
Turnpin La SE10 33 G2
Turnstone Cl E13 20 D2
Turret Gro SW4 38 C1
Tuscan Rd SE18 35 F1
Tuskar St SE10 34 B1
Tustin Est SE15 33 A2
Tweedale St SE15 40 A1
Tweedmouth Rd E13 20 E1
Tweezer's All WC2 6 J3
Twelvetrees Cres E3 19 G3

Twilley St SW18 37 C5
Twine Ct E1 26 A1
Twisden Rd NW5 10 C1
Twyford Pl WC2 6 G1
Twyford Rd, Ilf. 14 E2
Twyford St N1 10 F5
Tyas Rd E16 20 C3
Tyburn Way W1 23 G1
Tyers Est SE1 25 D3
Tyers Gate SE1 7 H5
Tyers St SE11 31 F1
Tyers Ter SE11 31 F1
Tylehurst Gdns, Ilf. 14 E2
Tyler Cl E2 18 E1
Tyler's Ct W1 6 C2
Tyler St SE10 34 B1
Tylney Rd E7 13 F1
Tyndale Ct E14 33 F1
Tyneham Rd SW11 31 A5
Tynemouth St SW6 30 D5
Type St E2 19 B1
Tyrawley Rd SW6 30 C4
Tyrone Rd E6 21 B1
Tyrrell Rd SE22 39 F2
Tyrwhitt Rd SE4 40 E1
Tyson Rd SE23 40 A5
Tyssen Pas E8 11 E3
Tyssen St E8 11 E3

U

Uamvar St E14 19 F4
Uffington Rd NW10 8 C5
Ufford St SE1 24 G3
Ufton Gro N1 11 C4
Ufton Rd N1 11 C4
Ullswater Rd SW13 29 C3
Ulundi Rd SE3 34 B2
Ulverscroft Rd SE22 39 E3
Ulysses Rd NW6 9 A2
Umbria St SW15 36 C4
Undercliff Rd SE13 40 E1
Underhill Rd SE22 39 G4
Undershaft EC3 7 H2
Underwood Rd E1 18 F3
Underwood Row N1 18 B2
Underwood St N1 18 B2
Undine Rd E14 26 F5
Union Ct EC2 7 H1
Union Gro SW8 31 D5
Union Rd SW4 31 D5
Union Rd SW8 31 D5
Union Sq N1 11 B5
Union St E15 12 G5
Union St SE1 7 C6
Unity Cl NW10 8 C3
Unity Way SE18 27 G4
University St WC1 17 C3
University Way E16 28 C1
Unwin Cl SE15 32 F2
Upcerne Rd SW10 30 D3
Uphall Rd, Ilf. 14 E4
Upham Pk Rd W4 22 A5
Upland Rd SE22 39 F3
Upney La, Bark. 14 G3
Upper Addison Gdns W14 22 G3
Upper Bk St E14 26 F2
Upper Belgrave St SW1 24 A4
Upper Berkeley St W1 16 G5
Upper Brockley Rd SE4 33 D5
Upper Brook St W1 24 A1
Upper Cheyne Row SW3 30 F2
Upper Grosvenor St W1 24 A1
Upper Grd SE1 6 J5
Upper James St W1 6 B3
Upper John St W1 6 B3
Upper Mall W6 29 C1
Upper Marsh SE1 24 F4

Upper Montagu St W1 16 G4
Upper N St E14 19 E4
Upper Pk Rd NW3 9 G2
Upper Phillimore Gdns W8 23 B3
Upper Richmond Rd SW15 36 G2
Upper Rd E13 20 D2
Upper St. Martin's La WC2 6 E3
Upper St N1 17 G1
Upper Tachbrook St SW1 24 C5
Upper Thames St EC4 7 C3
Upperton Rd W E13 20 F2
Upper Tulse Hill SW2 38 F5
Upper Wimpole St W1 17 A4
Upper Woburn Pl WC1 17 D2
Upstall St SE5 32 A4
Upton Av E7 13 D4
Upton La E7 13 D4
Upton Pk Rd E7 13 E4
Upton Rd SE18 35 E2
Upwood Rd SE12 41 D4
Urlwin St SE5 32 B2
Urlwin Wk SW9 31 G5
Ursula St SW11 30 F4
Urswick Rd E9 12 A2
Usborne Ms SW8 31 F3
Usher Rd E3 19 D1
Usk Rd SW11 37 D2
Usk St E2 19 B2
Uverdale Rd SW10 30 C3
Uxbridge Rd W12 22 D2
Uxbridge W8 23 B2

V

Vale, The SW3 30 E2
Valentine Pl SE1 25 A3
Valentine Rd E9 12 B3
Valentine Row SE1 25 A3
Valerian Way E15 20 B2
Vale Rd E7 13 E3
Vale Royal N7 10 E4
Valetta Gro E13 20 D1
Valetta Rd W3 22 A3
Valette St E9 11 G3
Valiant Ho SE7 34 F1
Valiant Way E6 21 F5
Vallance Rd E1 18 F3
Vallance Rd E2 18 F3
Valley Gro SE7 34 F1
Valliere Rd NW10 15 D2
Valmar Rd SE5 32 B4
Valonia Gdns SW18 37 A4
Vambery Rd SE18 35 E2
Vanbrugh Flds SE3 34 C2
Vanbrugh Hill SE3 34 C1
Vanbrugh Hill SE10 34 C1
Vanbrugh Pk SE3 34 C2
Vanbrugh Pk Rd SE3 34 C2
Vanbrugh Pk Rd W SE3 34 C3
Vanbrugh Ter SE3 34 C4
Vandome Cl E16 20 E5
Vandon St SW1 24 C4
Vandyke Cl SW15 36 F5
Vandyke Cross SE9 42 A3
Vane Cl NW3 9 E1
Vanguard Cl E16 20 D4
Vanguard St SE8 33 E4
Vanneck Sq SW15 36 C3
Vansittart Rd E7 13 C1
Vansittart St SE14 33 C3
Vanston Pl SW6 30 B3
Varcoe Rd SE16 32 G1
Vardens Rd SW11 37 E2
Varden St E1 18 G5

Varley Rd E16 20 E5
Varna Rd SW6 29 G3
Varndell St NW1 17 C2
Vassall Rd SW9 31 G3
Vauban Est SE16 25 F4
Vauban St SE16 25 F4
Vaughan Av W6 22 B5
Vaughan Rd E15 13 C3
Vaughan Rd SE5 39 B1
Vaughan St SE16 26 D3
Vaughan Way E1 25 F1
Vauxhall Br SE1 31 E1
Vauxhall Br SW1 31 E1
Vauxhall Br Rd SW1 24 C5
Vauxhall Gdns Est SE11 31 F1
Vauxhall Gro SW8 31 F2
Vauxhall St SE11 31 F1
Vauxhall Wk SE11 31 F1
Vawdrey Cl E1 19 A3
Veda Rd SE13 40 E2
Velletri Ho E2 19 B1
Venables St NW8 16 E3
Vencourt Pl W6 29 C1
Venetian Rd SE5 32 B5
Venn St SW4 38 C2
Ventnor Gdns, Bark. 14 G3
Ventnor Rd SE14 33 B3
Venue St E14 19 G4
Venus Rd SE18 28 B4
Vera Rd SW6 29 G4
Verbena Gdns W6 29 C1
Verdun Rd SW13 29 C2
Vereker Rd W14 29 G1
Vere St W1 17 B5
Verity Cl W11 15 G5
Vermont Rd SW18 37 C4
Verney Rd SE16 32 F2
Verney Way SE16 32 G2
Vernham Rd SE18 35 E2
Vernon Av E12 14 B1
Vernon Pl WC1 17 E4
Vernon Rd E3 19 D1
Vernon Rd E15 13 B4
Vernon Rd SW14 36 D1
Vespan Rd W12 22 C3
Vesta Rd SE4 33 C5
Vestry Ms SE5 32 D4
Vestry Rd SE5 32 D4
Vestry St N1 18 C2
Viaduct St E2 18 G2
Vian St SE13 40 F1
Vibart Gdns SW2 38 F5
Vicarage Av SE3 34 D3
Vicarage Cres SW11 30 E4
Vicarage Dr, Bark. 14 E4
Vicarage Fld Shop Cen,Bark. 14 E4
Vicarage Gdns W8 23 B2
Vicarage Gate W8 23 C3
Vicarage Gro SE5 32 C4
Vicarage La E6 21 B2
Vicarage La E15 13 B4
Vicarage Pk SE18 35 E1
Vicarage Pl SE18 35 E1
Vicarage Rd E15 13 C4
Vicarage Rd SE18 35 E1
Vicarage Wk SW11 30 E4
Vicars Cl E15 13 D5
Vicars Hill SE13 40 F2
Vicars Rd NW5 9 E2
Viceroy Rd SW8 31 E4
Victoria Dock Rd E16 20 B5
Victoria Dr SW19 36 F5
Victoria Embk EC4 6 G4
Victoria Embk SW1 24 D3
Victoria Embk WC2 6 G4
Victoria Gdns W8 23 B2
Victoria Gro W8 23 D4
Victoria Ind Est NW10 15 A2

Victoria Ms NW6 9 B5
Victoria Pk E9 12 C4
Victoria Pk Rd E9 12 A5
Victoria Pk Sq E2 19 A2
Victoria Pl SW1 24 B5
Victoria Ri SW4 38 B1
Victoria Rd E11 13 B1
Victoria Rd E13 20 D1
Victoria Rd NW6 9 A5
Victoria Rd W8 23 D4
Victoria Rd, Bark. 14 D3
Victoria Sta SW1 24 B5
Victoria St E15 13 B4
Victoria St SW1 24 C4
Victoria Way SE7 34 E1
Victoria Wf E14 26 C1
Victor Rd NW10 15 D2
Victory Pl SE17 25 B5
Victory Way SE16 26 C3
Viewfield Rd SW18 37 A4
Vigo St W1 6 A4
Viking Ct SW6 30 B2
Village, The W5 34 F2
Village Way SE21 39 C4
Villa Rd SW9 38 G1
Villas Rd SE18 28 E5
Villa St SE17 32 C1
Villiers Rd NW2 8 B4
Villiers St WC2 6 E4
Vincent Cl SE16 26 C3
Vincent Ms E3 19 E1
Vincent Rd SE18 28 D5
Vincent Sq SW1 24 C5
Vincent St E16 20 C4
Vincent St SW1 24 C5
Vincent Ter N1 18 A1
Vine Gdns, Ilf. 14 E2
Vine La SE1 7 J6
Vine Rd E15 13 C4
Vine Rd SW13 36 B1
Vine Sq W14 30 A1
Vine St W1 6 B4
Vine St Br EC1 17 G3
Vineyard Wk EC1 17 G3
Viney Rd SE13 40 F1
Vining St SW9 38 G2
Vintners Ct EC4 7 C3
Viola Sq W12 22 B1
Violet Cl E16 20 B3
Violet Hill NW8 16 D1
Violet Rd E3 19 F3
Virgil St SE1 24 F4
Virginia Rd E2 18 E2
Virginia St E1 25 F1
Virginia Wk SW2 38 F4
Viscount Dr E6 21 B4
Vista, The SE9 41 G4
Vivian Rd E3 19 C1
Voce Rd SE18 35 F3
Voltaire Rd SW4 38 D1
Voss St E2 18 F2
Vulcan Cl E6 21 C5
Vulcan Rd SE4 33 D5
Vulcan Ter SE4 33 D5
Vulcan Way N7 10 F3
Vyner St E2 11 G5

W

Wadding St SE17 25 C5
Waddington Rd E15 13 A2
Waddington St E15 13 A3
Wadeson St E2 18 G1
Wades Pl E14 26 F1
Wadham Gdns NW3 9 F5
Wadham Rd SW15 36 G2
Wadhurst Rd SW8 31 C4
Wager St E3 19 D3
Waghorn Rd E13 13 F5
Waghorn St SE15 39 F1
Wagner St SE15 33 A3
Waite Davies Rd SE12 41 C5
Waite St SE15 32 E2
Waithman St EC4 7 B2

Wakefield St E6 13 G5
Wakefield St WC1 17 E2
Wakeham St N1 11 C3
Wakehurst Rd SW11 37 F3
Wakeling St E14 19 C5
Wakelin Rd E15 20 B1
Wakeman Rd NW10 15 E2
Wakering Rd, Bark. 14 E3
Wakley St EC1 17 G2
Walberswick St SW8 31 E3
Walbrook EC4 7 F3
Walcot Sq SE11 24 G5
Waldair Wf E16 28 B2
Waldemar Av SW6 29 G4
Walden St E1 18 G5
Waldo Cl SW4 38 C3
Waldo Rd NW10 15 C2
Walerand Rd SE13 33 G5
Wales Cl SE15 32 G3
Waley St E1 19 C4
Walford Rd N16 11 D1
Walham Gro SW6 30 B3
Walker Cl SE18 28 E5
Walkers Ct W1 6 C3
Wallace Rd N1 11 B3
Wallbutton Rd SE4 33 C5
Wall End Rd E6 14 C4
Waller Rd SE14 33 B4
Wallflower St W12 22 B1
Wallgrave Rd SW5 23 C5
Wallingford Av W10 15 F4
Wallis Cl SW11 37 E1
Wallis Rd E9 12 D3
Wallis's Cotts SW2 38 E5
Wall St N1 11 C3
Wallwood St E14 19 D4
Walmer Rd W11 22 G1
Walmer Ter SE18 28 E5
Walm La NW2 8 F2
Walnut Tree Cl SW13 29 B4
Walnut Tree Rd SE10 34 B1
Walnut Tree Wk SE11 24 G5
Walpole St SW3 30 G1
Walsham Rd SE14 33 B5
Walsingham Pl SW11 38 A4
Walter St E2 19 B2
Walters Way SE23 40 B4
Walter Ter E1 19 B5
Walterton Rd W9 16 A3
Walton Cl SW8 31 E3
Walton Pl SW3 23 G4
Walton Rd E12 14 C1
Walton Rd E13 20 F1
Walton St SW3 23 F5
Walworth Pl SE17 32 B2
Walworth Rd SE1 25 B5
Walworth Rd SE17 25 B5
Wandon Rd SW6 30 C3
Wandsworth Br SW6 37 C1
Wandsworth Br SW18 37 C1
Wandsworth Br Rd SW6 30 C4
Wandsworth Common SW12 37 F4
Wandsworth Common W Side SW18 37 D3
Wandsworth High St SW18 37 B3
Wandsworth Plain SW18 37 C3
Wandsworth Rd SW8 31 D3
Wandsworth Shop Cen SW18 37 C4
Wanless Rd SE24 39 B1
Wanley Rd SE5 39 C2
Wanlip Rd E13 20 E3

Wansbeck Rd E9 12 D4
Wansey St SE17 25 B5
Wantage Rd E1 41 C3
Wapping High St E1 25 F2
Wapping La E1 25 F2
Wapping Wall E1 26 A2
Warback Rd W12 22 D2
Warburton Rd E8 11 G4
Wardalls Gro SE14 33 A3
Warden Rd NW5 10 A3
Wardens Gro SE1 7 D6
Wardle St E9 12 B2
Wardo Av SW6 29 G4
Wardour Ms W1 6 B2
Wardour St W1 6 C3
Ward Rd E15 13 A5
Wardrobe Ter EC4 7 C3
Wards Wf App E16 27 G2
Warfield Rd NW10 15 F3
Warham St SE5 32 A3
Warland Rd SE18 35 F3
Warley St E2 19 B2
Warlock Rd W9 16 B3
Warlters Rd N7 10 E1
Warmington Rd SE24 39 B4
Warndon St SE16 26 B5
Warneford St E9 11 G5
Warner Cl E15 13 B2
Warner Pl E2 18 F1
Warner Rd SE5 32 B4
Warner St EC1 17 G3
Warple Way W3 22 A2
Warren, The E12 14 A1
Warren La SE18 28 D4
Warren La Gate SE18 28 D4
Warren St W1 17 C3
Warren Wk SE7 34 F2
Warriner Gdns SW11 30 G4
Warrington Cres W9 16 D3
Warrior Sq E12 14 C1
Warspite Rd SE18 28 A4
Warton Rd E15 12 G4
Warwall E6 21 D5
Warwick Av W2 16 D3
Warwick Av W9 16 D3
Warwick Ct SE15 32 F5
Warwick Cres W2 16 D4
Warwick Dr SW15 36 D1
Warwick Ct SE15 16 C4
Warwick Ho St SW1 6 D5
Warwick La EC4 7 C2
Warwick Pas EC4 7 C1
Warwick Pl W9 16 D4
Warwick Pl N SW1 24 C5
Warwick Rd E12 14 A2
Warwick Rd E15 13 C3
Warwick Rd SW5 23 A5
Warwick Rd W14 23 A5
Warwick Row SW1 24 B4
Warwickshire Path SE8 33 D3
Warwick Sq EC4 7 C1
Warwick Sq SW1 31 C1
Warwick Sq Ms SW1 31 C1
Warwick St W1 6 B3
Warwick Ter SE18 35 F2
Warwick Way SW1 24 C5
Washington Av E12 14 A1
Washington Rd SW13 29 C3
Waterden Rd E15 12 E2
Waterford Rd SW6 30 C4
Water Gdns, The W2 16 F5
Watergate EC4 7 B3
Watergate St SE8 33 E2
Watergate Wk WC2 6 F5
Waterhouse Cl E16 20 E4
Water La E15 13 B3

Water La EC3 7 H4
Water La SE14 33 A3
Waterloo Br SE1 6 G4
Waterloo Br WC2 6 G4
Waterloo East E2 19 A1
Waterloo Gdns E2 19 A1
Waterloo Pas NW6 9 A4
Waterloo Pl SW1 6 C5
Waterloo Rd E6 13 F4
Waterloo Rd SE1 24 G3
Waterloo Ter N1 11 A4
Waterman St SW15 36 F1
Watermans Wk SE16 26 C4
Watermeadow La SW6 30 D5
Water Ms SE15 40 A2
Waterside Cl E3 12 D5
Waterside Path SW18 37 C2
Waterside Pt SW11 30 F3
Waterside Twr SW6 30 D2
Waterson St E2 18 D1
Water St WC2 6 H3
Waterview Ho E14 19 C4
Waterworks Rd SW2 38 F4
Watford Rd E16 20 D4
Watkinson Rd N7 10 F3
Watling Ct EC4 7 E2
Watling Gdns NW2 8 G3
Watling St EC4 7 D2
Watney St E1 18 G5
Watson Av E6 14 C4
Watson's St SE8 33 E3
Watson St E13 20 G1
Watts Gro E3 19 F4
Watts St E1 25 G2
Watts St SE15 32 E4
Wat Tyler Rd SE3 33 G5
Wat Tyler Rd SE10 33 G5
Wavell Dr, Sid. 42 G4
Waveney Av SE15 39 G2
Waverley Ct SE18 35 F1
Waverley Gdns, Bark. 21 G1
Waverley Pl NW8 16 E1
Waverley Rd SE18 35 E1
Waverley Wk W2 16 B4
Waverton Ho E3 12 D5
Waverton Rd SW18 37 D5
Waverton St W1 24 A2
Wayfield Link SE9 42 F4
Wayford St SW11 30 F5
Wayland Av E8 11 F2
Wayman Cl E8 11 G3
Waynflete Sq W10 22 F1
Weardale Rd SE13 41 A2
Wear Pl E2 18 G2
Wearside Rd SE13 40 F2
Weatherley Cl E3 19 C3
Weavers Ter SW6 30 B2
Weaver St E1 18 F3
Weavers Way NW1 10 D5
Webb Cl W10 15 E3
Webber Row SE1 25 A3
Webber St SE1 25 A2
Webb Rd SE3 34 C2
Webbs Rd SW11 37 G3
Webb St SE1 25 D4
Webheath Est NW6 9 A4
Webster Rd SE16 25 F4
Wedderburn Rd NW3 9 E2
Wedderburn Rd, Bark. 14 F5
Wedgwood Ms W1 6 D2
Weech Rd NW6 9 B1
Weedington Rd NW5 10 A2
Weigall Rd SE12 41 F5
Weighhouse St W1 17 A5
Weimar St SW15 36 G1
Weir Est SW12 38 C5

Weir Rd SW12 38 C5
Weir's Pas NW1 17 D2
Weiss Rd SW15 36 F1
Welbeck Rd E6 20 G2
Welbeck St W1 17 A4
Welbeck Way W1 17 B5
Welby St SE5 32 A4
Welfare Rd E15 13 B4
Welland St SE10 33 G2
Wellclose Sq E1 25 F1
Well Ct EC4 7 E2
Wellesley Av W6 22 D4
Wellesley Rd NW5 10 A2
Wellesley St E1 19 B4
Wellesley Ter N1 18 B2
Well Hall Rd SE9 42 B1
Wellington Gdns SE7 34 F2
Wellington Ms SE7 34 F2
Wellington Pl NW8 16 F1
Wellington Rd E6 21 B1
Wellington Rd E7 13 C1
Wellington Rd NW8 16 E1
Wellington Row E2 18 E2
Wellington Sq SW3 30 G1
Wellington St SE18 28 C5
Wellington St WC2 6 F3
Wellington Way E3 19 E2
Welling Way SE9 42 F1
Welling Way, Well. 42 F1
Wellmeadow Rd SE6 41 B5
Wellmeadow Rd SE13 41 B4
Wells Ho Rd NW10 15 A4
Wells Pl SW18 37 D5
Wells Ri NW8 9 G5
Wells Rd W12 22 E3
Wells St W1 17 C5
Wellstead Rd E6 21 C1
Wells St E9 11 G4
Well St E15 13 B3
Wells Way SE5 32 D2
Wells Way SW7 23 E4
Well Wk NW3 9 E1
Welsford St SE1 32 F1
Welshpool St E8 11 G5
Welstead Way W4 22 B5
Weltje Rd W6 29 C1
Welton Rd SE18 35 G3
Wemyss Rd SE3 34 C5
Wendell Rd W12 22 B3
Wendle Ct SW8 31 E2
Wendon St E3 12 D5
Wendover Cl SE17 32 D1
Wendover Rd NW10 15 B1
Wendover Rd SE9 41 G1
Wenlock Rd N1 18 B1
Wenlock St N1 18 B1
Wennington Rd E3 19 B1
Wensley Cl SE9 42 B4
Wentworth Cres SE15 32 F3
Wentworth Rd E12 13 G1
Wentworth St E1 18 E5
Wernbrook St SE18 35 E2
Werrington St NW1 17 C1
Werter Rd SW15 36 G2
Wesley Av E16 27 D2
Wesley Cl SE17 25 A5
Wessex St E2 19 A2
West Arbour St E1 19 B5
Westbere Rd NW2 8 G1
Westbourne Br W2 16 D4
Westbourne Cres W2 23 E1
Westbourne Gdns W2 16 B5
Westbourne Gro W2 16 B5
Westbourne Gro W11 23 A1

Westbourne Gro Ter W2 16 C5
Westbourne Pk Rd W2 16 B4
Westbourne Pk Rd W11 15 G5
Westbourne Pk Vil W2 16 B4
Westbourne Rd N7 10 G3
Westbourne St W2 23 E1
Westbourne Ter W2 16 E5
Westbourne Ter Ms W2 16 D5
Westbourne Ter Rd W2 16 D4
Westbridge Rd SW11 30 E4
Westbrook Rd SE3 34 E4
Westbury Rd E7 13 E2
Westbury Rd, Bark. 14 F5
Westbury St SW8 31 C5
Westbury Ter E7 13 E3
West Carriage Dr W2 23 E1
West Cen St WC1 6 E1
Westcombe Hill SE3 34 D1
Westcombe Hill SE10 34 D1
Westcombe Pk Rd SE3 34 B2
West Cotts NW6 9 B2
Westcott Rd SE17 32 A2
Westcroft Cl NW2 8 G1
Westcroft Sq W6 22 C5
Westcroft Way NW2 8 G1
West Cromwell Rd SW5 23 A5
West Cromwell Rd W14 23 A5
West Cross Route W10 22 F1
West Cross Route W11 22 F1
Westdale Pas SE18 35 D2
Westdale Rd SE18 35 D2
Westdean Cl SW18 37 C4
Westdown Rd E15 12 G1
Westdown Rd SE6 40 E5
West Eaton Pl SW1 24 A5
West Ella Rd NW10 8 A4
West End La NW6 9 B5
Westerdale Rd SE10 34 D1
Western Gateway E16 27 D1
Western La SW12 38 A5
Western Rd E13 13 E3
Western Rd SW9 39 A2
Western Way SE28 28 F4
Westferry Circ E14 26 D2
Westferry Rd E14 26 E2
Westfield Cl SW10 30 D3
Westfields SW13 36 B1
Westfields Av SW13 36 A1
Westfield St SE18 27 G4
Westfield Way E1 19 C2
West Gdns E1 25 G1
Westgate St E8 11 G5
Westgate Ter SW10 30 C1
West Gro SE10 33 G4
West Gro La SE10 33 G4
West Halkin St SW1 24 A4
West Ham La E15 13 B4
West Ham Pk E7 13 D4
West Hampstead Ms NW6 9 C3
West Harding St EC4 7 A1
West Hill SW15 36 F5
West Hill SW18 37 B3
West Hill Rd SW18 37 B4
Westhorne Av SE9 41 F4
Westhorne Av SE12 41 D5
Westhorpe Rd SW15 36 E1

West India Av E14   26 E2
West India Dock Rd
E14   19 D5
West La SE16   25 G3
Westleigh Av SW15   36 D3
Westmead SW15   36 D4
Westminster Br
SW1   24 E3
Westminster Br Rd
SE1   24 E3
Westminster Gdns
SW1   24 G4
Westminster Gdns,
Bark.   21 G1
Westmoor St SE7   27 F4
Westmoreland Av,
Well.   42 G1
Westmoreland Pl
SW1   31 B1
Westmoreland Rd
SE17   32 B2
Westmoreland Rd
SW13   29 B4
Westmoreland St
W1   17 A4
Westmoreland Ter
SW1   31 B1
Westmoreland Wk
SE17   32 C2
Westmount Rd SE9   35 B5
Weston Ri WC1   17 F1
Weston St SE1   25 C4
Westover Rd SW18   37 D4
West Parkside SE10   27 E3
Westport Rd E13   20 E3
Westport St E1   19 B1
West Quarters W12   15 C5
West Rd E15   13 C5
West Rd SW3   30 G2
West Rd SW4   38 D3
West Row W10   15 G3
West Smithfield EC1   18 H4
West Sq SE11   25 A4
West St E2   18 G1
West St WC2   6 D4
West Tenter St E1   18 E5
Westvale Ms W3   22 A2
Westview Cl NW10   8 B2
Westview Cl W10   15 F5
Westville Rd W12   22 C3
West Warwick Pl
SW1   24 B5
Westway W2   16 B4
Westway W9   16 B4
Westway W10   15 G5
Westway W12   22 C1
Westwick Gdns
W14   22 F3
Westwood Gdns
SW13   36 B1
Westwood Pk SE23   39 G5
Westwood Rd E16   27 E2
Westwood Rd
SW13   36 B1
Wetherby Gdns
SW5   23 D5
Wetherby Pl SW7   23 D5
Wetherell Rd E9   12 B5
Wexford St SW12   37 G5
Weybridge Pt SW11   31 A5
Weyman Rd SE3   34 F4
Weymouth Ms W1   17 B4
Weymouth St W1   17 B4
Weymouth Ter E2   18 E1
Whalebone Ct EC2   7 G1
Wharfdale Rd
SW10   30 C1
Wharf Pl E2   11 F5
Wharf Rd E15   13 A5
Wharf Rd N1   18 B1
Wharfside Rd E16   20 B4
Wharf St E16   20 B4
Wharton Cl NW10   8 A3

Wharton St WC1   17 F2
Whateley Rd SE22   39 E3
Whatman Rd SE23   40 B5
Wheat Sheaf Cl
E14   26 F5
Wheatsheaf La
SW6   29 E3
Wheatsheaf La
SW8   31 E3
Wheatsheaf Ter
SW6   30 A4
Wheatstone Rd
W10   15 G4
Wheelers Cross,
Bark.   21 F1
Wheelwright St N7   10 F4
Wheler St E1   18 E3
Whellock Rd W4   22 A4
Whetstone Pk WC2   6 G1
Whetstone Rd SE3   34 F5
Whichcote St SE1   6 J6
Whidborne St WC1   17 E2
Whinchat Rd SE28   28 F4
Whinyates Rd SE9   42 A1
Whiskin St EC1   18 A2
Whistlers Av SW11   30 E3
Whistler St N5   11 A1
Whiston Rd E2   18 E1
Whitbread Rd SE4   40 E2
Whitburn Rd SE13   40 F2
Whitby Rd SE18   28 B5
Whitcher Cl SE14   33 C2
Whitchurch Rd W11   22 F1
Whiteadder Way
E14   26 F5
Whitear Wk E15   13 A3
Whitechapel High St
E1   18 E5
Whitechapel Rd E1   18 F5
White Ch La E1   18 F5
White City Cl W12   22 C1
White City Est W12   22 D1
White City Rd W12   22 D1
Whitecross St EC1   18 B3
Whitefield Cl SW15   36 G4
Whitefriars St EC4   7 A2
Whitehall SW1   6 E5
Whitehall Ct SW1   6 E6
Whitehall Gdns SW1   6 E6
Whitehall Pl SW1   6 E6
White Hart La SW13   36 A1
White Hart Rd SE18   28 G5
White Hart St EC4   7 D1
White Hart St SE11   31 G1
White Hart Yd SE1   7 F6
Whitehead's Gro
SW3   30 F1
White Horse La E1   19 B3
White Horse Rd E1   19 C5
White Horse Rd E6   21 B2
White Horse Yd EC2   7 F1
White Kennett St E1   7 J1
Whitelegg Rd E13   20 C1
Whiteleys Shop Cen
W2   16 C5
White Lion Ct EC3   7 H2
White Lion Hill EC4   7 C3
White Lion St N1   17 G1
White Post La E9   12 D4
White Post La SE13   40 E1
White Post St SE15   33 A3
White Rd E15   13 B5
Whites Grds SE1   25 D3
White's Row E1   18 E4
Whitethorn St E3   19 E3
Whitfield Rd E6   13 H5
Whitfield Rd SE3   34 A4
Whitfield St W1   17 D4
Whitgift St SE11   24 E5
Whiting Av, Bark.   14 D4
Whitings Way E6   21 C4
Whitlock Dr SW19   36 G5
Whitmore Est N1   11 D5

Whitmore Gdns
NW10   15 E1
Whitmore Rd N1   11 D5
Whitnell Way SW15   36 F3
Whitstable Ho W10   15 F5
Whittaker Rd E6   13 F4
Whittaker St SW1   24 A5
Whitta Rd E12   13 G1
Whittingstall Rd
SW6   30 A4
Whittington Av EC3   7 H2
Whittlesey St SE1   6 J6
Whitton Wk E3   19 E1
Whitwell Rd E13   20 D2
Whitworth Pl SE18   28 D5
Whitworth Rd SE18   35 C3
Whitworth St SE10   34 B1
Whorlton Rd SE15   39 G1
Whyteville Rd E7   13 E3
Wickersley Rd
SW11   31 A5
Wickford St E1   19 A3
Wickham Cl E1   19 A4
Wickham Gdns
SE4   40 D1
Wickham Ms SE4   33 D5
Wickham Rd SE4   40 D2
Wickham Rd SE11   31 F1
Wickham St, Well.   35 D5
Wick La E9   12 E5
Wicklow St WC1   17 F2
Wick Rd E9   12 B3
Wickwood St SE5   32 A5
Widdenham Rd N7   10 F1
Widdin St E15   13 A4
Widley Rd W9   16 B2
Wigeon Path SE28   28 F4
Wigham Ho, Bark.   14 E4
Wigmore Pl W1   17 B5
Wigmore St W1   17 A5
Wigram Rd E11   20 E3
Wilbraham Pl SW1   23 G5
Wilby Ms W11   23 A2
Wilcox Cl SW8   31 E3
Wilcox Rd SW8   31 E3
Wild Ct WC2   6 G1
Wildcroft Rd SW15   36 E5
Wilde Cl E8   11 F5
Wildfell Rd SE6   40 F5
Wild Goose Dr
SE14   33 A4
Wild's Rents SE1   25 D4
Wild St WC2   6 F2
Wildwood Cl SE12   41 C5
Wilfred St SW1   24 C4
Wilkes St E1   18 E4
Wilkinson Rd E16   20 F5
Wilkinson St SW8   31 F3
Wilkin St NW5   10 B3
Willard St SW8   38 B1
Will Crooks Gdns
SE9   41 F2
Willenhall Rd SE18   35 D1
Willesden La NW2   8 F3
Willesden La NW6   8 F3
Willes Rd NW5   10 B3
William Bonney Est
SW4   38 D2
William Cl SE13   40 G1
William Dunbar Ho
NW6   16 A1
William IV St WC2   6 E4
William Gdns
SW15   36 D3
William Henry Wk
SW8   31 D2
William Morley Cl
E6   13 G5
William Morris Way
SW6   37 D1
William Rd NW1   17 B2
William Saville Ho
NW6   16 A1
Williams Bldgs E2   19 A3
Williamson St N7   10 E1
William St SW1   23 G4

William St, Bark.   14 E4
Willington Rd SW9   38 E1
Willis Rd E15   13 C5
Willis St E14   19 F5
Willoughby Pas
E14   26 E2
Willoughby Rd NW3   9 E1
Willoughby Way
SE7   27 E5
Willow Av SW13   29 B5
Willow Bk SW6   36 G1
Willow Br Rd N1   11 B3
Willowbrook Rd
SE15   32 E2
Willowfield Cl
SE18   35 G1
Willow La SE18   28 B5
Willow Pl SW1   24 C5
Willow Rd NW3   9 E1
Willow St EC2   18 D3
Willow Vale W12   22 C2
Willow Wk SE1   25 D5
Wilman Gro E8   11 F4
Wilmcote Ho W2   16 C4
Wilmer Gdns N1   11 D5
Wilmer Lea Cl E15   12 G4
Wilmington Gdns,
Bark.   14 F3
Wilmington Sq
WC1   17 G2
Wilmington St
WC1   17 G2
Wilmot Cl SE15   32 F3
Wilmot Pl NW1   10 C4
Wilmot St E2   18 G3
Wilmount St SE18   28 D5
Wilna Rd SW18   37 D5
Wilsham St W11   22 F2
Wilshaw St SE14   33 E4
Wilson Gro SE16   25 G3
Wilson Rd E6   20 G2
Wilson Rd SE5   32 D4
Wilsons Rd W6   29 F1
Wilson St EC2   18 C4
Wilton Av W4   29 A1
Wilton Cres SW1   24 A3
Wilton Ms SW1   24 A4
Wilton Pl SW1   24 A3
Wilton Row SW1   24 A3
Wilton Sq N1   11 C5
Wilton St SW1   24 B4
Wilton Ter SW1   24 A4
Wilton Vil N1   11 C5
Wilton Way E8   11 F3
Wiltshire Rd SW9   38 G1
Wiltshire Row N1   11 C5
Wimbart Rd SW2   38 F5
Wimbledon Pk Rd
SW18   37 A5
Wimbolt St E2   18 F2
Wimborne Cl SE12   41 C3
Wimborne St N1   18 C1
Wimpole Ms W1   17 B4
Wimpole St W1   17 B5
Winans Wk SW9   31 G5
Wincanton Rd
SW18   37 A5
Winchcomb Gdns
SE9   41 G1
Winchelsea Cl
SW15   36 F3
Winchester Rd
SW6   30 A3
Winchester Av NW6   8 G5
Winchester Cl SE17   25 A5
Winchester Rd NW3   9 E4
Winchester Sq SE1   7 F5
Winchester St W1   31 B1
Winchester Wk SE1   7 F5
Wincott St SE11   24 G5
Wincrofts Dr SE9   42 F2
Windermere Av
NW6   8 G5
Windermere Ct
SW13   29 B2

Winders Rd SW11 30 F5
Windlass Pl SE8 26 C5
Windmill Cl SE13 33 G5
Windmill Ct NW2 1 C2
Windmill Dr SW4 38 C3
Windmill La E15 15 A3
Windmill Pas W4 22 A5
Windmill Rd SW18 37 E4
Windmill Rd W4 22 A5
Windmill Row SE11 31 G1
Windmill St W1 17 D4
Windmill St SE1 7 A6
Windrose Cl SE16 26 B3
Windsock Cl SE16 26 D5
Windsor Gdns W9 16 B4
Windsor Rd E7 13 E2
Windsor Rd E10 8 D3
Windsor Rd, Ilf. 20 F1
Windsor St N1 11 A5
Windsor Ter N1 18 B2
Windsor Wk SE5 32 C5
Windsor Way W14 22 F5
Windsor Wf E9 12 D2
Wine Cl E1 26 A1
Wine Office Ct EC4 7 A1
Winford Ho E3 12 D4
Winforton St SE10 33 G4
Winfrith Rd SW18 37 D5
Wingate Rd W6 22 A4
Wingate Rd, Ilf. 14 D2
Wingfield Rd E15 13 B2
Wingfield St SE15 39 F1
Wingford Rd SW2 38 E4
Wingmore Rd SE24 39 B1
Wingrave Rd W6 29 E2
Winifred Gro SW11 37 G2
Winifred St E16 28 B2
Winkfield Rd E13 20 E1
Winkley St E2 18 G1
Winn Common Rd
    SE18 35 G2
Winnett St W1 6 C3
Winsham Gro SW11 38 A3
Winslade Rd SW2 38 D3
Winsland St W2 16 E5
Winsley St W1 6 A1
Winslow SE17 32 D1
Winslow Rd W6 29 E2
Winsor Ter E6 21 C4
Winstanley Est
    SW11 37 E1
Winstanley Rd
    SW11 37 E1
Winston Rd N16 11 C1
Winter Av E6 14 A5
Winterbrook Rd
    SE24 39 B4
Winterton Ho E1 18 G5
Winterwell Rd SW2 38 E3
Winthorpe Rd
    SW15 36 G2
Winthrop St E1 18 G4
Wise Rd E15 13 A5
Wishart Rd SE3 34 G4
Wisley Rd SW11 38 A3
Wisteria Cl, Ilf. 14 D2
Wisteria Rd SE13 41 A2
Witan St E2 18 G2
Witherington Rd
    N5 10 G2
Withycombe Rd
    SW19 36 F5
Wivenhoe Cl SE15 39 G1
Wixs La SW4 38 B2
Woburn Pl WC1 17 E3
Woburn Sq WC1 17 D3
Woburn St WC1 17 D2
Wodehouse Av SE5 32 E4
Woking Cl SW15 36 B2
Wolfe Cres SE7 34 G1
Wolfe Cres SE16 26 B3
Wolferton Rd E12 14 B1
Wolffe Gdns E15 13 C3
Wolffram Cl SE13 41 B3
Wolftencroft Cl
    SW11 37 E1

Wolseley Rd E7 13 E4
Wolseley Rd SE1 25 E3
Wolsey Av E6 21 C2
Wolsey Ms NW5 10 C3
Wolsey Rd N1 11 C2
Wolverton Gdns
    W6 22 F5
Woodborough Rd
    SW15 36 D2
Woodbridge St EC1 18 A3
Woodchester Sq W2 16 C4
Woodchurch Rd
    9 B4
Wood Cl E2 18 F3
Woodcocks E16 20 F4
Wooder Gdns E7 13 C1
Woodfall St SW3 30 G1
Woodfarrs SE5 39 C2
Woodfield Pl W9 16 A3
Woodfield Rd W9 16 A4
Woodford Rd E7 13 E1
Woodgrange Rd E7 13 E1
Woodhill SE18 28 A5
Woodhouse Gro
    E12 14 A3
Woodington Cl
    SE9 42 C4
Woodland Cres
    SE10 34 B2
Woodland Cres
    SE16 26 B3
Woodland Gro
    SE10 34 B1
Woodlands, The
    SE13 41 A5
Woodlands Pk Rd
    SE10 34 B2
Woodlands Rd
    SW13 36 B1
Woodlands St
    SE13 41 A5
Woodland Ter SE7 28 A5
Woodland Wk NW3 9 F2
Wood La W12 15 E5
Woodlawn Cl SW15 37 A3
Woodlawn Rd SW6 29 F3
Woodmans Gro
    NW10 8 B2
Woodmans Ms W12 15 D4
Woodman St E16 28 C2
Woodpecker Rd
    SE14 33 C2
Woodquest Av
    SE24 39 B3
Wood Retreat SE18 35 F5
Woodrow SE18 35 B5
Woodseer St E1 18 E4
Woodsford Sq W14 22 G3
Woodside Rd E13 20 F3
Woods Ms W1 24 A1
Woods Rd SE15 32 G4
Woodstock Ct SE12 41 D4
Woodstock Gro
    W12 22 F3
Woodstock Rd E7 13 F4
Woodstock Rd W4 22 B4
Woodstock Ter E14 26 F1
Woodvale SE23 40 A4
Woodville SE3 34 E4
Woodville Rd SE10 41 D3
Woodville Rd N16 11 D2
Woodville Rd NW6 16 A1
Woodwarde Rd
    SE22 39 D4
Wood Wf SE10 33 F2
Woodyard La SE21 39 D5
Woodyates Rd
    SE12 41 D4
Woolacombe Rd
    SE3 34 F4
Wooler St SE17 32 C1

Woolmore St E14 26 G1
Woolneigh St SW6 37 C1
Woolstaplers Way
    SE16 25 F5
Woolwich Ch St
    SE18 28 A4
Woolwich Common
    SE18 35 C2
Woolwich Ferry Pier
    E16 28 C3
Woolwich Foot Tunnel
    E16 28 C3
Woolwich Foot Tunnel
    SE18 28 C3
Woolwich Garrison
    SE18 35 B2
Woolwich High St
    SE18 28 C4
Woolwich Manor Way
    E6 21 B3
Woolwich Manor Way
    E16 28 D1
Woolwich Mkt
    SE18 28 D5
Woolwich New Rd
    SE18 35 C1
Woolwich Rd SE7 34 D1
Woolwich Rd SE10 34 C1
Wooster Gdns E14 20 A5
Wootton St SE1 24 G2
Worcester Dr W4 22 A3
Worcester Rd E12 14 B1
Wordsworth Av E12 14 A3
Wordsworth Rd N16 11 D1
Wordsworth Rd,
    Well. 35 G4
Worfield St SW11 30 F3
Worgan St SE11 31 F1
Worgan St SE16 26 B4
Worland Rd E15 13 B4
World's End Est
    SW10 30 E3
Worlidge St W6 29 E1
Worlingham Rd
    SE22 39 E2
Wormholt Rd W12 22 C1
Wornington Rd
    W10 15 G4
Woronzow Rd NW8 9 G3
Worship St EC2 18 C3
Worsley Gro E5 11 F1
Worsley Rd E11 13 B1
Worsopp Dr SW4 38 C5
Wortley Rd E6 13 G4
Wotton Rd NW2 8 E1
Wotton Rd SE8 33 D2
Woulwham Rd E16 20 C5
Wrekin Rd SE18 35 E3
Wren Av NW2 8 E2
Wren Path SE28 28 F4
Wren St WC1 17 F3
Wrentham Av
    NW10 15 F1
Wrexham Rd E3 19 E1
Wricklemarsh Rd
    SE3 34 E4
Wrigglesworth St
    SE14 33 B3
Wrights La W8 23 C3
Wrights Rd E3 19 D1
Wrottesley Rd
    NW10 15 C1
Wrottesley Rd
    SE18 35 E2
Wroughton Rd
    SW11 37 G4
Wroxton Rd SE15 32 G5
Wulfstan St W12 15 B5
Wyatt Cl SE16 26 D3
Wyatt Dr SW13 29 E3
Wyatt Rd E7 13 D3
Wycherley Cl SE3 34 C3
Wycliffe Rd SW11 31 A5
Wycombe Pl SW18 37 D4

Wye St SW11 30 E5
Wyfold Rd SW6 29 G3
Wyke Rd E3 12 E4
Wyleu St SE23 40 C5
Wyllen Cl E1 19 A3
Wymering Rd W9 16 B2
Wymond St SW15 36 E1
Wynan Rd E14 33 F1
Wyndcliff Rd SE7 34 E2
Wyndham St SE5 32 B3
Wyndham Pl W1 16 G4
Wyndham Rd E6 13 G4
Wyndham Rd SE5 32 A3
Wyndham St W1 16 G4
Wyneham Rd SE24 39 C3
Wynford Rd N1 17 F1
Wynne Rd SW9 31 G5
Wynnstay Gdns W8 23 C3
Wynter St SW11 37 D2
Wynyard Ter SE11 31 F1
Wythens Wk SE9 42 D4
Wythes Rd E16 28 A2
Wythfield Rd SE9 42 B4
Wyvil Rd SW8 31 E3
Wyvis St E14 19 F4

Y

Yabsley St E14 26 G2
Yalding Rd SE16 25 F4
Yardley St WC1 17 G2
Yarrow Cres E6 21 A4
Yateley St SE18 27 G4
Yates Ct NW2 8 F3
Yeate St N1 11 C4
Yeats Cl NW10 8 A3
Yeldham Rd W6 29 F1
Yelverton Rd SW11 30 E5
Yeoman's Row
    SW3 23 F4
Yeoman St SE8 26 C5
Yeo St E3 19 F4
Yewfield Rd NW10 8 B4
Yew Gro NW2 8 F2
Yew Tree Rd W12 22 B1
Yolande Gdns SE9 42 A3
York Br NW1 17 A3
York Bldgs WC2 6 F4
York Gate NW1 17 A3
York Gro SE15 33 A4
York Ho Pl W8 23 C3
York Pl SW11 37 E1
York Pl WC2 6 F4
York Rd E7 13 D3
York Rd SE1 24 F3
York Rd SW11 37 D1
York Rd SW18 37 D1
Yorkshire Rd E14 19 C5
York Sq E14 19 C5
York St W1 16 G4
York Ter E NW1 17 A3
York Ter W NW1 17 A3
Yorkton St E2 18 F1
York Way N1 10 E5
York Way N7 10 E5
Young Rd E16 20 F5
Young St W8 23 C3
Yukon Rd SW12 38 B5
Yuletide Cl NW10 8 A4

Z

Zampa Rd SE16 33 A1
Zangwill Rd SE3 34 G4
Zealand Rd E3 19 C1
Zenoria St SE22 39 E2
Zetland St E14 19 F4
Zoar St SE1 7 D5